de Gruyter Studies in Organization 56
Translating Organizational Change

de Gruyter Studies in Organization

Organizational Theory and Research

This de Gruyter Series aims at publishing theoretical and methodological studies of organizations as well as research findings, which yield insight in and knowledge about organizations. The whole spectrum of perspectives will be considered: organizational analyses rooted in the sociological as well as the economic tradition, from a socio-psychological or a political science angle, mainstream as well as critical or ethno-methodological contributions. Equally, all kinds of organizations will be considered: firms, public agencies, non-profit institutions, voluntary associations, inter-organizational networks, supra-national organizations etc.

Emphasis is on publication of *new* contributions, or significant revisions of existing approaches. However, summaries or critical reflections on current thinking and research will also be considered.

This series represents an effort to advance the social scientific study of organizations across national boundaries and academic disciplines. An Advisory Board consisting of representatives of a variety of perspectives and from different cultural areas is responsible for achieving this task.

This series addresses organization researchers within and outside universities, but also practitioners who have an interest in grounding their work on recent social scientific knowledge and insights.

Editors:

Prof. Dr. Alfred Kieser, Universität Mannheim, Mannheim, Germany

Advisory Board:

Prof. Anna Grandori, CRORA, Università Commerciale Luigi Bocconi,
Milano, Italy
Prof. Dr. Cornelis Lammers, FSW Rijksuniversiteit Leiden, Leiden, The Netherlands
Prof. Dr. Marshall W. Meyer, The Wharton School, University of Pennsylvania,
Philadelphia, U.S.A.
Prof. Jean-Claude Thoenig, Université de Paris I, Paris, France
Prof. Dr. Barry A. Turner, Middlesex Business School, London, GB
Prof. Mayer F. Zald, The University of Michigan, Ann Arbor, U.S.A.

Translating Organizational Change

Edited by
Barbara Czarniawska and Guje Sevón

Walter de Gruyter · Berlin · New York 1996

Barbara Czarniawska, Professor, School of Economics and Management, Lund University, Lund, Sweden

Guje Sevón, Professor, Swedish School of Economics, Helsinki, Finland

With 6 figures and 2 tables

Library of Congress Cataloging-in-Publication Data

Translating organizational change / edited by Barbara Czarniawska and Guje Sevón.
 − (De Gruyter studies in organization ; 56)
 Includes bibliographical references and index.
 ISBN 3-11-014869-2 (cloth ; alk. paper). −
 ISBN 3-11-014868-4 (pb. ; alk. paper).
 1. Organizational change.   I. Czarniawska-Joerges, Barbara.   II. Sevón, Guje.   III. Series.
 HD58.8.T725   1996
 658.4'06−dc20   96-286
                                                           CIP

Die Deutsche Bibliothek − Cataloging-in-Publication Data

Translating Organizational Change / ed. by Barbara Czarniawska and Guje Sevón. − Berlin ; New York : de Gruyter, 1996
 (De Gruyter studies in organization ; 56 : Organizational theory and research)
 ISBN 3-11-014868-4 brosch.
 ISBN 3-11-014869-2 Gb.
NE: Czarniawska, Barbara [Hrsg.]; GT

♾ Printed on acid-free paper which falls within the guidelines of the ANSI to ensure permanence and durability.

Typesetting: Converted by Arthur Collignon GmbH, Berlin. − Printing: Arthur Collignon GmbH, Berlin. − Binding: Mikolai GmbH, Berlin. − Cover Design: Johannes Rother, Berlin.

Acknowledgments

Barbara Czarniawska wishes to express her deep gratitude to the Swedish Council for Research in Humanities and Social Science for having financed the project and the School of Economics and Management at Lund University for having made it possible.

Guje Sevón is deeply indebted to the Foundation of the Swedish School of Economics and the school itself for financial and other support of this project. She is also grateful for the financial support from the Finnish Academy, which allowed for one sabbatical year, during which the final phases of preparation of this volume was taking place.

The editors own a special debt to the authors who through a period of four years and many revisions stayed loyal to the idea of producing high quality manuscripts for this volume. A special thank goes to Tony Spybey and his home institution, the University of Plymouth for hosting one of the workshops during which the authors met to exchange ideas and comments on the manuscripts.

Table of Contents

Organizational Imitation in Identity Transformation

Imitating by Editing Success:
The Construction of Organizational Fields

The Logic of Organizational Transformation: On the Conversion of Non-Business Organizations

Technical and Aesthetic Fashion

Introduction

Barbara Czarniawska and Guje Sevón

> Travel by this road, where you will see
> clear marks of wheels. To allow earth and
> heaven to share equally in your warmth,
> do not go low, nor yet force your way
> into the upper air: if you drive too high,
> you will set the dome of heaven on fire,
> and if you are too low you will scorch the
> earth. The middle way is safest (Ovidius,
> *Metamorphoses*, Book II [103–141]).

Was Phoebes advising Phaeton on how to accomplish an innovation or how to espouse conformity? How to reach success or how to avoid failure? Or both? Those who study organizational innovation are well aware of how inseparable those opposites are and how far those ideas travel which do follow the route advised by Phoebes.

Although the contributors to this volume come from several disciplines − sociology, political science, psychology, anthropology and management − we are all students of organizations. And, like most other students of modern organization, we tend to study it in relation to organizational change.

There are at least two reasons for concentrating on change. One is usually formulated in physicalist terms, borrowed from the theory of perception: only what moves is visible. Static pictures dull the senses, as the air traffic controllers know all too well. A smoothly run, well-routinized organization does not offer much insight to a researcher. Things go well because they go well; this might be due to successful routines or to a receptive market, and only a change can reveal the makings of success. It is like the optical illusion of a stable source of light where in fact a stroboscope is flashing at such a speed that the pause between one flash and the next cannot be detected.

The other reason needs to be formulated in terms of language for describing social phenomena. It has to do with the fact that, during periods of stability, people take their realities for granted, and are therefore unable to reveal their construction to themselves or to others. In times of change, old practices are destroyed and new ones are constructed, which invites the questioning and de-construction of the previous social order. Perhaps this is not a result of change, but rather change itself — change being the periods during which people begin questioning things that were previously taken for granted.

Luckily for those studying organizations, change abounds. One could almost speak of continuous change, which should not be surprising, as the social world undergoes constant construction although projecting a strong illusion of stability.

Once in the field, researchers search to understand changes, observing events as they develop, listening to the accounts provided by the actors who, often wondering about what is happening, do not mind doing it aloud, sharing their doubts and reflections with the researcher.

Unfortunately, these accounts rarely amount to any coherent description or unified explanation. In an organization where a new managerial technique is being introduced, the senior employees claim that they have seen it ten, even twenty years before. Organizations of the same type introduce identical innovations but, when queried by researchers, claim to have invented them themselves. Or the other way around: they claim to have imitated some solution or device, but the external observer fails to find similarities between the "original" and the "copy."

Usually, solving such puzzles begins by consulting already-existing theories of organizational change in search of explanations. There are several main ones, situated at different levels of analysis and taking different angles: the diffusion theory of innovation, the planned change and organizational development theories, the population ecology theory, to name a few. Some take no interest in what are perceived as micro-phenomena like those mentioned above. Others, however, have answers to all these contradictions. If one group of actors claim that a technique is new and another is old, look at the interest constellations behind: the two opinions serve two different interests. Alternatively, one group of actors may be more senior than the other (time factor) or else physically separated from the other (space factor). If the actors perceive their project to be similar to another, and the researchers do not, somebody must be wrong (usually the actors).

All these answers can be classified into two broad categories: when two statements or observations contradict one another, either one of them is incorrect or else there is a third statement which makes the contradiction apparent. These categories represent the time-tested way in which paradoxes are solved in language ruled by linear logic.

Solutions to linguistic paradoxes, however, have little if any bearing on organizational life. It may well be that those who claim to have seen the current reform a while before truly remember the events that younger people do not, but it also means that they cannot be expected to act with the same enthusiasm as younger people and, what is more important, that a rhetorical battle (smashing novelty or old hat?) will take place in the organization, most likely becoming the central event of the reform.

The contributors to this volume are thus united in the conviction that different theories are needed which do not so much attempt to "solve" paradoxes as they try to preserve them in order to understand their crucial role in the life of organizations (Czarniawska, 1996). However, given how the topic of "old-turning-new" permeates the whole volume, there is no intention of coming up with a "new theory" which will explain organizational change once and for all. The present times are tainted with weariness and suspicion of "meta-narratives" (Lyotard, 1987), stories that attempt to introduce a lasting order in one sweep. Instead, there is a growing preference for "little narratives," for partial interpretations which can be patched together in search of understanding, but equally well fragmented again to be put into another theoretical collage. In this volume, these fragments come mainly from two directions, and we shall attempt to present them in what follows.

On "Scandinavian Institutionalism"

As mentioned before, the contributors to this book come from different disciplines. What joins them is a common interest in the phenomenon of organizational change, but also a tendency to turn to theories which treat construction and deconstruction of institutions as the most fruitful way of conceptualizing social order. Specific theoretical formulations vary, however: with a common start in the work of Weber, different routes go via works of Durkheim and Mauss to Mary Douglas, via Parsons and Merton to Selznick, and from the Chicago School to Becker and Denzin, to name a few possible percourses. Although all of these (and more) can be traced in the essays constituting this volume, let us concentrate on one trend especially visible in organization studies − the so-called new institutionalism."

It has become customary to speak of "old institutionalism" in organization theory (see e. g. Powell and DiMaggio, 1991). Its main message, in a succinct formulation of March and Olsen (1989), can be formulated as follows: organizational action heeds the logic of appropriateness, and not, as the theory of rational choice would have it, the logic of consequentiality. Actions are decided on the basis of actors' classifications of the situation they are in and their own identity. Logic of consequentiality, or of rational choice, is used to legitimize the actions undertaken, especially when questioned.

"Old institutionalism" emphasized the central role of norms and socialization processes, of rule and role conflict, and pointed out that rules and identities are taken for granted in a "normal attitude." Institutions can be thus defined as collections of stable rules and roles, and corresponding sets of meanings and interpretations.

"New institutionalism," as presented by, for instance, Powell and Di-Maggio (1991), adopts the centrality of the logic of appropriateness in organizational action, and continues the emphasis on rules and roles, as well as the construction of meaning which takes place in organizations. However, it radicalizes older approaches by presenting identities as results of actions and not as their antecedents (see especially Meyer, 1986a); it dynamizes them by focusing upon the process of rule development (institutionalization); and it makes them more complex by nuancing the theory of conflict.

As pointed out by many critics, however, one issue that is not taken care of is the issue of change. It is understandable in the light of the fact that the main thrust of the institutionalist approach, the provocation achieved, depended on contradicting traditional organizational theory which, informed by rational choice theory, assumed change as an organizational norm. Stability, not change, was the norm, claimed the institutionalists.

Powell's (1991) defense against criticism does not fully answer this; it says, basically, that change must be treated as an exception rather than a rule. While this insistence on stability rather than change can be seen as a part of provocative program of the new institutionalism, a further glimpse into the "old" institutionalism reveals better reasons for such insistence. Institutionalism can be traced back to the Chicago school of pragmatism: Veblen, Dewey, but in the first place George Herbert Mead (Baldwin, 1986). One of the sources of the inspiration for Mead's understanding of the social world was Wundt, and, in the USA, Watson. The only dissension between Mead and Watson was over the fact that the symbolic meaning of communication was not included in Watson's behaviorism, which thereby failed to grasp what was truly human – the social. They agreed, however, that institutions are "natural" systems (see also Røvik in this volume). This biologistic way of construing social life led to the adoption of a theory of evolution which permits change only by mistake – mutations which are then reinforced by natural selection. Energy systems might be open, but information systems are closed – the genetic information is reproduced without variation.

Is this conception wrong? Of course not: unless we permit the existence of supernatural forces, all we know is natural; culture is the product of nature, like everything else. This, however, does not give us an explanatory apparatus of any power. On the contrary, population ecology is the only theory which makes sense in such a light. Unfortunately, this type of explanation does not allow us to interpret what we are, after all, witnessing in the field: that, although "planned change" never succeeds in full, people do manage to convince each other − to change their opinions, beliefs, and ways of acting − and not only by mistake.

This ambiguity concerning change is the focus of what can be called, for lack of a better term, a "Scandinavian institutionalism". Born mainly in contact with US authors such as James March and John Meyer, it originated in the works of Johan Olsen (for example *Petroleum og politikk*, 1989) and Nils Brunsson (see the recent anthology by Brunsson and Olsen, *The reforming organization*, 1993). The "Scandinavian" institutionalism espouses the basic tenets of the new institutionalism and addresses the issue of change in a different way, due to its closeness to the slightly different pragmatic tradition − that of Thurman Arnold. Change and stability together become an organizational norm, as the logic of appropriateness is seen as complementary to the logic of consequentiality.

Describing organizations as a combination of change and stability assumes paradoxicality of organizational life (in tune with Luhmann's theory of autopoetic systems). The dynamic focus is maintained: the processes which attract our attention are processes of identity formation and deconstruction, rule establishment and rule breaking, institutionalization and deinstitutionalization. The emphasis on the construction of meaning requires, however, a replacement of many concepts used to describe organizational change in the past. To be able to achieve this, we turned for inspiration in yet another geographical direction.

Constructionism in Studies of Science and Technology

A recent wave of symbolism in organization studies resulted in a certain neglect of the "hard" aspects of organizing: machines, technologies, buildings. Numerous variations of social constructivism engaged in a fight against scientistic realism concentrated on demonstrating that people, not nature, construct culture; objects were supposed to obey different laws than meanings. The picture of organizations became strongly idealist and organizational life perceived as filled with spiritual endeavors: organizational change seemed to consist of change in symbols and metaphors. This led to an unfortunate debate around the question of whether those "symbolic changes" were accompanied by "real changes," thus maintaining an unnecessarily dualist view of organizations and producing an unintended impression that symbolic changes are "unreal."

Does this mean that, in agreement with what we said in the previous section, we should turn to "naturalistic" ways of viewing social phenomena? Again, one can easily demonstrate that, as much as it makes sense to claim that everything is natural, it makes equally good sense to say that everything is cultural. After all, culture is the only thing we know, a "bubble" through which we perceive the world (Czarniawska-Joerges, 1991). What does not makes sense, though, is to contrast "nature" with "culture," in the vein of the 18th century scientists (Latour, 1992a).

The studies of science and technology as best represented by e. g. Latour and Woolgar (1979), Callon (1986), Callon and Latour (1981), Knorr-Cetina (1981; 1994), revealed that objects and facts are as much socially constructed as symbols, that all human knowledge is social, and that, as much as it is sensible and practical to believe that things exist even when nobody looks at them, it can never be "proven" or "demonstrated" that they exist. Thus the adjective "social" as in "social constructivism" is obviously redundant.

Constructionism requires, however, a much more careful and reflective use of metaphors, especially those taken from natural sciences. Once again, the matter is not to avoid "natural" metaphors or be true to "cultural" ones. The problem arises when metaphors are treated as analogies, where the creative leap between two different things that nevertheless throw a light upon each other is removed and the two things are treated as being alike. "Isomorphism of the field" (DiMaggio and Powell, 1983) is a beautiful metaphor; when taken as analogy, it becomes nonsense (what are the "crystals"?). As Morgan (1980) pointed out, there is nothing more ridiculous than an attempt to "operationalize" metaphors.

In the present context two such carelessly used concepts are of crucial importance: "diffusion" of ideas − until now the central concept in descriptions of transfer of innovations − and "power," another physicalist concept used to grasp internal aspects of organizational change processes. Both tow with them whole chains of assumptions, which usually remain unexamined in organization theory.

"Diffusion" suggest a physical process, subject to the laws of physics, and thus the explanation of phenomena denoted by this term provokes a further train of physical metaphors, like "saturation" or "resistance." Latour (1986) proposes to replace it with *translation* calling attention to the richness of meanings associated with this term, of which only some are evoked in everyday speech. The easy way to illustrate this is to quote the Oxford Dictionary definition, which gives it following meanings:

I. Transference; removal or conveyance from one person, place or condition to another. *b.* Removal from earth to heaven, *orig.* without death (...) *d. Physics.* Transference of a body, or a form of an energy, from one point of space to another.

II. 1. the action or process of turning from own language into another; also, the product of this; a version in a different language (...) *b.* The expression or rendering of something in another medium or form. *2.* Transformation, alteration, change; changing or adopting to another use; renovation (*The Shorter Oxford English Dictionary on Historical Principles*, Oxford University Press, 1973, p. 2347).

It is this richness of meaning, evoking associations with both movement and transformation, embracing both linguistic and material objects, that induced Latour and Callon, and the contributors to this volume after them, to borrow the notion of translation from a contemporary French philosopher, Michel Serres. As the reader will see later in this volume, translation is a key concept for understanding organizational change.

Another concept in need of re-definition is that of "power" which, although defined in a wide variety of ways (see Lukes, 1986), always assumes some kind of a property or potential attributed to some actors or groups of actors. For Callon and Latour (1981), "power" stands for range of associations: actors associate with other actors (including non-humans) and the more numerous and important their associations are, the greater is the power of the whole network thus created. In this sense, power is a result and not a cause, and it does not "belong" to anybody in particular.

This re-definition might look like the splitting of linguistic hairs, if not for the radical consequences it has for re-constructing the central distinction of the social sciences: that between micro- and macro-. The addition of "meso" just complicates the distinction somewhat, without questioning its underlying premises: that, in fact, there exist two social worlds which interact. The micro-world consists of individuals, be that persons or organizations. The macro-world consists of macro-actors such as state, society, market or United Nations. The two worlds coexist in a causal loop: macro-actors establish the constraints for micro-actors, whereas micro-actors change the macro-scene only by their aggregate action.

Described like this, the micro-macro distinction begins to sound like a caricature: after all, it would be hard to find any social scientist who believes that there is "another world," someplace "over there." And yet this is a vision which is taken for granted in most social analysis, and not only organization studies.

What Callon and Latour made us aware of is the fact that there is only one social world, but that it can be described in many different languages. Or, as a relativist might want to put it, there are as many worlds as there are languages to speak about them. The point is, claiming that two of these worlds happen to share the same existence is sheer metaphysics, very much like claiming that there is a heaven or hell parallel to and in interaction with the human world.

Micro-actors associate, creating networks. As the network's operation acquires a relative stability, the network begins to be perceived, or conceived of, as a macro-actor, by definition more powerful than any micro-actor. Market changes do not result in changes in a producer's behavior, and changes in consumer behavior do not result in market changes. They are one and the same, usually at different points in time: it is a consumer's

behavior yesterday which made constraints on the consumer's options today, and couched in a different language.

These are, then, some central concepts with which we hope to revitalize
the theory of organizational change, so that it might help us grasp the
complexity of organizational life without either reducing it to simplistic
models or replacing it with complication of the argument. It is up to the
reader to judge whether we have succeeded. We believe we have gathered
an exceptionally interesting collection of field studies – analyzed in theoretical terms – which aspire to deliver insights which can be of interest to both
scholars and managers looking for new ways of grasping the complexity of
their practice.

The Contents of the Volume

The first chapter, "An idea whose time/space has come. Organizational
change as translation," authored by Barbara Czarniawska and Bernward
Joerges, challenges the two most widespread models of organizational
change: that of planned change, complemented by a picture of "unintended
consequences," and that of determined change, as in all "adaptation to
environment" models. With a focus on organizational action based on a
collective apparatus of sense-making, the authors argue that change is a
result of a blend of intentions, random events and institutional norms, as
opposed to the idea of change as the result of strategic choice or environmental influence.

The chapter traces the route of translated ideas from their local "discovery" to their objectification into forms which can move in time and space,
ready to be exploited in the making of fashions. Successful fashions lead to
institutionalization. The process is circular, as local discovery requires the
existence of an objectified idea in global space. Similarly, travels of ideas
are continually being materialized into organizational actions in local space.

This first chapter introduces the central theme of the book – the paradox of change and stability – but also announces the remaining chapters:
the logic of stability and change from a local perspective (chapters 2–4),
organizations as agents for developing institutions (chapters 5–6), and institutional change in global space (chapters 7–8).

Chapter 2, "Organizational imitation in identity transformation," by
Guje Sevón, points out and problematizes the historically-assumed character of imitation as the opposite of innovation. The discussion dissociates
itself from the ostensive definitions of imitation, bringing to the fore its
performative character. Imitation is based on socially constructed framing,
in which reasoning by analogy plays the dominant role. What are learned

in the process are not only beliefs about the connection between action and its outcome, but also desires concerning outcomes.

This chapter deals with the interplay between action and identity, claiming that imitative action is central to theories of change. The chapter argues that change (imitation) is contingent on matching between situation and identity, based on appropriateness and sense-making. It is a process of learning from the experience and performance of other organizations, where imitation is an ongoing and never-completed accomplishment.

The chapter thus collapses the dichotomy of imitation/innovation as a product of a specific construction produced in a given historical period (colonialism) and reformulates it as an active learning process. Such an understanding of imitation has far-reaching implications for the comprehension of organizational identity and its development, and also of processes of organizational attention and interpretation of the environment.

Kerstin Sahlin-Andersson in her essay "Imitating and editing success. The construction of organization fields and identities" (Chapter 3) takes up cases of imitation known from field studies. Many such studies have shown that organizations are becoming increasingly similar. This chapter describes and suggests some explanations of the spreading of organizational forms and practices. To begin with, organizations tend to compare themselves to other organizations which are defined as similar, and to imitate those among them which are considered successful. The distance between the model-organization and the one which follows the model opens up a space for translations, fillings-in and various interpretations. Meanings ascribed to and derived from the models are then edited in accordance with situational circumstances and constraints. The chapter describes the "editing process" and the process of translation as happening against a set of "editing rules," arriving at a picture of imitation which is far from passive adoption.

As editing assumes change, so does change provoke further editing. When organizations change their identities, they also change their models. This chapter elaborates on the theme of the previous chapter, focusing on the topic of rule development. The author shows how new organizational identities are modified in a process of translation in local space.

Anders Forssell and David Jansson ("The logic of organizational transformation. On the conversion of non-business organizations," Chapter 4) start from the observation that organizational change sometimes means that an organization not only changes parts of itself, but transforms the whole of its organizational form. During the last decade there has been, for instance, a strong tendency for public organizations to become private. This privatization often meant more than a change in ownership. If an organization changes from a public agency to a business company, a new logic comes into play: profits, sales and market-shares become important, customers replace tax-payers, etc. Using empirical examples from three different kinds of organizations, this chapter shows how the transformation of non-business organizations into business enterprises can be explained from an intra-organizational perspective, and how a logic of such transformation can be discerned. In order to do this, the chapter discusses first how the organizational form of any organization is determined. The answer to this query, the chapter argues, is to be found in the existence of institutionalized forms that prescribe how operations are to be organized. Whenever an organization starts to redefine its operations (what it does, e. g. when a local government starts to define its operations as services), the logic of organizational transformation is put into action. If the previous organization form does not "fit" the organization's new operations, it is argued, a change of form — a transformation — is likely to occur. And although this process may take many years to accomplish, it is probable that it will be perceived as both natural and inevitable by most organizational actors.

This chapter argues that organizational changes occur as a consequence of following the logic of the "organization-as-a-tool" metaphor, and shows how the fact that this metaphor is taken for granted legitimates certain combinations of activity and form, but not others.

Chapters 5 and 6 illustrate the stability and change of institutions by discussing the phenomenon of fashion. Fashion is a good example of an institution that represents the paradox of stability and change; on the one hand, it incorporates the stabilizing principle, but on the other, it simultaneously depends on change itself. Eric Abrahamson in "Technical and aesthetic fashion" points out that while the influence of fashion on most areas of social life attracts both popular and scientific attention, the fashions in management techniques, albeit well known to observers of business practices, remain unanalyzed. This sustained inattention to management fashion occurs partly because organizational stakeholders assume that the realm of management is governed by rational thought, and partly because the mechanism of fashion is not well understood in the social sciences. This chapter addresses the social processes impelling the fluctuations of management fashion.

The discussion in this chapter asserts the existence of fashion-setting communities dedicated to discovering management techniques — management consultants, business schools, business mass-media organizations — which manufacture and disseminate a legitimating discourse that casts those techniques as the embodiment of management progress. It also examines the receptivity of fashion-users to this discourse.

"Deinstitutionalization and the logic of fashion" by Kjell-Arne Røvik (Chapter 6) revolves around the concept of "institutionalized standards," i. e. socially constructed and widely spread prescriptions of how to successfully organize parts of organizations. These institutionalized standards travel in time and space. They "hit" concrete organizations, stay there for a while, and then leave. Diffusion and adoption studies enlightened much of the first part of the process: the arrival of institutionalized standards to concrete organizations. What is missing is the knowledge about how they depart.

The chapter coins the concept of deinstitutionalization, as denoting the process by which institutionalized standards, which have gained a rule-like status within certain periods and certain organization fields, explaining the right way of organizing, gradually loose their position. Such a deinstitutionalization process may be revealed through a decrease in the speed of the diffusion process, or even a roll-back, in which organizations which previously adopted a standard try to get rid of it. Finally, the chapter discusses ways in which the ideas which turned unattractive may be stored in organizations for a possible future use.

This chapter continues and extends the previous one by looking at an often unnoticed social mechanism, which, however, has potential explanatory power in organizational analysis: how certain organizational practices and forms fall out of fashion, and what next happens to them.

The next chapter extends the analysis to the global space, at the same time illustrating the main theme of organizational change as a blend of intentions, random events and institutional norms, all processed in a collective apparatus of sense-making. Chapter 7 − Tony Spybey's "Global transformations" − addresses the notion of transformations in the reproduction of social institutions in terms of their increasingly global nature. A range of global institutions have arisen as the result of the attempts of the West to become the world's first truly global culture. The global communication system, the nation-state system, the global economy, the global military order and latterly the environmental movement all have provided conditions for our routine day-to-day reproduction of the structure of society. Indeed, it is impossible to enter into social interactions without some awareness of the global dimension. Therefore, it is argued, any meaningful study of social organization must take into account this process of globalization.

The chapter describes the emergence of global institutions, pointing out that it now makes sense to conceive of a social identity against a global background as well as to classify a particular situation in global terms. This phenomenon can be seen as resulting in the extension of western institutions beyond any earlier thinkable limits, but also in the homogenization of the repertoire of possible matches between situations and identities, therefore limiting the repertoire of action and thus possibly feeding the defeat of the present institutional order and the beginning of a new one.

Richard Rottenburg in "When organization travels" (Chapter 8) uses examples from African countries to analyze the clash between two institutionalized thought structures which meet on the organizational ground. The western rationalist model of organization encounters the local version of the organizing process, embedded in different kinds of institutions. The incompatibility of those two models leads to puzzlement and frustration on the part of western mandators, who act upon the premise of the universal superiority of their model. Disembedded from its institutional context, the rational model stands unconnected, supported only by the African political and managerial elite and by their Western sponsors. In a society with no industrial tradition and no relevant institutional arrangement, an introduction of formal organizational structures from a fundamentally different life-world is even less effective, if not downright abortive. Thus chapters 6 to 8 take up the negative side of the coin − the fall of old institutions and failures at establishing new ones − to complete this picture of ideas that travel globally and take root locally.

In the last chapter "Otherhood: The promulgation and transmission of ideas in the modern organizational environment," John Meyer comments on the earlier chapters. In addition he elaborates on factors involved in the development of the idea-creation and idea-transmission system in the environment and also particularizes the properties of ideas that enhance their potential to travel.

Travels of Ideas[1]

Barbara Czarniawska and Bernward Joerges

What is "an organizational change"? A different pattern of practice, as noticed by the observers from the outside, a vision of a leader who wants to transform a faulty reality, or both? And why just this change and not any other? Why do ideas that have been with us for decades, if not for centuries, as not more than figments of vivid imagination, all of a sudden materialize in organizational action? Why are organizational environments seen as changing in a given way? Why do managers or other employees come upon certain ideas at a given time? Why don't they implement what they had decided? Where did the "unintended consequences" come from? Such questions were posed since organization theory emerged as a field of inquiry in its own right, and many an answer has been submitted.

We will begin by reminding readers of the more familiar answers, in order to contrast them with a sample of puzzling phenomena which attracted our attention but failed to find an explanation within the existing body of theory. We attempt to interpret these phenomena by scrutinizing the inclusive, ongoing process of materialization of ideas, of turning ideas into objects and actions and again into other ideas.

Presenting organizational change, the crux of organizational life, as a story of ideas turning into actions in ever new localities, we hope to approach the question of how local action emerges and becomes institutionalized on a more global scale in a way which goes beyond received models of change. In particular, we hope to go beyond the characteristically modernist opposition of materialism and idealism and the dichotomies which follow from it: social/technical, intentional/deterministic, subjective/objective. The roadposts leading beyond this dual landscape: the notions of "idea," "localized and globalized time and space," "translation," "organizational fashion," "institution." We then proceed to recontextualize phenomena of organizational change with the help of these notions.

---

[1] This is a substantially revised version of the essay "Winds of organizational change: How to translate into objects and actions," published in Samuel Bacharach, Pasquale Gagliardi, and Brian Mundell (eds.), *Research in organizational sociology,* Vol. 13. Greenwich: JAI Press, 1995.

Received Images of Change

The modernist dichotomies mentioned above find their reflection in two dominating images of organizational change: as a planned innovation and as an environmental adaptation. Under the first label approaches such as strategic choice, decision-making and organization development may be grouped; under the second, contingency theory, population ecology and, at least in certain variations of neoinstitutionalism, institutional theory.

Yet the image of organizational change as presented by these two schools of thought is constantly contradicted by organizational practice. Yes, we can see actors and groups learning and making conscious choices, carefully designing programs of change, but those very programs leave us (and them) with a heap of "unintended consequences" and "unexpected results" that are supposed to be disposed of in the next step, but somehow never are. As a result of a constant critique from the environmentalists, more sophisticated rational models and concepts like "bounded rationality" and "opportunism" were advanced.

There are similar problems with adaptionist approaches, whether mechanistic or organic type. Practical and political problems are involved: if everything is determined from outside, what can researchers contribute to managers' attempts to do their job? Shall we recommend a Hindu-type of fatalism, or shall we try to sell what McCloskey (1990) calls the snake-oil story, i. e. present ourselves as possessors of a secret that will help the chosen few to control the world? There are also serious problems concerning theoretical developments: what are the social mechanisms which are commensurate to biological mechanisms? We know (or at least we think we know) what is isomorphism when it comes to crystals, but what exactly does its equivalent in an organization field look like? Is it an analogy or a metaphor, and if a metaphor, what does it illuminate? Another contentious issue is which evolutionary persuasion to adopt: Lamarckian ideas of functional evolution, largely rejected in biology but still very attractive to social scientists, or some geneticist version, resorting to something as metaphysical as "memes"?

There is a certain comfort in the fact that the two schools criticize each other, leading to improvements and achieving a kind of balance. But this balance seems to have been static for a while now, resembling more a stalemate than anything else. We are not the first to seek a way out from this stalemate: it is enough to mention the enormously impressive and, at the time of its emergence, revolutionary "garbage-can model" (Cohen and March, 1974; March and Olsen, 1976; March, 1988) which moved in the direction of accepting both contingency and control as elements shaping the process of change. In this sense our attempt is close to the garbage-can, but we differ in at least two respects from this perspective.

The first difference is that we do not go along with the model's behaviorist distance towards the actors involved, the distance which results in largely disregarding their intentions and attempts to make sense. We hasten to add that such readings of others' texts are, of course, very risky. In fact, Cohen and March's (1974) recommendations on how to influence a garbage-can decision making process seem to suggest that the authors give priority to intentional action − even in the face of randomness. However, the fact that intentions fail does not prove that they are irrelevant for understanding the outcomes. Thus our stance is one at the same level with organizational actors: we sit inside, or in any event within listening range to the garbage-can, in order to follow how the actors try to put together ideas and actions that come to them, in their never ending activity of sense making.

This leads to the second difference. Garbage-can and related theories, even when they allow for reflexivity, still aim at establishing a meta-level explanatory discourse, not readily accessible for the actors studied. Theorists know better − and different.

In contrast, we suggest an approach where the organizational theorist does not don a stance of categorical superiority but rather a kind of sideways perspective (which would be very impractical to take for practitioners of organizing). This involves in the first place listening closely to, and later talking back to, organizational actors. Not because *they* know better, but because they know.

A point of research philosophy enters here. It would be a mistake, as Rorty observes, to privilege actors' own accounts of their doings and cultures as epistemically superior, because they may be good accounts, but then they may be not. But it would not be a mistake "to think of [them] as morally privileged." According to Rorty, social scientists have a duty to listen to actors' (in this case organizational practitioners') accounts, not because they are privileged accounts of their cultures "but because they are human beings like ourselves" (Rorty, 1982, p. 202).

Rorty continues by proposing that social scientists should act as *interpreters* − in order to facilitate a conversation between groups who do not have the same language. Thus, if we seem to know more than a specific actor does, it is not because we are omniscient, but because we have had the chance to look at many garbage cans, have had the leisure to see them in a sequence, and to produce serialised accounts of what we saw. If we see things in a different light than actors do, it is because our *Sitz-im-Leben* is different. Their duty is to act, ours is to reflect and interpret, and although it would be silly to attempt to draw a strict line between the two, as everybody acts and (almost) everybody reflects. Nevertheless, there is a social division of labor between managers and researchers, where both sides would gain from perfecting their respective specialties and then engaging in a dialogue about them.

In other words, we have no intention to tell managers what to do in the face of a change or stagnation. We want to tell everybody who wants to listen a complex story of how changes come about and leave the actors to decide which conclusions to draw, fully expecting that managers might come to different conclusions than union stewards upon reading our reports. This means that we remain reserved in regard to control theories with their claim to superior usefulness, to law-like theories with their attractive elegance, and to a metalanguage with its hermetic rhetoric. The usefulness of such highly glossed accounts remains open to question, too. Organizational actors are perfectly capable of producing simplifications and stylizations − action theories − themselves. They are constantly engaged in what Luhmann (1991) calls *Entparadoxierung,* or de-paradoxifying. We owe them a different type of assistance in tackling the irreducible complexity of organizational life, one we call *systematic reflection,* as a complement to action-induced simplifications.

In the present essay, we propose to complete familiar images of organizational change − as a series of planned moves from one state to another or a continuum of reactive adaptations − with the image of materialization of ideas. This process (which might, but does not have to, become incorporated in some agent's attempt to achieve control) can be observed when, out of the myriads of ideas floating in the translocal organizational thought-worlds, certain ideas catch and are subsequently translated into substance in a given organization, often barely touching the bureaucratic apparatus of planned change. More likely than not, it is the same ideas which materialize in similar organizations around the same time, indicating that mechanisms are at work which are best seen as akin to fashion. This process is explored from a constructionist perspective, drawing in equal measure on narrative and logo-scientific knowledge in organization theory and research (on the distinction between the two, see Lyotard, 1979; Bruner, 1986).

When Ideas Go Places

What made us interested in alternative conceptualizations of change? A phenomenon which can be called "travels of ideas," and which is a focus of this volume as a whole. It has been observed, and will be again and again in this book, that many organizations introduce the same changes at about the same time (Zucker, 1977; March and Olsen, 1983b; Forssell, 1989; Powell and DiMaggio, 1991). To explain this by saying that they do so hoping to gain strategic advantage would be trivial: of course they do not introduce change to attract losses. In fact, one could argue that the omnipresence and simultaneity of agendas of organizational change in such situations tend to reduce its competitive edge for a given organization. A search for entirely novel solutions would seem more promising. But conventionality seems to have a competitive value of its own. Confronting this puzzle we will begin with a series of examples of organizational changes illustrating the issue.

Public Administration Reforms

In 1977, the local authorities in one Swedish municipality decided to decen-
tralise their political decision-making and to do it in the form of sub-municipal committees (Czarniawska-Joerges, 1988). Two other municipalities followed their example and in 1979 the Swedish Parliament introduced a Local
Bodies Act, permitting and encouraging municipalities to experiment with
various forms of local democracy. sub-municipal committees (SMCs) were
the most popular form and the original experimenters soon served as consultants to those who wanted to exploit their experience. In many such
cases the potential followers, when asked why they wanted to introduce the
reform, looked perplexed and answered: "Doesn't everybody?" As it turned
out, this was not the case. Furthermore, when the Minister of Civil Affairs,
who was enthusiastic about the changes and did much to propagate them,
proposed a bill introducing the reform for all municipalities, Parliament
said "no." By 1988, 25 municipalities had introduced SMCs, 65 rejected the
proposal, 3 withdrew from change which was already well advanced, 26
were still experimenting, while 166 did not reveal any interest in the reform
(Johansson, 1988). The wave came, affected some places, and left others
without much trace.

However, this is only one possible version of the course of events (ours).
When asked, the actors involved presented many other interpretations. One
was that the whole process started already in the 1940s and was simply
continuing, searching for optimal forms of local democracy – SMCs was
just the most recent form. Proponents of another version claimed that the
reform was a reaction to defects felt in local democracy as a result of previous, administrative-type reforms (where the changes were ordered from
above) which merged small municipalities into large administrative and political units. Still another attributed the reform to initiatives from a given
party (there were at least three possible candidates). Yet another version
would have it that the first municipality thrives on attracting attention and
therefore always leads all possible experiments, which are then followed by
other, like-minded opportunists. There were also suggestions that the whole
idea came from the central government, and more specifically from the
Ministry of Civil Affairs, whose Minister, ironically nicknamed "the Knight
of Light," wanted to make it his contribution to posterity.

The only thing those interpretations had in common was that they all
mentioned some *plot* which accounted for spreading of ideas: political response to societal need, imitation, subordination, fashion-following, or
sometimes all of them together. In fact, when all such schemes seem to
operate in the same direction, the interpretations can be combined. But
who is right if some contradict others?

Beckman (1987) studied another public sector reform: introducing Research and Development units and other organizations at the regional level,

with the aim of improving regional co-operation between research and higher education institutions on the one hand, and business companies on the other. The author suggested an interpretation according to which the new units were a result of a conscious central policy, based on a specific perception of the present situation (increased co-operation between the public and private sectors as one solution for a potential unemployment problem); a policy which followed a fashionable theory of regional industrial development (innovation and product cycle theory) and imitated international solutions.

The regional actors, however, did not see the developments as steered by central government. In their opinion, solutions emerged as a result of an organic, down-to-earth, anarchic and unstructured decision process. Beckman agreed that both processes took place and explained the difference in perceptions by the fact that what he called "value control" was not perceived as control. Administrative orders and check-ups are perceived as control, but not information spreading, idea-suggestions and persuasion.

We agree with Beckman that turning ideas into substance might take the form of a planned change. As it is now, however, organization studies tell us much more about planned change or "forced learning," and much less about materialization of ideas in general, or about unplanned change in particular. This might be interpreted as evidence that "ideas turning into substance" is a relatively recent way in which organizations change. More likely, though, is that organization theory has never paid much attention to such plots. Let us look at some other instances.

Development Projects and Technology

Speaking of turning ideas into substance inevitably transfer brings technology issues to mind. Development projects and technology transfers to so-called developing countries present particularly intricate cases of idea materialization (Joerges, 1976). Ideas are turned into things, then things into ideas again, transferred from their time and place of origin and materialized again elsewhere. How does it happen? Observing development projects, Hirschman (1967) noted something he called a "pseudo-imitation" technique: a method that is used to promote projects that would normally be discriminated against as too obviously replete with difficulties and uncertainties.

Projects are here presented as unproblematic replications of experiences that were successfully carried through in another, and then in yet another, place.

For example, for a number of years after World War II, any river valley development scheme, whether it concerned the Sao Francisco River in Brazil, the Papaloapan River in Mexico, the Cauca in Colombia, the Dez in Iran, or the Damodarn in eastern India, was presented to a reassured public as a true copy − if possible, certified expressly by David Lilienthal − of the Tennessee Valley Authority (Hirschman, 1967, p. 21).

Billing a project as a straight replica of a unquestionably successful venture in an "advanced" country (or organization) makes it acceptable even under very different conditions.

These are cases where a set of actions is already in the offing and an idea is needed to legitimately trigger it. A technology arrives, first as a nebulous idea, something only vaguely, in some minds, related to some actions, which then lands heavily on the ground, showing its nasty side, requiring still new investments and additional commitments. At worst, a new technology can break down a whole social system, as Trist and Bamford's famous study of coal-mining documented (Trist and Bamford, 1951). At best, in the course of the fitting process, the idea and the set of actions will get adjusted to each other in a new, unique combination.

One could object that in all the above cases we are speaking about simple planned changes which can be satisfactorily interpreted in terms of leaders' ingenuity and/or environmental pressure ("crisis management"). But what usually happens is that the materialization of a technical idea starts a chain-reaction of consequences which are not only unplanned, but sometimes undesirable as well. The Polish government decided to start building a metro system in Warsaw in the late 1940s: a wave of various financial crises made the project first unfeasible and then obsolete. Nobody, not even the experts of the World Bank could, however, achieve the termination of the project − one cannot simpy bury the underground structure as if nothing happens. Warsaw has its metro since 1995.

Planned changes are often sets of ideas which never materialize; whereas materialized ideas go down like avalanches, with almost no resistance, especially if they acquire the form of complicated machinery. But where do they come from? Where will they go? How can we follow them − with what metaphors − or vehicles?

Vehicles/Metaphors

On Ideas

Before we move any further, we will commit an act of reductionism and decide, for the purpose of this essay, how to conceive of "ideas."

Mitchell (1986), who faced a similar predicament, went back in etymology and observed that the word "idea" comes from the Greek word "to see" and is close to the noun "eidolon," central to Greek theories of physical perception. If we recall Rorty's interpretation of modern science as a mirror of nature (Rorty, 1980), we will realize even more clearly how close the discourses related to mental phenomena and to physical optics are to each other. To understand is to see; to see is to understand; "the innocent eye is blind," and so on.

In agreement with Mitchell, we find it worthwhile "to give in to the temptation to see ideas as images, and to allow the recursive problem full play" (Mitchell, 1986, p. 5). He classified images as graphic, optical, perceptual, verbal and mental, counting ideas among the latter, together with dreams and memories. We admit having problems with the classification: how do we know that a mental image exists before it has taken the form of words or pictures? What is the difference between "optical" and "graphical"? Let us simplify this classification by saying that ideas are images which become known in the form of pictures or sounds (words can be either one or another). They can then be materialized (turned into objects or actions) in many ways: pictures can be painted or written (like in stage-setting), sounds can be recorded or written down (like in a musical score) and so on and so forth. Their materialization causes change: unknown objects appear, known objects change their appearance, practices become transformed. This view accords with the pragmatist tradition which takes ideas to be "instruments that not only can become true by doing their job in inquiry, but can also transform the environment to which they are applied" (Hollinger, 1980, p. 87).

The "application" of ideas takes place through acts of communication. Tracing repeated communication, we ask where ideas travel, and although this question is formulated in spatial terms, the movement of ideas involves of course both time and space.

Local and Global and Their Relation to Time/Space; Particular/Universal; Micro/Macro

It has been pointed out many a time (e. g. Zey-Ferrell, 1981) that much of organization theory is ahistorical. While macro-developments are plotted over historically long periods of time, organizational change studies customarily stress temporality. First there were losses, and then there was an plan of change, and then there was an implementation, which led to unexpected results... Or, in another variation of the same story: an organization was born, and then the environment changed, and then the organization adapted/failed to adapt and survived/died. Spatial considerations, in contrast, play a minor role: although the company executives might be travelling thousands of miles per day, "the organization" seems to be situated in one point, unless it expands.

On this score, organization theory remains fully in tune with the modernist melody. Listen to Foucault who early on voiced the new, "postmodernist" concern for place and space. The great obsession of the nineteenth century, he said, was history, "with its themes of development and of suspension, of crisis and cycle, themes of the ever-accumulating past (...) Space was treated as the dead, the fixed, the undialectical, the immobile. Time, on the contrary was richness, fecundity, life, dialectic." The present epoch, he added, may turn above all into an epoch of space and simulaneuos networks (Foucault, 1980, p. 70).

This sentiment is widely shared in most reflections on postmodernity (see e. g. Gergen, 1991). One of the typical reasons given is the "shrinking" of space due to transportation and communication technologies. We, too, insist on the travel metaphor – and yet we think that we can also explain why time is and remains to be so irreducibly important in all that is being said about social life. Time – is sequentiality, the plot of every narrative, which remains to be our central mode of knowing (Bruner, 1986; 1990), language games and postmodernist experiments nevertheless. Sequentiality implies causality – in terms of both objective causes and human intentions – and is the basic glue which holds together our narratives. On the other hand, all kinds of displacements in space and time are better captured using metaphors, this central element of the paradigmatic (i. e. scientific) mode of knowing. We therefore need notions which will allow us to grasp time *and* space simultaneously, like in *localized time* and, by contrast, in *globalized time*.

The everyday use, however, prefers the essentialist adjectives "local" and "global." We shall mostly follow the common use for simplicity sake, asking the reader to keep in mind that these are not ostensive but performative properties: people *make* something into local or global; they localize or globalize. And they do it at different time intervals, of course.

Contemporary language in general is ill-suited for Einsteinian reflections. Verbs stand for time, and nouns stand for space. One can combine them, but not join them in one expression. And yet it probably would not be difficult to convince everybody that these phenomena exist only together: "movement" occurs in time/space, and in every instance when we accentuate space or time, the other aspect is still present, although hidden.

Thus we can speak of a dominant idea – in a given time/space. In this sense, Foucault can be seen as saying that dominance of time-metaphors gives room (in time) to space-metaphors. It is of course no use to fight against common usage, but it is interesting to point out what it obscures. Also, we will try to illustrate the usefulness of such notions as space/time continua. In order to do this, we shall first approach two other dichotomies which are closely related to the local/global distiction: cultural universals vs. particulars, and macro- vs. micro-actors.

Cultural universals, much debated in anthropology since Kroeber (1948), seem to be taken for granted by mainstream anthropologists as much as they have come under attack by the discipline's "reflective" dissenters. It was perhaps Geertz's collection of essays *Local Knowledge* from 1983 which firmly established the grounds for the position that there are no universals, only particulars, and that local knowledge is the only knowledge that there is. Since then, this topic was taken up both in the Diltheyan tradition of romanticizing the unique, as in the more complex stance of "modernist anthropology" (Clifford and Marcus, 1986; Marcus, 1992).

Closely related to this is a reformulation of the micro-macro problem undertaken by Callon and Latour (1981; see also *Introduction* to this volume). In an article aptly named "Unscrewing the big Leviathan: how actors macro-structure reality and how sociologists help them to do so," they point out that no macro-actors exist: there are only micro-actors who associate with other micro-actors constructing networks that appear to be of a super-human size. What we call "global economy" is a network of many local economies, which thus acquire an unprecedented scale and scope of action.

But it is as important to say what "global" is not: it is not "total," in the sense including everybody on earth. It would be safe to guess that actually the majority of the inhabitants of the globe are not connected into this net, which does not mean that they are not influenced by it, directly or indirectly. In this last sense, though, "global" becomes trivialized and has nothing to do with the present era: acid rain was always global, whether produced by East German factories or by the outer space object which made the Yucatan crater and extinguished dinosaurs. Also, "global" is not an extra-entity, nothing "above" or "beyond" local: *its is a hugely extended net work of localities.*

Taking our cue from these critiques of the mostly spatial metaphors of the universals/particulars and the macro/micro debates, we can now, carefully, introduce the notions of *localized time/space* and *globalized time space* which should really be named "translocal," in the sense of interconnecting localized time/spaces. In this context, global and local do not form an irreducible dichotomy, but a continuum. Local time is a sequence of moments spent in a unique place, its antonym being not global or time, but "momentary space" or "co-temporary space," an ensemble of places accessed at the same moment (e. g. the reach of your cable television). Similarly, the antonym of global time is "lasting space," or historic space, large ensembles of places permanently accessible − in reality, the Earth, in science-fiction, many other planets or satellites.

We begin by tracing ideas along the course of local time/space: how, at a given moment, do individuals and groups at certain place happen to notice an idea? Of course, the beginning of the story is arbitrary, but we see a point in beginning just there, because it is a narrative, a story that we want to spin. We watch ideas become quasi-objects, transgressing the barriers of local time and entering translocal paths, becoming "disembedded," in Giddens' (1990) terms. We watch them again, landing in various localities, becoming "re-embedded," materialized in actions, and — when judged successful — becoming institutions, only to occasion anew the generation of ideas.

Translation

How to build a device mediating between local and global time/spaces so that "global" retains sense which does not suggest a metaphysical idea of something beyond and above the localized time/space, a device that allows us to demonstrate how ideas can travel? How might one conceive of idea-objects moving in space and time?

Idea-spreading is traditionally discussed in terms of "diffusion" (see for example Rogers, 1962; for a review Levitt and March, 1988). Like other field metaphors, this has an economic value, rendering the less known in terms of the more familiar, the immaterial in material terms. But adopting the metaphor for our purposes takes us up an impasse. It may be plausible to say that ideas move from "more satiated" to "less satiated" environments, but by doing so we also suggest that the law of inertia applies to ideas as to physical objects. But does this offer a convincing interpretation of phenomena in question? If we look at phenomena such as braindrain, we notice that the reverse is more apt: ideas travel from less satiated to more satiated environments, so that one has to save face by evoking another physical metaphor, that of "critical mass" which "attracts." Rather than adding new physical metaphors to defend one another (a very smart political move at times), we could substitute them instead.

Latour contrasts the diffusion model with another one: that of translation, according to which

> the spread in time and space of anything — claims, orders, artefacts, goods — is in the hands of people; each of these people may act in many different ways, letting the token drop, or modifying it, or deflecting it, or betraying it, or adding to it, or appropriating it (Latour, 1986, p. 267).

The translation model (see also *Introduction* to this volume) can help us to reconcile the fact that a text is at the same time object-like and yet it can be read in differing ways. Also, it answers the question about the energy needed for travelling: it is the people, whether we see them as users or creators, who energize an idea any time they translate it for their own or somebody else's use. Ideas left in books left on shelves do not travel, and no amount of satiation will help to diffuse ideas from closed libraries. Watching ideas travel, "[w]e observe a process of translation — not one of reception, rejection, resistance or acceptance" (Latour, 1992b, p. 116).

It is important to emphasize, once again, that the meaning of "translation" in this context far surpasses the linguistic interpretation: it means "displacement, drift, invention, mediation, creation of a new link that did not exist before and modifies in part the two agents" (Latour, 1993, p. 6), that is, those who translated and that which is translated. This explains why the concept is so attractive to us: it comprises what exists and what is created; the relationship between humans and ideas, ideas and objects, and humans and objects − all needed in order to understand what in shorthand we call "organizational change."

But as presented above, translation sounds like a micro-process, something that happens between two people or maybe three: is that enough energy to send an idea all around the world? Basically, yes, but in the course of hundred years or so. However, we know that ideas travel at the speed of light-waves. Translation is speeded up, made continuous and magnified by technology: more specifically, by mass storage, mass reproduction and mass media technologies. It is this hybridized humans/technologies network which is the material basis for more complex translation mechanisms: fashion and institutionalization.

Fashion/Institution

Fashion was until recently a phenomenon treated with disdain and neglect in social theory and organization studies.[2] Part of the blame goes to critical theorists: "Fashionability allows individuals who follow the imperatives of fashion to abandon the responsibility to make history and shape culture" (Finkelstein, 1989, p. 144) is only one of the more recent examples of modern critique of fashion coming from that school. However, blame should be also directed to the dominating masculine culture of the social sciences, where war, sport and technology are worth serious scrutiny and become a source of unproblematic metaphors; not so events and phenomena perceived as coming from feminine realms.

To us, a metaphorical and literal understanding of fashion seems to be the key to understanding many puzzling developments in and between organizations. The concept can importantly complement another phenomenon which has attracted much more attention, namely institutionalization. We want then not only to redeem the importance of fashion, but we also want to put it together as the unseparable part of the "iron cage" of institutions, paradoxical as it may sound.

We can put it as follows: much as fashionability and institutionalization seem to be opposites, one standing for temporality and frivolousness and

---

[2]   Several essays in this volume are dedicated to the reversal of this situation, see e.g. Abrahamson and Røvik.

the other for stability and seriousness, it seems more fruitful to see them as interconnected and interdependent. Fashion is the fringe, the margin, the challenge to the institutionalized order of things, but its durability in time and mobility in space, indeed, its use of technologies which are required for that scope, depends on its firm institutionalization in the contemporary western world. Similarly, much as fashion seems to sabotage and threaten established institutions, it is also an institutional playfield: new practices can be tried out and disposed of − or institutionalized, thus revitalizing the existing institutional order. Although it has been tried many a time, it is hard to show a fashion that brought about a revolution; it would be easier to show that totalitarian systems suffocate fashionability.

We can probably achieve a tentative agreement of our readers for this reasoning, only because it will permit them to ask the next question: which ideas brought about by fashion are institutionalized, and which are not? This is an honorable question that produced many an answer. Mary Douglas, for instance, says that, "[to] acquire legitimacy, every kind of institution needs a formula that founds its rightness in reason and in nature" (1986, p. 45). In the context of the invention of the camera, Mitchell concludes that: "What is natural is, evidently, what we can build a machine to do for us" (1986, p. 37). In organizational thought-worlds almost all ideas are, or can be presented as, based on reason and nature. Hence: those ideas which can be presented as natural (for example, by showing that they can be materialized into tangible machines), lend themselves to be institutionalized.

The answer to the question does not lie, in other words, in inherent properties of ideas, but in the success of their presentation. The same question can actually be put earlier on: which ideas become fashionable and which remain for ever local? We think that, on their way to become institutionalized practices, ideas are turned around and about, in this process acquiring object-like attributes, becoming quasi-objects, more like crawling ants than free-floating spirits. Organizational actors, like a collective ant-eater, catch many, spit out most, and savor some, presumably on the grounds of relevance to some organizational problem. But the match does not lie in the attributes of an idea or in the characteristics of the problem. It can hardly be claimed that the inventor of the camera did it to solve the problem of taking pictures. The perceived attributes of an idea, the perceived characteristics of a problem and the match between them are all created, negotiated or imposed during the collective translation process. All three are the results, not the antecedents of this process. With some exaggeration, one can claim that most ideas can be proven to fit most problems, assuming good will, creativity and a tendency to consensus. It is therefore the process of translation that should become our concern, not the properties of ideas.

Figure 1 is a simplified scheme of the process we intend to present.

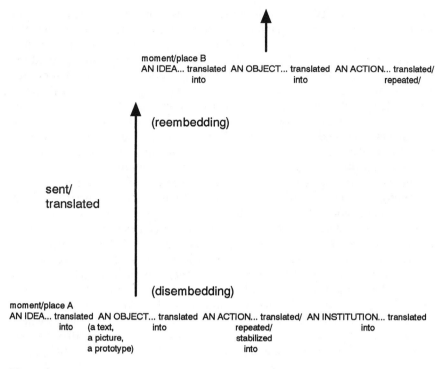

Figure 1

An Idea Is Objectified

The circumstances in which an idea arose in the local time/space or, even more important, how and when it decisively came into the span of attention of a given group of organizational actors, are usually unknown. More likely than not, it was a meaningless event at that point in time/space. On the other hand, ideas do not arrive out of the blue: one can argue, as Merton did in "On the Shoulders of Giants" (1985), that all ideas circulate most of the time, at least in some places. Therefore it is more appropriate to discuss processes of *attention* rather than of information in relation to ideas that appeared in a given place/moment.

When the translation of ideas into actions is well advanced, the actors involved feel a need to mythologize by dramatizing origins. They say things like: "I remember when X went to Brussels for this special course and came back with that extraordinary idea..." or "When consultants came, they entranced us with an idea that we are living in and by chaos..." But other actors quote other incidents or deny the initiating importance of this or that particular incident, which makes the observer wonder whether "the idea from Brussels" or the notion of "chaos" were important as such. In his study of industrial policy in Sweden, Jacobsson (1989) found actors in the Ministry of Industry claiming that they had learned from experiences which, under scrutiny, had apparently never taken place. It might well be that, in the reconstruction of the past, an event is chosen or invented because it is rhetorically convenient (a "logical" starting point for a story that is being told).

Alternatively, the incidental and disruptive character of the initial events is stressed to demonstrate the incredible touch of luck in the idea's timely arrival. The idea fell on unprepared ground, as it were; but soon its upshots were seen as it rapidly connected to important currents in organizational life.

Both types of memories serve the same purpose: to tie, meaningfully, the arrival of an idea to present problems experienced by people in organizations or attributed to the organizations themselves. Often there is an attempt to portray the process as functional: this particular idea was spotted and adopted because it served well in resolving a specific difficulty or in creating a new opportunity in situations of stagnation. The idea of attention as a social product serves well to tie together the variety of events constituting this process.

Attention as a Social Product

Attention, or more properly speaking perceptual readiness (Bruner, 1957) has been most frequently studied in the context of tangible objects and their attributes, where "objects" stand both for objects of perception and organs of perception, understood physiologically. Burner's more general theory of perception shows a deep understanding of the social character of perception. According to him, perception involves an act of categorization, that is, placing or giving an identity to an object, event or an idea. Such acts of categorization are usually "silent" or implicit: "we do not experience a going-from-no-identity to an arrival-at-identity, but (...) the first hallmark of *any* perception is some form of identity" (Bruner, 1957, p. 125).

Categorization, then, takes place against a system of categories, or, as Schütz would have put it, "typifications" built in the course of the life experience. This means that we cannot perceive something unless it somehow relates to what we already know. People reading the same texts see in them different ideas, depending, partly, on what they expect to see, and partly on what they are able to notice in terms of categories accessible to them. This explains why unfamiliar ideas take such a long time and so many repetitions to be observed. It also illustrates, in accordance with the postulates of hermeneutics, the initial requirement of translation: we cannot translate what is wholly unrecognizable.

When categories are all in place we focus attention on some, but not on others — why? Schütz' notion of "the purpose at hand" can be of use here. At any moment of our daily lives, we find ourselves in a "biographically determined" situation, that is "in a physical and socio-cultural environment as defined by him, within which he has his position, not merely his position in terms of physical space and outer time or of his status and role within the social system but also his moral and ideological position" (Schütz, 1973, p. 9). Any biographically determined situation includes specific possibilities of future action: this is what Schütz denotes as "the purpose at hand." And the purpose at hand selects "those elements among all the others contained in a situation which are relevant for this purpose"(Schütz, 1973, p. 9).

Thus the managers of prosperous organizations look for something that seems different and exciting; those in crisis look for salvation; those who are already engaged in a program of action look for something that can be used as a "guiding idea" (Czarniawska-Joerges, 1990). What is more, organizational units in modern corporations are constantly fitted, as it were, with a "purpose" (goals, visions, business idea) which, especially in good times, changes them from slow ant-eaters into veritable idea-vacuum-cleaners: they will inhale everything that fits the tube (Meyer, 1990b). If they see what they inhale as more of the same of what they already had, nothing happens; so many "changes" are just celebrations of status quo. But certain encounters with ideas actually lead to a reformulation of the purpose at hand (Rorty, 1991). This is why many practitioners consider evaluating of the results of change in terms of its goals as superfluous: more often than not, the main achievement of a change program is the reformulation of its initial goals.

In such a context, Bruner (1961) speaks of a *discovery*, following on the spoor of Vygotski, a Soviet psychologist and contemporary of Schütz. Discovery is not the act of finding out something which was previously unknown, but the act of obtaining knowledge for oneself by using one's own mind.

> Discovery, whether by a schoolboy doing it on its own or by a scientist cultivating the growing edge of his field, is in its essence a matter of re-arranging or transforming evidence so reassembled to additional new insights (Bruner, 1961, p. 22).

Similarly, Rorty speaks of "reweaving our web of beliefs," or "recontextualization" (1991), whereas Latour (1992a) of the change in the translator and in the translated. Thus a cognitive psychologist, a pragmatist philosopher and a sociologist of knowledge all agree in this account: we approach an idea in terms of what we already know, and sometimes the encounter barely confirms it; at other times, an idea re-arranges our beliefs and purposes as we translate it; the act of discovery creates a new idea and a new actor. This is the meaning of change on the phenomenological level (see also Margolis, 1987).

However, even if a person or a group make a discovery, there are still many other people who have to participate in the process if the idea is to materialize. How can they be persuaded to continue the chain of translations?

Social Context

An obvious place to start looking for answers is the context of organizational decision-making. Discussing this, we will do well by beginning with what is invisible: the influence of taken-for-granted political arrangements (call it structure if you must). Thus, gender studies for instance tell us that in group-meetings ideas coming from a woman usually have to be re-proposed by a man in order to be noticed. If they are noticed at the first utterance, they are often incorrectly attributed to some man present at the gathering.[3] Females who are tokens in all-male groups need external accounts for their ideas to gain influence (Taps and Martin, 1988). The same phenomenon can be observed in most gatherings where high-status people are asked their opinions more often, talk more, receive more positive comments and are more likely to influence the group's decisions (Smith-Lovin and Brody, 1989).

Such taken-for-granted political structures can be accompanied by taken-for-granted cultural ones. We use this term to cover what Bachrach and Baratz (1963) called "non-decisions" or "agenda setting." Certain issues will not appear on an agenda unless a serious disruption of taken-for-granted social reality takes place. A long experience within a certain type of cultural structure leads to cultural color-blindness. Thus managers are usually power-blind, men are gender-blind, and social scientists are ideology-blind.

But the fact that certain things are not consciously noticed does not mean that they are not pragmatically exploited. The greatest advantage of the taken-for-granted is, indeed, that it can be put to use without too much ado (Jansson, 1989). For example, when the issue of power and politics in academia comes into the focus of a discussion, academics tend to deny its relevance (with honorable exceptions such as Sederberg, 1984, or Agger, 1991). This, however, does not prevent them from acting in ways which invite political interpretations. Hendriks and Kalishoek (1987), for instance, described the decision-making on staff cut-backs at Dutch universities. A

---

3   Working and writing together, we lack no opportunity to collect illustrations of this phenomenon.

person or a group with an idea goes around and "anchors" it with potential allies. When the decision is formally taken, it only confirms what is already irreversible. But when a plan developed by one person or a small group is all of a sudden presented to a decision-making body, it will be sent back for elaboration or accepted but simply left unimplemented, no matter how ingenious it was. In other words, an idea might strike an individual like the legendary apple which supposedly struck Newton's head,[4] but not a group. One plants ideas into a group, one does not hit it with them.

The example also shows how one can create new structures through taken-for-granted processes. In the case of Dutch universities, the "lobbyists" did not, of course, try to anchor their ideas with those who would become potential victims of their plan. This weakened the latter's possibilities of fighting back and opposing the "decision" when it emerged. Similarly, Jansson (1989) described the way certain investment decisions are promoted through the skillful use of procedures which are taken-for-granted. Decision making seems to play a peculiar role in the materialization of ideas: it is mostly a legitimizing ritual. As Rorty puts it, "poetic, artistic, philosophical, scientific or political progress results from the accidental coincidence of a private obsession with a public need" (1989, p. 37), not from decisions made. Yet decision rituals need be performed, too.

Ideological Control

This is not to deny the role of intentional influence. We would like to emphasize the role of ideological control in this context, that is control which takes place by influencing ideologies held by organizational actors, shaping their ideas about what reality is like, how it should be and how to achieve the desired state (Czarniawska-Joerges, 1988). Teaching (directed learning) can be seen as one way of exerting such influence (other possible ways being public debate, straightforward offers of ideologies, rituals and so forth).

Bruner (1961) speaks of two teaching modes: *expository* and *hypothetical*. In the former mode, the relationship is unidirectional and all responsibility resides with the teacher. Truth is exposed to the "learner," whose only task is to assimilate it. In the hypothetical mode, the teacher and the learner go together through various "as if" states of affairs until the learner discovers the one that widens her or his understanding; it might or might not be a discovery already made by the teacher.

Ideological control in organizations tends to be of the expository kind: it is the authority of the "teacher-leader" and not the motivation of the "learner-follower" that gives weight to an idea. Ideas are noticed because

---

4   This is a good example of how a folktale explains the phenomenon of inspiration by help of reification: an idea must be a thing if it "strikes."

that is what the leadership wishes; there are also official translations. But the ideas noticed by leaders often fail to materialize in practice. In many cases, though, the two modes blend into each other: an idea may be "rediscovered" by shop-floor actors and can thus be materialized "spontaneously," that is, by a series of non-official translations. We claim that discovery, either spontaneous or guided by a skillful teacher, is always important for the materialization of ideas. Exposing people to ready-made ideas pre-empts translation and therefore does not create the mobilization needed for action.

Another use of ideological control is the adoption of an idea already well entrenched, after the action has been carried out. Ideas are often appropriated and disowned. At the persuasion stage, it is convenient to present ideas as impersonally derived, from God, destiny or the *Zeitgeist* (on the assumption that ideas are greater than people.) When an idea has caught on, those with control aspirations try to appropriate it for control purposes, or, in the event of failure, to get rid of it by attributing it to somebody else, as is often the case in unsuccessful technology transfers.

Thus an event which takes place in a given time, is in fact related to many similar events happening more or less simultaneously in other places, although the actors need not be conscious of it all the time. In fact, as Meyer points out, an excess of consciousness and reflection prevents the easy adoption of ideas and builds up a resistance to ideological control (Meyer, 1990). This may be why Beckman's (1987) interlocutors insisted on their disconnectedness, their independent discovery, as described in section "Public administration reform." But nobody can deny at least one connection, the one created by mass media.

Public Attention

Organizational actors are forced to pay attention to issues which arise not only in the marketplace but also in society at large. Politics is the proper arena for this, but the voices of modern politics would not be heard without amplifiers: politicians together with the mass-media construct the problems which demand attention. There seems to be a limit, however, to the number of issues people notice and react to, regardless of their acuity. As Edelman notes, "[t]he logic that explains official, public and media attention to political problems does not turn on their severity but rather upon their dramatic appeals." And these appeals, in turn, "are vulnerable to satiation of attention and to novelty" (Edelman, 1988, p. 28). Similarly, Downs (1972) claimed that public reaction to problems is subject to "issue-attention cycles" where problems suddenly leap into prominence, remain in the center of attention for a short time, and then gradually fade from it. News is a form of entertainment competing with other types of entertainment — especially in the U.S.A., but also in other western countries. Because of this, a problem must be dramatic and exciting in order to maintain public interest, that is, to survive in the translocal time/space.

As long as a problem is in the focus of attention, all the ideas which can be related to it have a greater chance of being realized. All already existing actions that can be represented as coupled to it have a greater chance of being legitimized.

> Little wonder, then, that interest groups try to shape the content and the form of television and printed news, for to create a world dominated by a particular set of problems is at the same time to create support for specific courses of action (Edelman, 1988, p. 29).

The same reasoning can be transferred to the domain of organizational fashion, discussed later, where mass-media play an analogous role. It is thus time that we tried to conceptualize the ways in which ideas are made ready for travel.

Selected Ideas Translated into Objects

Ideas that have been selected and entered the chain of translations acquire almost physical, objective attributes; in other words, they become quasi-objects, and then objects.

The simplest way of objectifying ideas is turning them into linguistic artifacts by a repetitive use in an unchanged form, as in the case of *labels, metaphors, platitudes* (Czarniawska-Joerges and Joerges, 1990). This is an attempt at a reproduction, a mechanical translation, intended to minimize displacement effects. Local labeling, for instance, is especially important in cases where ideas must be fitted into already existing action patterns, as it reflects the broader, societal categorizing. A river valley program fits any river (which has a valley), decentralization can be almost any change in organizational structure, but by labeling actions in such ways, desired associations are created to master-ideas (see below) such as modernity and community help in the former case, democracy and autonomy in the latter. Words are turned into labels by frequent repetition in an unquestioning mode in similar contexts, so that a possible "decentralization, why?" will give way to "decentralization, of course!" and therefore decentralization will become what we happen to be doing in our organization. Even intellectual progress, that is, the development of ideas in itself, depends on the literalization of certain metaphors, so that new ones are needed (Rorty, 1989). The most successful labels turn into institutional categories themselves.

Another way of turning ideas into things is design; putting images into a graphic form. Adrian Forty's book *Objects of Desire* (1986) develops this theme on various levels, but we shall take just one example out of his many. *Lucky Strike,* the ultra-American cigarette, originally had a packet showing the Lucky Strike sign against a green background, it had a different back of the packet and the word "cigarettes" in liberty-style lettering. Raymond Loewy redesigned it giving it a white background, repeated the pattern on the back and modernized the lettering. The designer later suggested that by introducing "the impeccable whiteness," he had managed to influence the way people thought of cigarettes ("Freshness of content and immaculate manufacturing").

Forty offers another interpretation, emphasizing the fact that the redesign took place in the 1940s, when cigarettes were not yet thought health-damaging. He suggests two distinct factors as lying behind the enormous success of the packet "within a particular society at a particular point in history," namely, first, the "ideas of cleanliness and Americanness signified by the design belonged in the minds of all Americans and cannot in any way be said to have been an innovation of the designer," and secondly, "the way in which an association between ideas of whiteness, cleanliness and America was set up by the means of a single image." This latter image can be said to have been the creation of the designers, and Forty pays appropriate tribute to Loewy and his office: they certainly deserve credit for their skill in devising a form that conveyed the association so effectively. "No design works unless it embodies ideas that are held in common by the people for whom the object is intended" (Forty, 1986, p. 245).

We linger on this example because it depicts a literal process of the materialization of an idea, revealing the complexity of the whole process, the mixture of chance, social mood and intention. Beyond this, we see that even after having become an object, the idea did not become entirely "objective" and unambiguous, as the difference of interpretations by Loewy and Forty indicates.

Ideas are *communicated images,* intersubjective creations, and therefore a "property" of a community rather than of a single person (although individuals tend to appropriate ideas and the narratives attribute them to heroes). It has been suggested that in place of the traditional image of subsequent generations standing "on the shoulders of giants," it is the giants who are standing "on a pyramid of midgets" (Merton, 1985). Their collective character makes it possible to conceive of them as of things; everything that can be "seen" by more than one person acquires "objectivity"; this miracle of shared perception is in fact due to the already mentioned process of categorization according to the legitimate categories of a given time/space (Douglas, 1986; Meyer, 1990). The simultaneous collective and material character of ideas is especially interesting: we recognize an idea as "the same" or "different" because our social categorization tells us what to see, but at the same time we create a physical body to incorporate the idea, so that we know what to put into categories.

An Idea Travels

We can now depict a chain of translations, which gets speeded up as the ideas become more and more object-like and can be carried by modern transportation/communication technologies. And we shall try to say something more about travels: where from and where to?

Fashion Revisited

In a classic article, Blumer (1969) postulated that fashion is a *competition mechanism* which influences the market and distorts the demand and supply curves, both using and serving the economic competition. Its important element is a collective choice among tastes, things, ideas; it is oriented towards finding but also towards creating what is typical of a given time. We tend to agree with Blumer in basic views, but want to add that fashion, together with a free market, operates at institutional fringes. On the one hand, its variety is limited by the "iron cage" of existing institutions, which fashion actually reproduces; on the other, fashion is engaged in a constant subversion of the existing institutional order, gnawing ant-like at its bars. This is the first paradox connected to fashion: its simultaneous unimportance and saliency.

The translation mechanism helps to understand the second paradox: fashion is created while it is followed. It is the subsequent translations which at the same time produce variations in fashion and reproduce it. Hence the third paradox: fashion followers act differently due to the attempt to act in the same way. But what makes people follow fashions?

Fashion is the expression of what is *modern,* of what the community to which one belongs recently chose as the most valuable or exciting. It is worth adding that "belonging" ceased to be determined by birth and even by a permanent location. In globalized worlds, where people mass commute to work or to marriage between Tokyo and San Francisco, the notion of "community" acquires a new ring (Gergen, 1991).

For people in high organizational positions who perceive their mission as being that of bringing progress to organizations, to follow what is modern feels often like a duty (Forssell, 1989). However, this obligation is only part of their mission. Their duty is, equally, to protect organizations from what might be just a passing fad. One of their tasks is therefore to keep a distance to "mere" fashion. As Sellerberg observes, one might say that fashion's double nature − distance and interest − together constitute self-awareness.

> Those who stay at fashion's frontlines and participate in fashion's competitions must, naturally, be especially self-aware. This concerns also some companies. They invest in the current image, a profile matching the times (Sellerberg, 1987, p. 66, translation BC).

Following fashion can thus be, in a private enterprise, a way of keeping abreast of the competition, and in public administration a way of keeping up with the times in the interest of the people by being in the forefront of novelty. But one other aspect must be emphasized as well. Fashion, as a collective translation process, also functions as a release from the responsibility of individual choice (Sellerberg, 1987). To follow fashion is to be conformist *and* creative. In this sense fashion (like translation) stands for change, as opposed to tradition (literal imitation). But, as fashion is also repetitive, in a long range perspective it stands for tradition, too. Tarde, the classic imitation analyst, contrasted the control of the "timeless society" with the control of "times we live in," a time-collective, as Sellerberg (1987) interprets it.

An interesting observation made in one of the early fashion studies was that fashion is not related to progress. According to Agnes Brook Young, fashion is evolution without destination.

> The world generally considers that progress in material things consists in changes that make them more useful, or better looking, or less expensive. In the long run fashion never attains these objectives. Fashion is a slow, continuous change, unhampered by the restrictions of either aesthetics or practicality (1937/1973, p. 109).

We would claim, then, that the concept of fashion concerns ways of changing, as an alternative to the notion of progress, and that it is descriptive rather than normative in character. Agnes Brook Young's observation makes the paradoxical character of change more obvious: fashion operates through dramatized "revolutions," but "... in a real sense, fashion is evolution..."

Fashion, then, transpires as a highly paradoxical process. Its constitutive paradoxes: creation *and* imitation, variation *and* uniformity, distance *and* interest, novelty *and* conservatism, unity *and* segregation, conformity *and* deviation, change *and* status quo, revolution *and* evolution are only variations on the basic duality of communal life: the collective construction of individuality *and* the individual construction of collectivity. Separately, the two processes are often tackled, even within organization theory. But as a whole, understanding the process of social construction in the Berger and Luckmann's (1966) perspective remains largely a theoretical claim. And yet it lies at the very heart of organizational life and action.

In organizational context the most important is that fashion (together with other processes like control or negotiation) introduces order and uniformity into what might seem an overwhelming variety of possibilities. In this sense fashion helps to come to grips with the present. At the same time, it "serves to detach the grip of the past in the moving world. By placing a premium on being in the mode and derogating what developments have left behind, it frees actions for new movement" (Blumer, 1969, p. 339). It also introduces some appearance of order and predictability into preparations for what is necessarily disorderly and uncertain: the future. Fashion, in its gradual emergence, eases up the surprises of the next fashion, tunes in the collective by making it known to itself, as reflected in the present fashion and in the rejection of past fashions.

Between Fashions and Institutions: Master-Ideas

Individuals cannot create fashion, but they may try to influence it, and often successfully. Obviously, there are such fashion leaders, or market leaders in the organizational world as well. The study of municipal reforms revealed leading local governments who were accustomed to being first with any change in the local authority system. Hinings and Greenwood (1988) observed the same phenomenon in the British public sector. The leading local authorities popularized their translations via the Association of Local Authorities (the same in Sweden), by professional associations, and by the transfer of personnel through a career-system. DiMaggio and Powell (1983) speak, in this context, of "central organizations."

It is interesting that there seem to be "idea-bearing" organizations and professional roles which deal mainly with translations. This is, to an increasing extent, the role of professional consultants. Like traveling salesmen, they arrive at organizations and open their attaché-cases full of quasi-objects to be translated into localized ideas (Czarniawska-Joerges, 1990). Often they bring in the whole equipment needed for the materialization of an idea, but almost always they spill some extra ideas which might then materialize through some local translation − or might not. They are designers and distributors, wholesalers and retailers in ideas-turned-into-things, which then locally once more can be turned into ideas-to-be-enacted.

How do they know what to market? The final say in the selection of ideas, even for fashion, is often given to the *Zeitgeist* who, like all the holy spirits, has the double virtue of being invisible and all-encompassing. We shall, however, try to be a bit more specific and speak instead about legitimating narratives, such as metanarratives of modernity (emancipation and progress, Lyotard, 1987). Although they need not be evoked in their entirety, they give rise to a multitude of master-ideas, blueprints, paradigms which dominate a given period (with many other present, waiting for their turn). Therefore we agreed with Forty (1986) when he argued that, in a sense, an idea cannot catch on unless it already exists for some time in many people's minds, as a part of a master-idea in a translocal space/time.

Master-ideas serve as focus for fashions and build a bridge between the passing fashion and a lasting institution. Where does a new set of master-ideas come from? It seems that it comes from the narratives of the past (MacIntyre, 1981), which are translated into the present set of concepts, and are projected into the future, often in opposition to the present. Is not postmodernism building on the sophists and on Nietzsche? It is not that their ideas were non-existent during all that time; but all the texts which are now industriously studied were meaningless to most social scientists, dedicated for so many years to what is now sweepingly called "positivism." Positivism, in its turn, came as a reaction to a certain kind of metaphysics, and so forth. What is important to understand is the sequential, step-by-step character of para-digm-forming and paradigm-dissolution. Kuhnian "paradigm-revolutions" are rather non-revolutionary (although in personal discovery they might in-cense the neophyte). As Rorty observes, "Europe did not *decide* to accept the idiom of Romantic poetry, or of socialist politics, or of Galilean mechanics." In his view, this sort of shift occurs neither through acts of will nor through arguments. "Rather, Europe gradually lost the habit of using certain words and gradually acquired the habit of using others" (1989, p. 6).

There is a loop-like relationship between the ideas of the past and of the present; between metanarratives and master-ideas; between the mainstream and the fringe. A paradigm is a product and a producer; and probably never more influential than at its end, when its master ideas enter the glob-alized time/space and therefore their capacity of endowing local events with unique meaning is exhausted. Hirschman (1977) pointed out that this phe-nomenon is well known in intellectual history, exemplifying his point with the acceptance of the concept of "interest." Once the notion of interest acquired paradigmatic status, most of human action was explained by self-interest, and nobody bothered to define the notion with any precision. The power of master-ideas resides in the fact that they are taken for granted, unproblematic and used for all possible purposes. At the beginning of the rule of a paradigm, it is its power to excite, to mobilize and to energize that is most noticeable; toward the end, it is its unquestionability, obviousness and taken-for-granted explanatory power.

Although our story is about change and therefore about ideas which succeed[5], it is worth mentioning here that a ruling paradigm has a deadly power to reject ideas which are perceived as challenging it. In their study of urban reform, Warren et al. (1974) described how what they called "an institutionalized thought structure" repelled any idea suggesting an innova-tion in the paradigm itself, even within a massive program of innovation. To understand how this is possible, we need to introduce the notion of organization fields.

Institutionalization

Not all organizational ideas which are in fashion at a given time are tried out by all organizations in a given space-frame; fashion has its niches, merchants of meaning cultivate their specialties. Yet organizations form

---

5   See Røvik, Spybey and Rottenburg in this volume for negative examples.

time- and space-collectives, acquiring more or less similar practices. Fashion always operates against a background of seeming stability and unchangeability. The war of skirt-lengths presupposes the global practice of wearing skirts.

How do such collectives arise and delineate their boundaries? A useful concept here is that of the *structuration of organization fields* (Giddens, 1979; DiMaggio and Powell, 1983). Four elements constitute the process: an increase in interactions among organizations in a given field; the emergence of interorganizational structures of domination and coalition patterns; obligatory (and increasing) information exchange between the organizations of the field; and the development of a "field consciousness" − an awareness among participants that they belong together (DiMaggio and Powell, 1983). Structuration may come as a consequence of economic competition, the influence of the state (or some other political authority), and the pressures cutting across professional networks. Once a field has been structured, forces arise which prompt the organizations in the field to become more alike. DiMaggio and Powell speak of *coercive isomorphism* (organizations are forced or encouraged to be alike by actors from outside the field), *mimetic isomorphism* (organizations imitate one another when faced with uncertainty) and *normative isomorphism,* related to professionalization.

One wonders, however, whether the implicit determinism of a concept such as "field forces" is at all necessary. After all, actors might want to segregate their organizations from those outside the field, and will call it "coercion" in an act of self-justification; and to link themselves with those inside the field (uncertainty is a human condition, too unspecified to serve as an explanation). Seen this way, the first two "forces of the field" are not extraneous to the actors and recall the functions of fashion described by Simmel (1973): to unify a community by conforming to what is accepted and to separate by differentiating from all others.

The third "force," normative isomorphism, on the other hand, can be seen as a kind of mimesis itself, operating within different but partly overlapping fields (organizations versus professions), or else, and more truly following DiMaggio and Powell's intention, as a conscious imitation based on value choice (this interpretation, however, collapses the difference between mimetic and normative isomorphisms).

From our point of view, a time-and-space collective constantly selects and de-selects among a common repertoire of ideas plans for action, and the ideas repetitively selected acquire *institutional status.* Fashions bring in a variety of ideas; organizations within a field try them out, creating fashion by following it, but also creating institutions by persevering in certain practices, by refusing to reject previous fashions, or by hailing a new fashion as the final solution. Generally, one might say that what remains unaffected, after one fashion has changed into another, acquires the status of institutionalized action, the more so the longer it survives. One aspect of this is an increased attractiveness at the local level. Local actions conforming to existing institutions gain in what is the gain of institutions: the economy of effort, stability, order and control, the source of identity for individuals and groups (Berger and Luckmann, 1966; Douglas, 1986).

Presented like this, institutions seem to be just the opposite of fashion. How can one claim that institutions arise from fashion, and that the two mechanisms are complementary? It might be easier to accept if we scrutinize the other side of institutionalization. The economy of effort provided by institutionalization creates room for new ideas, which will eventually upset old institutions; a strong identity provides a basis for innovative experiments and social control creates, among other effects, social unrest and disorder. Creativity grows out of routine. Rationality breeds irrationality.

So we claim that fashions give birth to institutions and institutions make room for other fashions. The meaning of both forms of change is equally vexing: a new local action means, of course, a change in practices existing in a given place and moment, even if it recreates an old institution at another time, elsewhere. What was imitative for Beckman (1987), was new and original to his respondents. But as the re-creation process was idea-mediated and then transplanted onto different material ground, the institution was indeed new − even when compared with its original. On the other hand, when an idea legitimizes an already existing practice, this is possible precisely because the idea already has the status of an institution carrier and therefore is expected to transfer this status to existing actions. Such processes, described here from the local perspective of organizational collectives, can be seen, then, from the translocal view, if such is possible, as resulting in institutional isomorphisms within the organization field.

An Idea Is Enacted

We began our story in local time/space − an idea is objectified at a given place and moment − and then followed it through different moments and places into a global time/space, speculating about the means by which it travels. Now we come again to a local time/space: an idea has been objectified, has traveled, and has arrived at a new place ready to be translated into action. The journey approaches completion (before the idea will get on its way again) and we shall now watch the next stage of the story.

Ideas onto Actions

Many actions take place because they form a routine and nobody really remembers what their meaning originally was. Some were initially undertaken for ambiguous reasons and need to be legitimized by having commonly accepted motives ascribed to them. Others are expressions of an energy overload on the part of certain actors ("let's do something!") and, again, require ongoing legitimation. All can acquire respectable meanings by being successfully related to fashionable ideas. The institution of "culture city" gave many a European city a required lift. Giving a name to what is already being done is a major step in history-making: now we know what we have been doing all along and we will be able to tell the story. In the present, we "muddle through" hardly seeing the light, but we shall be able to acquire the appropriate distance, and a searchlight, once we discover an idea that suits our endeavors. Matching ideas to actions will change both, but this is a part of translation process.

A process of idea-materialization clearly operates in structuring future events and present happenings, as studies of large projects show (Sahlin-Andersson, 1989; Spetz, 1988). There seems to be a magic attraction to big projects, used as umbrellas for many actions already in existence, giving meaning and legitimacy to those about to begin, and providing a space for plans, dreams and designs. Big projects are in search for big ideas: Sahlin-Andersson's scrutiny of many such projects reveals a quantitative orientation of the search: with some exaggeration, it can be said that it does not seem to matter so much what the idea is, it is the scale that matters. Thus large buildings are more appreciated than small buildings, big research projects better looked at by foundations than small projects, and long range plans appear as more serious than the short term ones. Big is beautiful here.

The same idea can be used in both ways: either to give a name to past and present action or to initiate a new set of actions. In Gherardi and Strati's (1988) example of introducing Computer Aided Design in two engineering companies, one company interpreted the concepts as one step in a long, ongoing process of replacing of manned by automated technology while the other chose to see it as a beginning of a change towards a new way of working. This example shows once again that neither the attributes of the idea nor those of the action are decisive for the way the two will be matched − the match is a result and not the cause of the translation process.

Ideas into Actions

How can ideas be put into action at all? Obviously, to be put into action an idea must be supplied with an *image of action,* a verbal of graphic picture of possible action. Ideas that were for centuries considered unrealizable slowly acquire an action-image resulting from the changes in other ideas and in things (technology). But an image of action is not yet an action, a design for a machine is not yet a machine, and stage-set instructions are not yet a stage. How are they materialized?

Not by decision as an act of choice, as Brunsson (1985) observes with insight: competing ideas paralyze action. Hamlet puts himself in a hopeless situation with his ill-formulated question. Rather, it is a decision as an act of will, prompted by positive expectations concerning the process itself ("let's be!"), its results, or both. Indeed, the positive emotions concerning cognitive and material aspects of action must be taken for granted − why else should an idea be put into action at all? It must invoke an exciting, promising or aesthetically pleasing feeling. The cognitive process, prompted by acts of will, moves then towards calibrating "images of action" into something more like detailed "plans of action" (Miller et al., 1960) and then into deeds. "In places, all ready, run!" And they run. This magic moment when words become deeds is the one that truly deserves to be called materialization, whether performed mostly by human actors or mostly by material artifacts.

Sooner or later, a river valley project has to encounter the concrete river, the specific valley, the given groups of people and interests, the available machines and resources. Inevitably, it will turn into something different than expected and than planned, as the planners of Warsaw metro can well see 50 years after their plans were conceived. Our present research project, on city management, shows that even constructing a metro system, acquiring the equipment and running it, does not end the chain of translation. Discussions continue: is this the same metro as planned in the 1940s or a completely different one? Is it the same city which needed the metro? Is a metro an appropriate solution for the city transportation problems in the 21st century? If not, why metro? We heard a young journalist proposing a system of zeppelins flying over the city − a daringly new idea or an old, discredited one? The tangible fit between a tunnel in the ground, a technology and a city is no less socially constructed than the political and cultural "matches" discussed so far; it is simply − and surprisingly − even less discussed in the context of organizational studies. And this is a drawback, because even if it is just one moment-place through which an idea must pass, it is a crucial one in producing change. Soon the new object will provoke new ideas or a resurgence of old. Most ideas always float in between time/spaces; it is their repetitive touch downs in local places/moments which make the difference. The idea of space travel is as old as humanity, but compare Icarus' chariot with the Apollo or Mir spaceships. Ideas into objects, and then into actions, and then into ideas again...

Some Complications Introduced...

At this juncture one could rightfully point out that we make the process sound only too easy: an idea arrives in an objectified form, lands on the ground only to be readily translated into an action, even an institution. An essay like this one is of course always a simplification. Nevertheless at least two complications can be usefully introduced: that it takes a lot of ideas to accomplish even a simple action, and that ideas tend to produce counter-ideas, which then travel along through time and space.

Take an example familiar to every schoolchild: trains as transportation medium, conventionally traced from the epochal discovery of the English engineer Stephenson in 1829. Any schoolchild ambitious enough to consult *Encyclopedia Britannica* (1989), however, will soon discover that we are speaking about at least three ideas, each of them encompassing hosts of smaller ideas, going back in time, most likely, all the way to the caves, as the three following quotes illustrate:

> *Railroads* were first constructed in European mines in the 16th century, one of the earliest being that used in the mines at Leberthal, Alsace, in about 1550. Mining railroads in England date from about 1603 or 1604.(...)

> The earliest mining railroad cars were pulled by men or horses, and it was not until the first steam locomotive appeared in 1804 in Wales that the modern railroad emerged. Early locomotives were handicapped by the weakness of iron rails and the inefficiency and unreliability of their apparatus, but improvements in track materials and design and the technical advances made by such engineers as George Stephenson soon made railroads practical. The Stockton and Darlington Railway, which began operations in September 1825, was the first to carry both freight and passengers. It was followed by the Liverpool and Manchester railway in 1830, which, with the introduction of Stephenson's locomotive "Rocket," can be considered the beginning of the railroad era. By 1841 there were more than 1,300 miles of track in Britain.

> Railroads grew quickly in the 19th century, becoming a major force in the economic and social life of nations throughout the world. (...) Railroads reached their maturity in the early 20th century, as trains carried the bulk of land freight and passenger traffic in the industrialized countries of the world. By the mid-20th century, however, they had lost their preeminent position. The private automobile had replaced the railroad for short passenger trips, while the airplane had usurped it for long-distance travel...

> *The Watt engine.* While repairing a model Newcomen steam engine in 1764 Watt was impressed by its waste of steam. In May 1765, after wrestling with the problem of improving it, he suddenly came upon a solution − the separate condenser, his first and greatest invention. Watt had realized that the loss of latent heat (the heat involved in changing the state of a substance, *e. g.* solid or liquid) was the worst defect of the Newcomen engine and that therefore condensation must be effected in a chamber distinct from the cylinder but connected to it. Shortly afterward, he met John Roebuck, the founder of the Carron Works, who urged him to make an engine. He entered into partnership with him in 1768, after having made a small test engine with the help of loans from Joseph Black. The following year Watt took out the famous patent for "A New Invented Method of Lessening the Consumption of Steam and Fuel in Fire Engines."

Locomotive, any of various self-propelled vehicles used for hauling railroad cars on tracks... The first locomotive to do actual work, the "New Castle" built in 1803 by Richard Trevithick for a Welsh tramroad, was too heavy for the iron rails of the time. The first practical locomotive was built in 1812 by John Blenkisop, an inspector at the Middleton colliery near Leeds, Eng. Two vertical cylinders drove two shafts that in turn were geared to a toothed wheel that meshed with a rack rail.

By 1829 the English engineer George Stephenson had developed a locomotive, "the Rocket," that was a prototype for the modern steam locomotive. (...) In the United States John Stevens ran the first locomotive in 1825 on a three-rail track, the center rail engaging a toothed wheel on the engine.

These are, as we said, just examples of how many interrelated ideas went into the idea which we recognize as "locomotion by steam engine." This multiple idea produced in turn a whole batch of counter-ideas, like in the following excerpt from an expertise produced by *Königlich Bayrisches Obermedizinalkollegium* in 1835:[6]

> Locomotion with the help of any kind of steam engines should, in the interest of public health, be prohibited. The rapid movements cannot fail to produce in the passengers mental unrest, i. e. "delirium furiosum." Even conceded that travelers voluntarily undergo this danger, the state must at least protect the onlookers, since the view of a locomotive, which races along in full speed, suffices to elicit this terrible sickness, It is therefore paramount that on both sides of the rails a fence is raised of at least six feet height.

The steam locomotive and its true or imaginary dangers seem to belong to the past. But ideas do no cease to travel and, in spite of *Britannica*'s authoritative opinion that "railroads ... by the mid-20th century... had lost their preeminent position," they are back with us, now as an idea of the speed train. A collection of ideas encompassing this particular set would surpass by far the confines of this essay. Readers may rest assured, however, that the counter-ideas travel along:

> The Transrapid and other high-speed trains doing 500 km/h or more undoubtedly are high-risk technologies. Not only in terms of landscape and energy consumption – these features they share with conventional technologies. New is their unprecedented impact on the well-being of living nature, both human and non-human, both passengers and spectators. The cost of controlling environmental threats of these new technologies, in particular the extreme noise levels that must be expected, almost certainly cancels out the benefits promised by the industry promoting them.

---

6   The following two quotes are excerpted from Joerges (1994) where they are put to a somewhat different purpose.

The cost-benefit-speak replaced "delirium furiosum," but otherwise it is easy to recognize the same idea, down to a fence ... or is it completely different? As the spiral of translation continues, it is time for us to conclude our essay.

An Idea Whose Time/Space Has Come

> Greater than the tread of mighty armies is an idea whose time has come (Victor Hugo, quoted in Kingdon, 1984, p. 1).

In our terms, Victor Hugo spoke of an idea whose time/space has come through many interconnected chains of translation. On its trajectory from an idea to an object, to an institution, to an action and to an idea again, ideas go through many transformations and necessary passage points in the course of subsequent translations.

We started our narrative with ideas that take root in local knowledge (sometimes just in one head). As more and more people are persuaded to translate the idea for their own use, it can be materialized into a collective action. In order to become public knowledge, though, an idea must become objectified, made into a quasi-object: only then can it travel between local places and moments so as to move into translocal (global, collective-historical) time/spaces.

This process can be bolstered by willing political agents, but it is also shaped by contingent events and little controlled processes such as fashion. The actors involved, however, rarely see more than one or two stages of the entire process, framed as they are by the fictions created in local time/space. Thus in a given municipality, regional authority, city or government agency, some group of people "discover" an idea: having submunicipal committees, or a laboratory (R&D units), a metro or a steam engine as a means of locomotion, or a river valley project. The idea may appear new, sometimes shocking, even revolutionary.

The idea is then enacted: other people are persuaded to join in, decisions are formally made, municipalities divided into subparts, laboratories called to life, prototypes built and shown, licenses bought and applied. In order to solidify, to legitimize the idea-become-material, signals are sent to the wider community: dramatizing, justifying, marketing, selling, propagating. An idea, locally translated into action, is reified into a quasi-object that can travel: a book, a picture, a design, for purposes of non-local communication, recognizable in terms of a translocal frame of reference.

All these signals contribute to the creation of a wave, a fashion, which sometimes survives subsequent fashions and turns into an institution: public administration reforms, the TVA developmental model, or the trains. Such sedimented institutional patterns enable the next municipality, next region, next city, next country to notice easily idea-objects that have passed the tests of local action. Institutions are exchange networks through which properly packaged and blackboxed representations of ideas onto/into action are passed on constantly.

The limits of local vision obscure the fact that, if ideas are to be translated onto/into a local action, all of this must already have happened. Global time/space operates spirally, and those stretches of local time/space which did not enter the spiral are replete with ideas whose time has not come. They are asynchronic. In the local parlance they are experienced, very appropriately, as a "waste of time."

The Swedish municipal reform, for instance, "caught on" to the degree it did because there were earlier decentralization episodes in the translocal history of municipalities, a new municipal law and a preceding public debate: it was "fashionable." Reform partly failed because the transition into institutionalization was not achieved (had been prevented by a legislatory body). Or take the difference of interpretations between Beckman (1987) and the actors in regional units. This too was a difference in time perspectives. Typically, researchers aim at reconstructing unfolding events in translocal time and space whereas the actors, naturally, are bound to their local place and time as their frame of reference.

Ideas and Change

The time has come to end the story-telling and come to a point, which in our genre comes usually in a form of a summarizing metaphor. Here is ours: words substituted by a picture (Figure 2).

Figure 2, created by a combination of ours and Macintosh's drawing skills, is animated by an ambition to keep the theoretical cake and to eat it, too; to point out the illusionary character of "choices" within dichotomies of modernism. Dichotomies are logical devices meant to de-paradoxify: they apportion in two what is known as a whole. Although many such apportioning can be made with great success, the ensuing privileging of the one part at the expense of the other raises our doubts. It cannot be done without paying a price, which has to be paid in anticipation of action; a manager is expected to make up her mind whether to introduce a planned change or to wait for automatic adaptations to take place. No such decision is necessary in research, dedicated as it is to reflection. Therefore we propose to combine what is usually kept disjointed.

Contingency and Control

Does the image of organizational change as resulting from travels of ideas reconstruct change as a contingent process or the result of control processes? Both.

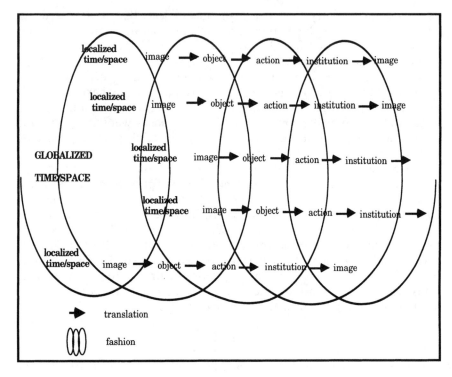

Figure 2

In the first place, planned organizational change, which is an attempt at controlled production of desired results, does not have to concern only the ideas which are the bestsellers on the translation lists. In most of our examples, organizational change happened as a result of some peripheral idea acquiring substance as a side-effect. In the case of Swedish municipalities, the leading idea was to decentralize political power, in the case of the Swedish regional boards, the idea was to experiment with new forms of industrial policy, in the case of TVA-like projects the ideas were many, ranging from political to technological to social, and in the case of the Watt engine the main idea was, allegedly, to prevent the waste of steam. Many of the translators may never have thought of contingent organizational changes (at least if one listens to what the rank-and-file employees have to say afterwards). Each attempt at a "planned change," however, might have inadvertently provoked (caused, pulled, pushed, driven, occasioned) a string of changes: restructuring, introduction of new structures, reshuffling of responsibilities, and so on. In relation to planned change, idea-materialization processes are like avalanches compared to a stone thrown on the ground.

This leads to many surprises in situations where a seemingly new idea is adopted as a label for an already existing practice, the intention being precisely to maintain the status quo. But the result usually encompasses much more change and innovation than was desired. Materialization of ideas can be also spontaneous or random. The concept of translation is useful to the extent that it captures the coupling between arising contingencies and attempted control, created by actors in search for meaning.

This reasoning can be as well reversed. Actually, we show change as adaptation to the institutional requirements of the environment. But such an adaptation is far from unconscious or passive: it activates the intentional processes of the creation of meaning. Presenting those processes in a translocal view as populations in motion has a certain metaphorical value, but offers insights of a very little pragmatic value. Any intentional action originates on the phenomenological level and all pragmatic knowledge must concentrate on how individual action become collectivized and the other way around. Describing actions of collectives and individuals as separate realms is as futile as the common wish to build bridges between them afterwards. The picture we want to convey is not dualistic: it is an image of how contingency is made meaningful (sometimes downright functional) by interpretation.

Explanations and Interpretations

The mixture of intentional and contingent effects that ultimately shapes change in any and all organizations vexes many, if not all, students of organizations. Usually, an analyst chooses one of two paths to follow: the "positive" one of looking for "objective" explanations which should eventually lead to formulation of "universal laws," or the "hermeneutic" one of looking for "subjective" interpretations which will end with the celebration of the particular and the unique. We do not want to follow either road.

Instead, we shall follow a route, marked by many others before us, where narrative knowledge, this mainstay of everyday life, freely mixes explanations with interpretations, opening causality to negotiation (Bruner, 1990). Planning to act at a distance requires the objectification of the target in order to produce strong explanations. Being acted upon elicits interpretations in terms of intentions of those who are acting upon you. Acting upon the world, we expect to change it objectively, but the knowledge about both methods and results of change will always remain enclosed in language. The crucial point is the choice of vocabulary, and here we opt to be disloyal to the ideal of science in which we have been schooled because we find blurred genres (Geertz, 1980) more receptive to grasping the complexity of organizational life.

Where is the place of the present attempt of blurring narrative and logo-scientific genres in the processes we describe? Do our ideas stand any chance of going translocal? Reflexivity of the kind we endorse has become fashionable, but not institutionalized in social research. Our organization field turns ideas into publications which count as materialization. Will our ideas become translated into others' publications? Will these be translated into other quasi-objects that can travel into other organization fields, for example outside the academia?

We have tried to cast a logo-scientifically phrased issue in the narrative form. This is, in a sense, the opposite of what structuralists and formalists theorists are after. In fact it is very much what the transition from school to life, say from Business School to a management, requires; thus there might already exist a need for stories like ours. But as the results of the translation process cannot be deduced from the idea itself, we will wait and see what happens next. The intentional part ends here.

Organizational Imitation in Identity Transformation

Guje Sevón

Western society applauds its winners. It is a competitive civilization in which the successful nation-states, firms and individuals are praised. Mary Douglas (1986) compares this society to a hierarchy that celebrates its patriarch, and the sect which commemorates its martyrs. Not only do Western people and organizations praise their heroes, they imitate them. The great popularity of books describing successful firms (see for example Peters and Waterman, 1982) is one indication of this trend. Firms imitate seemingly successful business strategies (going international), policies (applying strategic human resource management), organizational structure (divisionalizing organizations), technologies (adopting best practices, just-in-time-management), preferences (focusing on ecological management), and products. Products now routinely counterfeited include chemicals, computers, drugs, fertilizers, pesticides, medical devices, military hardware, and food, as well as parts for airplanes and automobiles. It is estimated that up to $600 billion in annual world trade is in fakes (*International Business Week*, December 16, 1985).

The intent of this essay is to introduce and develop the notion of organizational imitation. The objective is to define and discuss imitation in such a way that multiple research questions become visible. A main argument is that organizations are socially transformed in a process of imitation. Organizations are defined as social constructions; they are sets of collective action. For the discussion it is however useful to metaphorically describe an organization as a legal person an actor in the modern institutional order. This actor will be seen as a superperson, borrowing the argument from Czarniawska-Joerges (1994) that organizations are often metaphorically seen and taken for granted as superpersons: decision makers, leaders, and sometimes management groups or collectives. Here, an organization will be treated as an actor which is capable of cognitive action (although the actor not necessarily reflects upon its own capability): to attend to the environment, to make comparisons and judgments, to reason about causality and to act according to desires. An actor (in this essay exemplified by a corporate organization, a work unit, and a nation-state) is also able to conceive of itself and others as having identities. Based on the assumption that imitation is principally described as action by organizations as superpersons, literature on human actors will be referred to along with literature on organizations as actors.

Ostensive and Performative Definitions of Imitation

Imitation can be defined and understood in different ways. Imitation in most current literature is seen as an equivalent term to copying, namely reproducing or transcribing an original product. This literature puts stress on the effort which goes into finding a good model to imitate. The remaining process becomes a mechanical adaptation; one simply imitates (see the discussion below about literature on diffusion of innovations).

Imitation, especially if it is seen as a product that is a copy of an original, has been and still is a frequent object of study, especially when the original is seen as an innovation. In many of these studies, the focus has been on the spread of innovations where imitation has been treated as a cause of diffusion, as the mechanism that facilitates a diffusion of a certain object or idea. Borrowing Latour's (1986) classification of definitions, this research tradition has applied an ostensive definition of imitation. It implies that what is to be imitated is seen as a *given* phenomenon, as something that is objectified. It is seen as something immutable born with some impetus that propels it across a social area or space with various degrees of resistance.

These traditional models emphasize three elements in the process of diffusion (Latour, 1986). The first element is the initial energy (initiative, order, quote command, instruction) which usually is connected to power and leadership and seen as coming from an individual source (Czarniawska-Joerges, 1994, p. 208). This energy is seen as a trigger of movement, and it constitutes the only energy for diffusion. The second element is the inertia that conserves this energy, and the third is the medium through which the something is diffused. From this ostensive perspective, what spurs research interest are questions of why some object, idea or behavior is not perfectly transmitted, and why there is resistance (like lack of communication, ill will, opposition of interests groups, perception errors, indifference, et cetera) which hinders the diffusion. Typical inquires into these studies look at how frequent, how fast, how accurately, and to whom something is transmitted.

Imitation as ostensively defined has been examined by scholars from many disciplines who often have given it different labels. Scholars in marketing (e. g. Rogers, 1962) traditionally have looked upon imitation as a process of diffusion by which consumer products or technologies (more seldom administrative technologies) are adopted within a community. A similar focus exists in early work of economists; Tarde (1903) suggested that the cumulative number of adopters of a new idea follows an S-shaped distribution over time. Contemporary economists mainly study speed, costs/time trade-off, and information spillover in diffusion processes of innovations (Mansfield et al., 1981; Reinganum, 1983; Dasgupta, 1988). Business strategy researchers (e. g. MacMillan et al., 1985) look at imitation response time of competitors. In developmental psychology there is an interest both in imitation as a cognitive skill (e. g. Piaget, 1951) and in motoric imitation among neonatal children (e. g. Maratos, 1973). Among contemporary students of organization theory, imitation is a central notion in institutionalization and mimetic isomorphism (e. g. DiMaggio and Powell, 1983; Tolbert and Zucker, 1983). There is also an interest in imitation among students of anthropology (e. g. Durkheim, 1915; Linton, 1936; Douglas, 1986), and of psychoanalytic theory (Girard, 1977). Imitation as copying of original work is furthermore a popular object of study in the disciplines of literature, art history, and religion.

Contrary to most of the literature on imitation, which assumes that there is an immutable something which is carried by an autonomous impetus that diffuses across actors, I will see imitation as a process in which something is created and transformed by chains of translators. From this it follows that ideas or practices do not force themselves on organizations which then have to adopt them. The impetus for imitation must come from the imitators themselves, from their conception of situation, self-identity and others' identity, as well as from analogical reasoning by which these conceptions are combined. Imitation, hence performatively defined (Latour, 1986), becomes a process of translation with a specific focus on conceptualizing. This performative definition fosters description of an organization picking up an idea, translating it into something that fits its own context, and materializing it into action. The result of this action may or may not be similar to the idea that was originally conceptualized by the imitating organization. In other words, whatever is spread is not immutable; it may change in an ongoing process of borrowing ideas or practices in a chain of actors. Latour states that:

> According to [the model of translation]..., the spread in time or space of anything claims, orders, artifacts, goods is in the hands of people; each of these people may act in many different ways, letting the token drop, or modifying it, or deflecting it, or betraying it, or adding to it, or appropriating it. The faithful transmission of, for instance an order by a large number of people is a rarity in such a model and if it occurs it requires explanation (Latour, 1986, p. 267).

The image of imitation as an ongoing translation of transforming organizations differs from the diffusion model: in a translation model the initial force of the first actor in the chain is no more important than the hundredths. Furthermore, it is not possible to know where or when the process concludes; parts of an idea that is spread in time and space may turn up in quite new circumstances. Furthermore, it becomes less meaningful to distinguish between new (discovery, original, innovation) and old (copy), as the model of diffusion does. The arbitrary labeling of action as either copying or discovery is less useful in discussion about imitation as translation (for an extensive discussion about what is an original and what is a copy, or a fake, see Eco, 1990) because in both copying and discovery one uses bits of one's own and others' experience: I may sometimes be copying what you are doing (presumably by using bits of actions I already know); or I may have recognized the whole pattern of yours as one I already know, or similar to one I already know. According to Margolis (1987), in the latter case, I am not really copying the outside. Rather I am navigating through a now-recognized pattern from my own repertoire in a new context. Alternatively, there may simply be some (chance or characteristic) feature made salient by the very encounter with this context that cues the novel use of a pattern already in the repertoire. Whether the product of this interaction should be called copying or discovery has to do with how much and how important own parts are and how much is borrowed from others. For this essay such a quantitative distinction is not important. I see imitation as a process of identity transformation that is neither solely a copy nor a totally new invention, but something between these ideal types.

Elements in the Imitation Process

To imitate is to act like someone else with the more or less conscious intent to achieve the same, or similar, consequences. It is a way of learning from others' experience of having done and achieved something. Imitation may be considered a good strategy both by individuals and organizations as a strategy that saves time and resources: one does not have to use a trial-and-error strategy, or one may even avoid mistakes altogether. However, imitation as a strategy for saving resources and achieving desired identity may also be considered to have pitfalls. One of them is situated in the reasoning about connections between others' actions and identities. In situations of perceived uncertainty and uncomplete knowledge, organizations might feel that they do not know for sure what caused the desired states of others and whether the same magic will work once again, for themselves.

Imitation as a rationale for organizational change has been discussed by March (1981). This rationality which he calls the logic of appropriateness includes a judgment of what is a rational, or appropriate action. The judgment is based on comparison (matching) with others: *Who am I?*, *What situation is this?*, and consecutive action is based on the perceived action and achievements of other actors. Borrowing the main idea from this model, imitation will here be described as a process based on (1) matching of identifications and situations, (2) construction of desire to transform, and (3) institutionalized action.

A match is a judgment that something is similar to something else. In a process of matching questions and answers are posed and stated: *What am I like? (I am like X)*. Identity transformation starts when the organization asks *What would I like to be?* and answers *(I would like to be like Xa)*. In principal, as I see it, when an organization is positively matched in identity type and situation with another actor, it is possible to learn from this other's experience.

Identity is a modern institution, i. e. temporal and local (Meyer, 1986; Czarniawska-Joerges, 1994). It is taken for granted that organizations, like individuals, have identities. Meyer points out that a modern identity includes self-respect, efficiency, autonomy, and flexibility. In a positive match with another actor Xa, who is seen as having a similar type of identity, but is still more successful, more efficient, more autonomous, et cetera, a desire to change own identity may arise. The match may trigger new questions: *How can I become more like Xa?*, *What situation is this?* and *What is the appropriate action for me in this situation?* The analogical reasoning which follows is: If I do as Xa does, I may become more like Xa. The subsequent action taken in consideration of the result of the matching (acting like Xa) is a legitimate, appropriate action in an effort to transform one's own identity. It is borrowing the experience of this other actor acting in an institutional manner.

As organizational imitation may aim at becoming similar to some other organization in identity, crucial for the discussion about organizational imitation is, therefore, a statement that organizational identity is not seen as a stable, essential feature but rather as a conception of a feature that develops in an ongoing and never-completed accomplishment: The identity of an organization is a description of an individual identity *emerging from interactions* between actors rather than existing as a form of an essence that is consequently exhibited (Czarniawska-Joerges, 1994, p. 200).

Selective Attention in Organizational Imitation

Among modern organizations there is a taken-for-granted idea that it is desirable and possible to engineer social events in order to achieve features of modern identities, like self-respect, efficiency, autonomy, and flexibility. A firm with a good reputation (seen as having a desired identity) may become a model for imitation, and ideas about how to act be borrowed from this actor's repertoire. When there is uncertainty about what is proper action, information about what the majority of firms do may also serve a similar guiding function. A firm might search for a reliable recipe for good achievement when the context is changed for the firm, for example when the firm is newly established (new in the field), or when its performance is below average within the industry. Knowledge of others is not always available, though, and when there is a felt need to get ideas about action and practices from other firms, firms which are close, and therefore well-known, may also serve as models. Firms sometimes perceive market changes and changes among competitors that trigger changes in own strategy. These strategic action are often imitations of organizations which are seen as similar. Business strategy scholars (Porter, 1980; Huff, 1982; Rumelt, 1987) argue that key decision makers monitor rival organizations and formulate strategies to achieve desired competitive success. Outside the arena of competitive dynamics, organizations also nevertheless continuously monitor, perceive, and interpret what is going on in the environment; they pay attention to changes (Daft and Weick,1984).

An organization does not imitate every other organization, and neither does it imitate all the time. Let us focus on instances when an organization imitates a comparable entity, perhaps in similar surroundings, from which there seems to be something to be learned. This are instances where an organization imitates when it has more confidence in the history of others than in its own (the other knows better), that is, when it perceives uncertainty or ambiguity about how to act given its own experience. Examples of perceived uncertainty are discussed by Abrahamson (1991). He points out that imitating organizations are uncertain about environmental impact, goals, or technical efficiency. He argues that imitation is therefore expected (in literature) to be more frequent in some areas than in other depending on this uncertainty: for example, as administrative technologies produce unclear output but certain production technologies output which is less so, imitation of administrative techniques should be more common (see also Meyer and Rowan, 1977).

An organization's span of attention also determines what can be imitated. How organizations come to attend to certain parts of their environment is not at all a trivial issue. Generally, we can expect firms to attend more to changes than to non-changes; movement attracts attention (Bateson, 1979). For example, a firm may perceive a change in its market share, but not know how large a market share it has. Not all changes are perceived, though. An organization has a span of attention; it cannot attend to everything that can be considered its whole environment. Imitation, seen as a result of matching focused on identity, is normally assumed to occur in organization fields (DiMaggio and Powell, 1983).[1] Within an organiza-

---

[1]   A notion related to organization field appears in industrial economies. See, for example, Fligstein (1985), who states that industries are good theoretical proxies for environment.

tion field thoughts are shared[2] and diffused among organizations. That has to do with shared frames of meaning; an organization's attention to the environment is based on available interpretative frames that are constructed within the social space in which it operates. An organization field is for example an activity field which comprises organizations with a similar activity definition. These organizations have the same thought world. When imitation is the result of matching that is focused on identity transformation, the organizations attend to changes in the thought world. Let us assume that when imitation is a result of matching which is less focused on identities but more on desired outcomes (when it does not matter who I am, but only that I want the same outcome) we can assume that imitation occurs mainly in networks of action. These are organization fields which comprise organizations that usually interact. However, the distinction between a network of action and a thought world is blurred. Desired outcomes and desired identity are closely related, and it is evident that imitation also occurs across thought worlds in organization fields. Forssell and Jansson (this volume) describe a case in which local governments want to act like the financial giants they meet in their organization field.

An organization mostly perceives changes in its organization field. Perceived changes in actions, practices and achievements may trigger imitation. As thoughts are shared within a field, one would expect many organizations to imitate the actions and practices of field members. This in turn might increase the homogeneity of the field. DiMaggio and Powell consequently argue that (large) organizations are likely to come to resemble one another. The process behind this, they claim, is the professionalization of managers that tends to create a particular world view of appropriate organizational behavior. In that sense, networks of action become also thought worlds. But, as professionalization is a socialization process that makes actors perceive and act in a similar manner, how is it then possible that over time not all organizations in a field become clones of one organization with admired actions or practices? An answer to this question is available if we depart from the traditional perspective of institutional theory and look at imitative action from a performative perspective.

When organizational imitation is seen as translation rather than as copying of a stable feature, or as a spread of this feature within an area, the imitative action and the resulting outcome may as well vary between actors

---

[2]   The idea of shared meaning within a social space, or a society, is, however, older than the notion of an organization field in institutional theory. Fleck (1935) introduced the concept thought collective (cf. collective group, Durkheim and Mauss, 1963; Durkheim, 1915) and thought style (cf. Durkheim's collective representation) to describe what leads and exercises cognition and produces a stock of knowledge within a society.

and change over time and space. As a result, thought worlds and networks of action may transform, too. The variation between actors comes from the fact that actors may differ in what they learn from others and how they learn. Thus, the professionalization of actors within an organization field is not perfect. Moreover, organizations often borrow only certain features from another organization, and not the whole pattern, and they modify the borrowed idea in order to adjust it to their own conditions. Organizations conceive of themselves not only as similar to others but also as exclusively different. Consequently, to some degree they sometimes act differently, and end up as partly different from one another. Therefore, the result of imitation as a process of translation is that the fields are to some degree heterogeneous, and to some degree homogeneous. Furthermore, new fields may appear as a result; both organizations and organization fields change over time as a result of processes of translation.

A very distinct example of imitation seen as translation is given by Westney (1987) who studied Japan during the Meiji period, 1868–1912, when it experienced a most remarkable social transformation. During this period, Japan emulated many organizations from Britain, France, the United States, Germany and Belgium. Japan developed its navy, army, postal system, primary school system, judicial system, police system, and more. The police system was an emulation of the French system, but also partly of Japan's own traditions. From Paris was borrowed the system of financing, the formal regulatory structure, the political role of the chief, and the functions, size, and formal roles of differentiation and specialization. Such borrowed ideas were emulated in concert with Japanese characteristics and experiences. Japanese traditions contributed with ideas concerning the control of individual performance, orientation to public education, vertical administrative unit differentiation, training and education, information, and weaponry. Instead of choosing the French police recruitment system, Japan choose to continue the tradition of the Samurai and the Satsuma, who performed functions similar to those of the police but who were outside of the society. Japanese policemen were therefore recruited heavily from areas outside the population in which they were to function. The system for education and training of policemen was also taken from old Samurai traditions. From this mixture of attributes of the French police system and their own traditions, some innovations were born: the upper-level career patterns, the spatial dispersion, and the utilization of new communication technology.

Westney claims that the most important factor in deliberate departures from the original organizational model is the social context into which the organization is introduced when it is transferred out of the institutional environment in which it developed. The differences between Japanese and French society made it natural to modify the French system when adopted by Japan. This reminds us that an accomplished imitation does not imply a true and total copying. When Westney argues that the successful imitation of foreign organizational patterns requires innovation, she implies that an organization has many different desires, related to its different attributes (and desired belongings), and in the ongoing transformation of the organization a blend of these desires guides both deliberate and unintended changes. This triggers another less common discussion about the premises of the variability between organizations: that organizations may have more than one identity that controls their attention, and that they may also possess the desire to acquire the identities of others. To this I will later return.

Organizational Self-Identification: What Am I Like?

Matching of identities demands self-identification, an answer to the question: *What am I like?* One cannot make a self-identification, i. e. a social labeling applied to oneself, without reference to others. It is possible to only label oneself in relation to others. This implies that self-identification also demands at least indirectly the social labeling of others' identities. The question *What am I like?* becomes *Whom do I look like?* In cases of imitation, an organization may label itself with reference to and in comparison with, for example, high-reputation business firms. Such firms are, I suppose, most probably seen in the thought collective, to which the organization belongs. One reason for this is that the collective has a shared language for labeling and comparison, e. g. an organization might be seen as relatively high-reputational and, for example, small, progressive, and risk-seeking. The language and mental models of organizations is however not necessarily limited to business language. A thought collective can also offer language and mental images about a non-social world; in which case matching may also be made with non-human actors, as in: *What do I look like?*

The rhetorical strategy that organizations choose in order to present their identities seems to focus on three aspects: central character, temporal continuity, and distinctiveness (Albert and Whetten, 1985). A *central character* distinguishes the organization on the basis of something important and essential. *Temporal continuity* means that the identification includes features that exhibit some degree of sameness or continuity over time, and *distinctiveness* implies a classification that identifies the organization as recognizably different from others. Statements of ideology, management philosophy, culture, and rituals may be chosen in the rhetoric of an organization as a strategy to define its uniqueness. In those cases in which a distinctive identity is prized, a chosen strategy may be to select uncommon dimensions of interorganizational comparison as well as uncommon locations along more widely employed dimensions. Rhetorical statements may include habitual strategic propositions for example, a known willingness to take high risks, as may be the case for a company that is distinctively presented as entrepreneurial (Albert and Whetten, 1985). As imitation starts from the idea that there is something a similar entity has or shows which is worth taking on an as ideas for one's own action; we should expect firms that prefer to claim their distinctiveness to be less prone to imitate. Imitation is probably more common among firms that describe themselves by stating their central character.

As organizational self-identification is based on a process of matching with something else, the part of an identity which becomes salient therefore rests on what the organization compares itself with. A judgment of similarity is dynamic and context-dependent, and the perceived properties of an organization may vary as a function of what it is compared to (Medin, Goldstone and Gentner, 1993). It is easy to accept this statement in the case of individuals. For example, a manager may possess several unrelated self-identifications at the same time, and may refer to several social collectives simultaneously as well. Which of these identities and self-descriptions becomes salient depends however on the current context. A manager's identification and action may be more mother-like at home and more business-like at work. As a consequence, she may describe herself in reference to the class of women, the class of mothers, and the class of managers, but during working hours see herself mainly as a manager, or as a female manager (see also Elster, 1985; Leiser, Sevón and Lévy, 1990).

Likewise, an organization may identify itself in more than one way. A business firm may describe itself as a member of the class of international firms, the paper and pulp industry, family firms, and firms heavily burdened by debt.

Self-identification varies with reference group, and choice of reference group depends on the salient context at the moment. When the environment changes, the task at hand varies, the market situation turns, or the experience of the organization otherwise develops, the context may shift, which may in turn lead to a matching with entities different than those before, and, consequently, a reformulation of the identity. New labels may be added to earlier ones, because important features of an earlier identification persist in the structure, philosophy, strategy, et cetera. This is clearly shown by Westney (1987) in her description of Japan during the Meiji period. Sometimes, however, the identities form a hybrid organization, meaning an organization whose identity is composed of two or more types that would not normally go together. Examples include a bank which is operated by a religious organization (Albert and Whetten, 1985) and a state organization which is both the master of the public and the public servant (Czarniawska-Joerges, 1994).

Perhaps because few studies have until now focused on the process of organizational imitation from a performative perspective, there are barely any studies of implicit theories of how a business organization might answer the question of what it looks like, which classes of phenomena it belongs to. Neither are there many studies of changes in such self-descriptions. It seems as if such striving towards a consistent self-description is aimed less at finding "true" identity and values and more towards developing a suitable identity. Explicitly stated self-identity is also often the result of many years of self-assessment, often with help from outside, such as consulting firms.

Despite little research, and few known implicit and explicit self-labels, some examples of self-description are well known and widely shared. It is common to talk about firms as belonging to a certain industry. It is also popular to discriminate more specifically between international and domestic business and to differentiate firms according to products and services. Turnover is also a common feature of identification: "we are a large, international business firm in the paper and pulp industry." Self-identification may serve as a statement about the central character of the organization, important in a certain context. Sometimes, such a claim of identity may have another purpose, but it is generally meant to distinguish the organization from other organizations.

Imitation of Desires: What Would I Like to Be?

One prerequisite for organizational imitation is a self-identification like the type of self-identification experienced and broadcast by others. Perceived likeness of identity and/or context with an imitated model seems to be necessary, both for the attention to and the development of beliefs about what is correct, true and desired, and for judgment about whether it is possible to obtain a similar outcome. However, it would be meaningless to imitate an organization that is considered to be identical in all aspects, and in their rhetoric, organizations also state, in addition to their central characteristics, features of identity that make them distinctive.

The striving to be similar but also different is a dilemma that has been touched upon by scholars of organization theory. Institutionalists claim, on the one hand, that strong pressure exists to imitate organizations, or more specificly, organizational forms that have been successful (Hannan and Freeman, 1977; DiMaggio and Powell, 1983). But students of competitive dynamics, on the other hand, claim that the superiority of an organization comes from creating and sustaining attributes that are not easily imitated (Porter, 1980; Rumelt, 1984; Peteraf, 1993). However, this literature does not discuss the matter of what ends up being considered as successful achievement by an organization, and therefore desired. It is obvious that in organizational imitation, a constituent element of an organizational identity is its system of desires the collection of values concerning what is beneficial and to be sincerely wished for.

Where do these desires come from? They are not deducible from needs. Organizational desires, like individual ones, are socially constructed. Howe (1994) claims that (individual) desires can be characterized as cognitive phenomena which are heavily influenced by social learning. He summarizes his view:

> Human desire is something which is ultimately directionless a mere force, a potential for action or movement. (...) Direction must be given to it through learning, through being taught, implicitly, to place certain values on things. In some cases, such as eating, this is just a matter of being conditioned to identify food as being that which relieves the pain of hunger. In more interesting cases, it comes about by observing others and thereby learning what *they* value, which then seems to have a value in itself (Howe, 1994, p. 4).

Howe claims that one learns to desire something by adopting the desires of those around. Desires for a certain identity are also socially learned. One special case of imitating desires in order to obtain a closer likeness in identity is described by Girard (1977). He studied rivalry, specifically the imitation of the rival from a psychoanalytical perspective. His focus may also be relevant in the context of organizational imitation, because firms pay attention to and compare themselves with their competitors (Huff, 1990). Girard claims that rivalry does not arise because of the fortuitous convergence of two desires on a single object; rather, the subject desires the object because the rival desires it. Girard states that in desiring an object the rival alerts the subject to the desirability of the object. The rival, then, serves as a model for the subject, not only in regard to such secondary matters as style and opinion but also, and more essentially, in regard to desires. Girard writes:

> In human relationships words like sameness and similarity evoke an image of harmony. If we have the same taste, (...) surely we are bound to get along. But, the model, even if he has openly encouraged imitation, is surprised to find himself engaged in competition (Girard, 1977, p. 146).

Girard concludes that the disciple has betrayed the confidence of the model by following in his or her footsteps. Simultaneously the disciple feels both rejected and humiliated, judged unworthy by the model of participating in the superior existence that the model enjoys. In business societies, unlike among people, similarity between firms may not be seen as a state of harmony. On the contrary, competitiveness between members of the society of firms is predominantly part of the formula; competitors are rivals, and they fight for the same objects. This is an important aspect of corporate action. Also, Fligstein (1985) claims that every theory of organizational change must take into account the fact that the leaders of organizations watch one another and adopt what they perceive as successful strategies for growth and organizational structure. Stories in business magazines tell about these successes, and appoint the winners in the competition among companies. The winners gain distinction, and the losers perhaps envy.

Reasoning About Appropriate Action: Analogical Thinking

Imitation is a process which begins with identification and results in transformation. A link between the two is causal reasoning: what is before causes what is after; what is visible should be coupled together; great outcomes are caused by great events; et cetera. Business life is full of causal reasoning; reasoning about causes and effects is seen as necessary in order to behave in a rational way. Business people think that setting goals makes sense only if supported by ideas about how it is possible to reach goals, and, that diagnosed problems can be dealt with only if there is knowledge about what caused the problems. Examples of causal reasoning in business are connections perceived between a risk-taking propensity and a technical innovation, between a divisionalized organizational form and growth in turnover, and between employing a certain consultant in quality management and a subsequent turn-around.

For causal reasoning about what is appropriate action, analogies may be used. What analogy is chosen for a matching with one's own situation then becomes a crucial issue concerning what is imitated. There are several aspects of analogies which are interesting: the domain that the analogical model describes and the form and place of this description.

Analogical reasoning enhances the interpretation of a new situation. Actors use analogies to map the set of transition rules from a known domain into one which is a new, thereby constructing a mental model that can generate inferences in the new domain. Any system whose transition rules are reasonably well-specified can serve as an analogical model for understanding a new system (Collins and Gentner, 1989). Douglas (1986) and Quinn and Holland (1987) claim that there is however an advantage with analogies from the physical world. This advantage rests on the nature of the physical world itself, and the manner in which physical properties and relations are comprehended by human beings.

Identifying with and Imitating Non-Human Actors

Organizations may consider themselves metaphorically in terms of non-human actors and organizations; it is well known that organizations are engaged in metaphorical thinking (Morgan, 1986). One example of the use of metaphors from the non-human world is delivered by semiotic scholars: in order to gain insights about its identity an organization may compare itself to an animal, such as a lion, or to a car, such as a Volvo. Although metaphorical thinking is an important element in identity construction (Czarniawska-Joerges, 1994), it is less important in the case of imitation. What I wish to instead take up are interesting cases of matching in which the reasoning looks metaphorical but is in fact analogical.

When an organization perceives a similarity between itself and the features of a structure or an object in the non-human world it is engaged in analogical reasoning. The power of analogical reasoning vis-à-vis the non-human world is shown in a field study of international joint R&D ventures (Sevón, forthcoming).

Some project managers' descriptions of their R&D organizations were not stated in traditional organization terminology. Rather, the organizations were described as similar to the product or the scientific process that was the concern of the daily R&D work. Not only were they described as cases parallel to a physical world; organizational structures and processes that seemed important to the project managers were also designed similarly to physical ones. The study shows that this reasoning was used for making sense of organizational structure and action and of important organizational features. Maybe it also illustrates an interplay between analogical models and designing of an organization. The field study was, however, not focusing on this aspect, so we have to leave this issue open to speculation. In any case, the study indicates that the identity description and formation of an organization may originate from inference about a physical entity rather than from project organizations. Let me illustrate this.

The aim of one project organization was to develop compound electrical component systems. The total project included many subprojects, and it involved 39 participating firms. These partners developed different components which were to become part of larger systems. Therefore, the success of the total project was seen as mostly contingent upon the ability to coordinate the participating firms.

The organization of this large project was complex, with many different relationships between the partners. For example, in one subproject one partner dominated, while in others all partners were equal. As the partners did not necessarily trust each other, in some projects the R&D work was smooth, while in others it experienced difficulties. The competitiveness in the electricity industry is hard; partners in the same subproject even hesitated to inform each other about the latest development in the work. Although these conditions for a joint venture seem very problematic for scholars of organization design, a project organization had been set up that was considered adequate and efficient. What then would an organization look like that can perform during such problematic circumstances, and how might it be described? The project manager of one partner gave the answer:

> The collaboration between the firms is organized by one of the partners, Coordina, whose only function is to control and support the collaboration. Coordina has a main role as transmitter of information and stimulator of the R&D work. This agency acts as a central junction, with a female engineer who also works as a secretary for all projects. We all get information from her about what is simultaneously going on in the other projects. This is important because the progress of all projects is relatively interrelated. Coordina scans the work of all partners; it makes sure that everybody keeps to their deadlines. Coordina also gives administrative support.

The project is interesting in the way its organization is conceived. The project manager, an engineer and himself a researcher in the project, uses a component system analogy to describe the project organization. It is described as a structure consisting of different components that fit together by a centrally-located coordination and control office. This constructed reality of the project organization matches its products; the whole project is organized analogously to the systems of components that it develops. The competitiveness between partners that implies a low level of trust is compensated by the design of a neutral organizing and controlling partner, Coordina, which has nothing else at stake but the success of the whole project.

The case illustrates how a model from the physical world can function as the model in an organizational transformation as it creates beliefs about what is proper and desirable. Although the engineer himself was not aware of his analogical reasoning, the case tells us how an engineer might utilize his acquaintance with a technical system to make sense of the organizational world. The engineer did not offer an alternative model that could be found in traditional management literature. It seems to me that he used well-known products as a parallel case that allowed him to generate predictions about what would happen in various situations in a complex project organization. The case illustrates how people may intuitively use a picture from the domain in which they are skilled to map onto the domain of organizational structure, which is less well-known to them. And, simultaneously, the organizational structure may become perceived as the structure of an electrical component system. We can imagine that the project manager as an R&D engineer had faith in the idea of a component system. I got the impression from the project manager's description that for him an ideal organization consists of subunits which contribute to the whole organization with information transmitted in accordance with fixed rules, and of a communication center acting as the agent responsible for the efficiency of the information flow.

The structures of other R&D project organizations studied were different from those in this case. One project aiming at developing chemical products consisted of only two partners. The project manager of one of the partners described the relation as trustful, very close and reciprocal. He stressed that the most salient attribute was the good chemistry between the researchers of the two partners. In addition to the R&D project, a friendship development subproject was developed. This project, that was taken very seriously, was aimed at entertaining the other partner and strengthening the ties between the two partners. The Finnish partner arranged smoke-sauna baths with sauna diplomas for survivors, the Danish partner arranged crayfish parties on a ship in the North Sea. This subproject of friendship development can be analogically described as a catalyst aimed at fostering the success of the work developing chemical compounds.

These two cases indicate that a comparison with non-human entities sometimes makes sense. It makes sense, for example, when an organization type is uncommon and it may be difficult to ascertain to which class of organization it belongs. Also, if the organization knows little about organization fields, it may be difficult to tell to which group of organizations it belongs. As for ad-hoc organizations, like project organizations, which are led by people who have little knowledge about the management of organizations and are not always likely to be able to use the language of managers, the use of images and language from a non-organizational world may be a rather feasible alternative. For a project manager in a high-technology project organization, which is usually run by natural scientists who do not have much experience in business management, the immediate source for making sense of the project organization may derive from the natural science paradigm that occupies its daily scientific work. By analogical reasoning appropriate in the thought collective, the organization may be understood as a case parallel to the non-human world; the organizational pattern and functioning may in this case be perceived as similar to the physical. For other organizations, as with business organizations led by professional managers, the use of images from this domain may however be less customary. The managers of these organizations may prefer to rely on analogies that describe social organizations, and consequently imitate social action and patterns.

Agents of Organizational Imitation

In business life, analogical reasoning often appears in the costume of narrative structures which are communicated in story-telling. Story-telling or gossiping has an entertainment value but it also focuses attention on organizational agents and actions, and on organizations' history, rules, values, and morals usually by pointing at failures to satisfy them (March and

Sevón, 1988). Also, Bruner (1990) adds that as good stories, which should have some exceptional features, narratives are often about dramatic phenomena, about the successful or unsuccessful actions and outcomes of members of the society of organizations. He refers to Brown (1973) who told how young children in their first speech already show that they especially notice human interaction: agent-and-action, action-and-object, agent-and-object, action-and-location, and possessor-and-possession. This interest in stories about agents and actions does not disappear with age. Adults in business organizations teach each other stories about agents and actions. This activity is considered important. Business firms observe and describe the behavior of other firms because their own existence depends on the competitors' achievements, but also because getting ideas from others may save energy and time and reduce uncertainty and ambiguity.

Story-telling contributes to institution maintenance and the maintenance of exclusivity (March and Sevón, 1988). It states what the natural norms, rules, properties and contexts are. Narratives about organizational life teach us about how to interpret situations and the identity of others and oneself. Indirectly, they suggest answers to questions like *What kind of situation is this?*, *What am I like?*, *What would I like to be?*, and *What is appropriate for me in this situation?* The narratives may also suggest answers like *We are like X*, *We should want to be like Xa*, and *We should act like Xa*. The answers may be supplied by a recipe. An industrial recipe is grounded on taken-for-granted aspects that govern what are proper narrative themes, and it embodies shared believes about rational action for firms within an industry (Spender, 1989).

The channels for distributing recipes in narrative form are many. Newspapers print stories daily. Business consultants are influential agents as they construct and spread stories about organizational life (Huff, 1982; Czarniawska-Joerges, 1990; March, 1991). They use narratives to help define visionary statements for the identification of their clients. They also offer methods for organizational change, such as benchmarking, reengineering and adoption of best practice, that fully appreciate the usefulness of learning from others, and they write about them (for example, see Hammer, 1990). Business leaders write biographies. Some leaders who are judged successful write books to make their exclusivity publicly known (for example, Lee Iacocca, see Iacocca and Novac, 1984), and explain the problems they have experienced. Management training courses diffuse information about the experiences of various firms, and the social interaction during such courses is often an important occasion for gossiping. Also, communication networks among professionals from different organizations, and movement of personnel from one firm to another, as when there is a change of manager, promote the flow of narratives.

Concluding Remarks

To conclude, given the breadth of the topic of imitation so central to human and organizational action no work of the scope of the current piece can hope to be conclusive, but ideas and arguments have been introduced which should at least give pause for thought. The pivotal ideas presented have grown out of a perspective of imitation as a process in identity construction. When organizational imitation is viewed, as here, as learning from others, it means that imitating organizations answer the following questions: *What am I like?* (identification of one-self and others), *What would I like to be?* (a question about desire and the construction of desire), *What kind of situation is this like?* (analogical reasoning), and *What is appropriate for me in this situation?* (institutionalized action). The answers concern identification of oneself and others and how it is possible to become as one would desire. The organizational reasoning behind these answers is facilitated by analogical models borrowed from the human world, but also from the non-human. These models offer ideas about what is true and best. They are often shared among organizations in the same thought world or network of action. The models are often spread as narratives through the work of agents of different kinds.

Merton (1985) states that we live in a world where nothing is absolute new, where there are no absolute original ideas or actions. In such a world, every act is related to one's own and others' ideas, experiences and actions. At the same time, however, no idea or action is completely a copy from other organizations, as organizations pick up ideas and translate them into something that fits their own context. In this way, action, although imitated, may become different. Imitation is an ongoing and never-completed action. Through imitation, ideas, experiences and actions are constructed and spread over time and space thereby transforming ideas, mental models, actions, organizational forms, and organization fields.

I have stated that this perspective for discussing organizational imitation is rather uncommon. There are not many field studies which have so far focused on imitation from this viewpoint. A question of central interest concerns how an organization identifies itself, and therefore also with whom or what it compares itself. That means that studies of organizational attention and taxonomic mental models are needed, because these may tell from where an organization picks up ideas that it translates according to its own conditions. I have claimed that comparison with others is context-dependent, and therefore also variable. Field studies are needed to get illustrations of how identifications and perceived contexts change. Furthermore, the dynamic of an organization field is itself interesting to study. I have claimed that two processes occur in fields which are interesting results of organizational imitation: increases in homogeneity (see Abrahamson, this volume, for an extensive discussion) and increases in heterogeneity. The latter process has been less frequently focused upon in earlier literature, but is discussed at length in this volume (see Røvik and Abrahamson, this volume). For the discussion about organizational imitation it would be of great interest to learn more from field studies that focus on how organization fields are transformed and how this is connected to changes in organizational identifications.

Imitating by Editing Success: The Construction of Organization Fields[1]

Kerstin Sahlin-Andersson

Are Organizations Becoming Increasingly Similar?

Organizations frequently imitate other organizations. Often, when reforms, new models for planning and managing and the like are introduced in organizations, the actors who introduce the models refer to others' experiences, evaluations or effects. Those experiences are often described as successes.

Even organizations that operate under quite different circumstances are frequently shaped and presented in similar ways. Several researchers have noted that there is "a startling homogeneity of organizational forms and practices" (DiMaggio and Powell, 1983, p. 148), which is seen as resulting from processes through which organizations are becoming increasingly similar. This homogenization of forms has been explained in metaphorical terms, such as diffusion, fads, fashion, contagion, etc.

All these metaphors emphasize that organizations follow or imitate each other, but give little explanation as to how the forms are diffused. The impression is that new organization models spread almost automatically; organizations are regarded as passive entities which simply react and adapt to the latest trends. If we acknowledge that organizations consist of thinking and acting persons, and that each change in organizational practice or organizational form requires that people act, we will find that the mechanical explanations leave unanswered most of the questions about why organizations adopt new trends.[2]

If we are to talk about "diffusion" of organizational forms and practices, it is reasonable to ask what it is that is spreading. From the metaphors above, one gets an impression of "packages" of ideas, forms, or policies

---

[1] An earlier version of this paper was presented at the workshop "New Organizational Perspectives for Public Administration," 10th EGOS colloquium in Vienna, July, 1991.

[2] Such criticism of institutional analysis has been reported in several volumes published during the last years (see especially Powell and DiMaggio, 1991: Chs. 1, 8, 10 and 12; Strang and Meyer, 1994).

flying around and sticking to organizations. It is assumed that nothing happens to these ideas during the process of diffussion – a reified notion, but also a static one as far as the spreading of ideas or forms is concerned. While in the field, however, one easily finds that ideas which are supposed to be the same – or at least very similar – are presented in a great variety of ways. The actual processes of organizing might reveal an even greater heterogeneity than the one found by looking at presentations or labels used for various forms, reforms and practices. In order to make sense of the fact that organizations simultaneously reveal a striking homogeneity and heterogeneity, we need to understand both how the "diffusion" happens and how forms and practices are shaped and reshaped in various stages of this process: we need to follow how ideas travel.

In this essay I describe how organizational forms and practices circulate. I suggest explanations as to why organizations seek to imitate others and furthermore how forms and practices are circulated, adopted and handled in the local organizations. In the first section I claim that, from the perspective of the local actor, change processes are problem-based, and thus, in order to understand why and how actors attend to new forms and models we need to know how problems are constructed in the local setting. The explanation suggested here is that local problems are constructed through comparing the local situation with that of other organizations. These others are organizations with which the local organization can identify and moreover organizations that possess characteristics which seemingly make them successful. The gap between the local situation and the one to which it is compared is then defined as a problem. Another cause for imitation is identity crisis. When the present organizational identity is threatened one of the reactions might be to look for "idols" – once again, organizations which are judged successful.

In the following section of the essay I describe the circulation of models as an editing process. The editing process is a process of translation. Imitated "successes" are formulated and reformulated as they are circulated.[3] Similarities are emphasized while differences that might lead to a conclusion that the imitated prototype does not fit in the local setting are played down. In order to attract attention, imitated prototypes are reformulated in more dramatic terms. In such processes of translation, new meanings are created and ascribed to activities and experiences.

At first glance, such processes might seem to be creative and open-ended. However, the process of translation is restricted by implicit editing rules. It

---

[3] Sevón (in this volume) proposes an understanding of imitation as a dynamic process, where neither the starting point nor the outcome are given at the outset. The present chapter continues this thought by showing in detail, what is imitated, and how the translation proceeds.

is a process characterized by social control, conformism and traditionalism. The examples provided reveal a number of editors and editing rules that restrict and direct the translation in each phase of the circulation of proto-types.

After prototypes have been edited and imported into the local setting, new expectations for and new meanings ascribed to the organizational activities may result from the language and comparisons the imitation entails. Thus imitation of successes may result in transformed organizational identities.

Local Constructions of Problems

When I have interviewed managers about organizational reforms, they have described these reforms as ways to solve or handle a local problem. Members of organizations tend to describe and perceive such changes as locally-based and problem-driven even though researchers often find these processes to be solution-driven and solution-based, not in the local organizations, but in society as a whole or in the mutual relations among organizations.

From the perspective of the local actors, new models or practices are sought when the actors perceive that there are problems in the present situation. Why then are some situations perceived and described as problematic? One common definition of a problem is the difference between a desired state and a present state. The perception of a problem is thus a result of a comparison. For a long time organization theorists have stressed that organizations do not operate in a vacuum. One can go a step further by saying that organizations are neither experienced or presented in a vacuum.

In order to understand what an organization is, what it does, and how well it does, organizational actors compare their situations and their organizations with others. Actors tend to compare their organization with others considered to be similar in one way or another. Also, they compare organizations with other organizations or models that display some characteristics which seemingly make them successful or potentially successful. In other words, local actors compare their organizations with organizations which fit their hopes and expectations for the future. The difference between one's own situation and the one with which one is compared becomes then a definition of the problem. We will come back to the question of how organizations are compared with others, but let us start with an illustration of a locally constructed problem.

The illustration shows how a problem was defined as the basis for a regional development project carried out in the county of Stockholm. For many years the industrial sector in the southern part of the county was shrinking with a strained economy as a result. The city council discussed this under the label of "an unbalanced region" (Sahlin-Andersson, 1990; 1991). Such a labeling of the problem implied that what was defined to be the problem for the southern part of the county was the way in which it differed from the wealthier northern part. Once the problem was perceived in such terms, it followed that the designated solution was to do away with the differences between South and North: to make the southern parts of the county as much like the northern part as possible. One of the more obvious differences between the north and the south was that the airport, the university and most of the modern "high-tech" companies were found in the north. Thus, designated solutions for the observed problems were to build another airport in the southern part of the county, to build another university in the southern part of the county, and to arrange facilities attracting high-tech companies to the south.

When problems are defined through comparisons between one's own situation and a seemingly more successful organization and situation, problems and solutions tend to merge into each other. The problem is defined as the difference between the two organizations, and the solution is to eliminate these differences. Such changes cause organizations to become increasingly similar. In order to understand how organizations define situations and problems, we then need to find out with whom they compare themselves and with whom they are compared. This will tell us where organizational actors look for models and organizations to imitate, but it will also yield an understanding of how organizations are identified.

Organizational Identities Are Derived from Organization Fields

The identity of a subject – a person or an organization – is defined in relation to others; it is derived from its reference to and relationships with others. Such references are expressed in the way activities are presented and perceived. However, this does not mean that the identity is formed in each interaction or in each relationship. Expectations as well as interpretive schemes are anchored in societal institutions, generally known and taken for granted as objective knowledge. The identity represents an abstracted view of what is regarded as consistency and continuity in a person's, a group's or an organization's activities.

That identities are institutionally constructed does not mean, however, that they may be treated as being "out there." They become internalized and thus can serve to structure the individual's own consciousness (Berger, 1966). The identity is then produced and reproduced in a continuous narration where individual or organizational activities are accounted for and made sense of (Czarniawska-Joerges, 1994). Such presentations of oneself are meaningless until they are understood by others. Hence, the identity of a subject is dependent on others' identification of this subject as a subject (Pizzorno, 1991). This identity is dependent upon what it is possible to recognize and name, with the help of typifications and classifications that others share.

Furthermore, when a subject is identified in relation to a particular group, certain aspects of that subject become taken for granted and acted upon, while other aspects seem irrelevant or unimportant. Thus, identity focuses attention both in the sense of directing attention towards certain criteria in the organizational operations, and of helping to determine what the organizational actors will attend to in the environment, i. e. what parts of the environment are seen as relevant. The organizational identity both follows from and is the basis for that with which the organization interacts and is compared. The single organization confirms or changes its identity through comparisons with, references to, and imitation of others. The subject is defined as part of a group, and it is adherence to the group which gives meaning and order to the collective, and thus defines individual identity (Garfinkel, 1967). When an organization is compared with a new and different group, its identity will change, and so will the definition of the problems that the organizations has.

Groups of organizations whose activities are defined in similar ways have been conceived of as shaping organization fields. The concept of organization fields, as defined in this way, has its roots in the notion of a field which is of central importance in the works of Bourdieu. In Bourdieu's terms a field consists of a defined group of actors − people and organizations − who fight or compete about something they have in common, and regard as important. Actors in the field need not necessarily have face-to-face interactions.

As DiMaggio (1983) emphasized, the extent of interaction in the field is always an empirical question. The field is an analytic construction and is demarcated by the eye of the observer.[4] There are no set boundaries. The field could rather be defined as a reference system, shaping the participants' attention structures and identities − what the participants view as impor-

---

[4] However, the use of the term "field" is far from consistent in organizational analysis. In the literature we often see the terms "networks," "fields," and "sets" used synonymously. What is more, the concept of field has often been used to describe all organizations and interactions within a certain geographical area (for example Warren, 1967) or a societal sector (for example Meyer and Scott, 1983). Such uses of the concept give the impression of the field as an entity with fixed meanings and fixed boundaries, an entity which can be measured by counting the number of contacts, exchanges and the like. For a presentation of the number of studies based on such a notion of fields as seemingly fixed physical entities see Scott (1987a).

tant issues (March and Olsen, 1993). The common belief in and adherence to the importance of the definition of what the activities are all about holds the field together (Bourdieu, 1977).

One example is the literary field, which is grounded in the common belief that it is important to produce good literature. The divergence of opinion within the field, and the struggle between actors in the field, may concern in what way this aim is important. In the literary field example, struggles may revolve around what good literature is and why good literature is important.

The field may also be described as a system of relations − relations which have evolved between the actors who define their activities as being concerned with similar issues. In the field a structure of central and peripheral positions evolves. Dominating organizations form reference points and models for the rest of the organizations in the same field. Actions taken by a single actor are orchestrated by the meanings, typifications and identities developed in the field. A coherent pattern of action and meaning develops without any single actor intentionally striving for coherence and conformism (Bourdieu, 1977). From this it follows that organizations in the field become increasingly similar as the actors try to change them.

The problem with the field concept as it is used by, for example, DiMaggio and Powell (1983) is that it may give the impression that the field exists objectively, and thus that similarities and differences exists objectively. Instead, as will follow from the illustrations given in this chapter, similarities, differences, and therefore organization fields are socially constructed and are constantly changing, in spite of the general impression of stability. This also means that we can identify processes where such similarities and differences are produced and reproduced. An organization which is seen as prototype is chosen on the basis of perceived similarities with the organization that wants to imitate. When organizations change identity they also change their minds about whom and what they will imitate. However, it works the other way, too.

It has been shown in examples of many decision making processes that solutions precede and dictate problems (Cohen et al., 1972). What is more, although several potential models to imitate are at hand, attention is limited, and therefore only models that attract other actors' attention become circulated. If organizational actors like a prototype, and decide that they want to imitate it, they may emphasize what seems to be similar and disregard differences between the settings. In such a way, similarities are constructed together with the problems that actors often in retrospect describe as that which motivated the adoption of the new model in the first place. This way not only the imitating organization, but also the imitated organization, may acquire a new identity.

Identity Crisis Leads to Imitation

The Swedish public sector has been seen as forming a distinct area of institutional life — an organization field. Actors in the field have been viewed and described — by themselves and by others — as a coherent group. Similar ideals and ideas have circulated among these organizations. The public organizations have been conceived of as different from private organizations. Such differences have been stressed within the educational system, in the organizing of research groups and research topics, in organizations' recruiting of personnel, in debates about organizational forms, etc. In earlier literature, when public and private organizations were compared, and when it was suggested that public organizations could learn from private organizations, etc., this was not seen as self-evident, but to instead be argued for. This was clearly shown in two books, written by older highly influential Swedish scholars — Heckscher (1921) and Thorburn (1974) — who argued that public organizations could become much more effective by being organized and managed in ways inspired by private organizations. Thus, even though it was questioned by these authors, the group of public organizations and the group of private organizations were seen and treated as distinctively different.

Actors in public organizations increasingly turn their attention to what they and others previously considered to be different fields, and seek to relate to, imitate and interact with organizations that were previously defined as being of a distant kind. Public organizations refer to and turn their attention to international examples and to the private sector (Czarniawska, 1985). Swedish public agencies have also sought more interaction with private companies through, for example, big joint projects (Sahlin-Andersson, 1989; 1990), through increasingly hiring staff with working experience from the private sector, and through frequent meetings with leading persons in private companies concerning various policy areas (Jacobsson, 1989).

The frequent comparison with private business brings with it a new language, and thus a new way of perceiving the activities as well as the mission of the organization. Similarities with business organizations are emphasized, and what is specific to the public agencies is either not attended to or, when mentioned, treated as a restriction or as a disturbance, preventing the organization from corresponding fully with the new ideal. As public agencies are increasingly compared with private companies, and private companies are generally perceived to be more successful, then the ways in which the public agencies differ from the private companies increasingly constitute the definition of what their problems are.

This increased interaction and identification with private organizations is an expression of an effort on the part of public organizations to change their identity. There is no longer a descriptive and normative discourse unique to the public agencies. The public organization field is dissolving and the agencies are adopting a terminology − a definition of problems − of essential or necessary solutions and activities taken from the field of organizations in general.

The group of public organizations is thus weakened as a distinct, recognized area of institutional life, and it turns to others rather than to its own background in order to define or make sense of its situation and its experiences. This has led to what Czarniawska-Joerges (forthcoming) termed its "identity crisis." Pizzorno described an identity crisis as follows:

> We do not know whether the meanings we intend to give our life plans anticipate what others will uncover in them. We become insecure. But this is not something happening within each of us. It is the language used around us to define identities that seems to escape our grasp. Not being clear about how others will evaluate the worth of our actions, we have difficulty communicating with others about ourselves − indeed, we have doubts about the meaning our actions could receive (Pizzorno, 1991, p. 222).

It has often been said that uncertainty drives imitation. This, however, as Sevón in this volume concludes, must be understood as uncertainty in one's own experience. In such states of uncertainty, actors search around for more reliable experiences and models to imitate. They search for new identities.

Today, there is no distinct, widespread language giving meaning to the specific activities carried out in public organizations. Public organizations lack ways to make sense of or relate their experiences to well-known and widely-accepted meanings. We may speculate differently about why this "identity crisis" has come about. It is sometimes explained by the growth of management education, or it is explained by political opinions.[5] The problem with such explanations is that they may give the impression that public organizations have changed while private organizations have remained unchanged. My focus in this paper on public organizations is not intended to reinforce such an impression

Seen in a broader perspective, one may conclude that the view of organizations as actors, with specific objectives, ideas and ideologies which ide-

---

[5]   Of course, it is an important research question to show the background to and the development of the present situation. Not too many years ago, the public agency partly served as a model for private enterprises, at least in an administrative sense. For example, the budgeting that was introduced in private companies was modeled after public organizations. These changes where one organizational type is perceived as a model, as the most efficient and legitimate form of organizing, reflects and effects institutional changes in the society as a whole. To explain such institutional changes broad historical studies of the rationalization of the western culture are needed (see for example Thomas et al. 1987; Brunsson and Hägg, 1992; Strang and Meyer, 1994). However, I shall not pursue that question further here.

ally cover all the members of the organization, is a rather recent phenomenon. Thus all organizations seem to have developed common identities, not based on what they produce, whom they serve, etc., but on the fact that they are identified as organizations.

What distinguishes an organization from just any group of people is that the organization is envisaged as having a more or less clearly defined objective, strategy, structure (including a division of labor), and a certain continuity, consistency and coherence in its activities. An organization is assumed to be controlled by a single "sovereign," i. e. it is led from the top. The organization is required to account for its activities, and reference is often made to a boundary between the organization and its environment. Thus, the organization exhibits an identity which distinguishes it from other organizations, and which defines in broad terms what is to be expected of it.

Modern society, it has been claimed by Meyer et al. (1987), Gergen (1991) and others, has changed the way in which we understand ourselves. The modern individual is assumed to be an actor, i. e. is assumed to have intentions, to be purposive, consistent, and, at least to some extent, rational, and to be aware of and able to control his or her activities. An actor is a decision-maker who is assumed to be able to make his own decisions based on intentional reasoning. An actor is also expected to be in some sense unique, or individual (Berger et al., 1973), so that actors and environments can be distinguished from one another.

Identity is predominantly a concept applied to individuals; the transfer of the concept to groups or organizations follows from the notion that not only individuals in our modern society, but also collectives such as organizations and nation states, are perceived and presented as actors (Meyer et al., 1987). Czarniawska-Joerges (1994), for example, claims that one of the most popular modern conceptions of organizations is that of a super-person. Organizations are perceived and presented as actors who think, reason and behave in a coordinated and consistent way (see also Brunsson, 1989).

Just as we expect individual people to know what they are doing, and expect their thoughts to be at least partly in control of their actions, so that they are not carried away by their limbs without the knowledge of their heads or thoughts, so do we also expect a modern organization to be controlled by its head, and we expect that its head can account for what the organization is doing. The concept of organizational identity implies the conception of the organization as an individual. Apart from this, we also expect an organization to have a task or an objective, as well as a clear division of labor and responsibility. From this it follows that in all organizations a lot of attention is focused on issues such as control, integration, strategies, accounting and the like, the idea being that similar principles about effective organization can be applied in any setting — be it a state debt-collection authority, a hospital, a car producer, a pharmaceutical company or a sports club.

One expression and possible intensification of such a development is that management consultants or organizational consultants are engaged in all kinds of organizations, and the argument for hiring them is not that they are experts on the specific operations carried out in the organization, but rather experts on organizational matters in general. Czarniawska-Joerges (1990) named these consultants "merchants of meaning," describing them as persons with tool-boxes and identity-kits that the public organizations used in their search for meaning. The tools and kits involve a number of labels taken from the private sector which are used more or less metaphorically in the public organizations that these consultants work with.

I took part in a meeting of managers from all different levels in a state debt collection authority.[6] The state-operated debt-collection authority is a regional authority whose task it is to collect unpaid private and public debts. A consultant had been called in to work with them on a new organization design. He started his speech, when presenting his main ideas, by emphasizing that he did not know anything about their operations, but had many years of experience from efficient industrial companies. Thus, what mattered was general knowledge about organization, not about the specific operations connected to recovering and collecting debts and taxes.

Another meeting that I attended, in a hospital, gave a similar impression. This meeting was held for the nurses, and this time there also was a speaker who did not stress the specifics of health care, but repeatedly stressed how the hospital or the hospital ward could be understood as any organization. When it came to terminology, I found myself thinking that I could have heard a similar speech in any organization. Even though the speech was held by a nurse, few specific health-care terms were used.

Imitating Success

Organizations seldom have direct experiences of the organizations or practices they imitate and refer to. What they imitate are rationalizations — stories constructed by actors in the "exemplary" organization, and their own translations of such stories. What spreads are not experiences or practices *per se*, but standardized models and presentations of such practices. The distance between the supposed source of the model — a practice, or an

---

6   The following two examples are based on a study of daily practices in two public organizations: a state debt-collection authority and a hospital ward. On various occasions over a year and a half, I followed the work of the staff of the organizations.

action pattern − and the imitating organization forms a space for translating, filling in and interpreting the model in various ways.

Success stories, i. e. accounts of specific examples defined as successes, have been conspicuous in the proliferation of science parks in Europe in the late 1980s and early 1990s. A Science Park is a planned area around a university where high-tech firms are located. For many regional planners in the late 80s, such parks were perceived as the solution to various regional and industrial problems. Success stories about science parks were also frequently written and related to. These stories took the form of "recipes" (Saxenian, 1988). They were usually circulated in consulting books, in journals, by consultants, in conferences and interaction between organizations.

When using such recipes, it seems that it should be important to take differences in conditions and contexts between the imitated and the imitating organizations into consideration. The planning of European science parks as modeled on the successes of Silicon Valley, Route 128, and similar examplars, has been criticized for a lack of such consideration. Numerous authors have argued that there are no − nor can there ever be − "success formulae" (Hall and Marcusen, 1985; Blakely et al, 1987; Saxenian, 1988). What leads to success in one situation might not be possible to duplicate in another situation. This argument is supported by the fact that almost every other science park planned and built in the USA has failed (Taylor, 1985; DesForges, 1986). It is not easy to find out very much about these failures, which may not come as a big surprise because, as Sevón writes in this volume, Western society celebrates its winners. It is the successes which draw attention and which are referred to. Less successful changes are seldom related in this context. Of course, certain aspects of all science parks can be defined as failures, but they are seldom mentioned. Certain features of the imitated example are usually not given any attention (Rogers and Larsen, 1984). And even if everybody knows that changes can never be fully controlled, changes accomplished in one place serve as a prototype, accompanied by an underlying assumption that this prototype can be imitated and implemented anywhere, and that it is possible to plan everything.

One research park was established in southern Stockholm in the late 1980s[7]. During the planning phase, frequent references were made to various famous research parks in the US, the UK and France. Listening to these, however, one could easily reach the conclusion, as I did, that what the planners of the research park in southern Stockholm imitated was not the frequently praised Silicon Valley, but rather the story about it, and more specifically, the success story of Silicon Valley. Interestingly enough, some aspects which were often mentioned in connection with the success story of

---

[7]   I studied how the research park was being planned and established. A more complete description of this project is to be found in Sahlin-Andersson (1990).

Silicon Valley, (for example, the nice weather, the scenic environment, and the existing industrial structure in the region) could not be copied and were left out of the references made.

Situation- and time-specific features and unplanned elements of change are seldom mentioned in references to "success models." As a specific course of events emerges as exemplary for many very different situations, it is disconnected from time and place and forms a context-free prototype. The likely result of such imitation processes is thus not exact copies but instead something which differs considerably from the imitated model. This is well described and analyzed by Westney (1987), who showed that the imitating organization often lacks first-hand knowledge about the organizations they imitate. DiMaggio and Powell provided a rationale for similar observations, writing that ."... institutional models are unlikely to be imported whole cloth into systems that are very different from the ones in which they originate" (DiMaggio and Powell, 1991, p. 29).

When the regional planners who were establishing the science park in southern Stockholm referred to internationally-known examples, they in fact referred to the stories about these examples. If we view prototypes as recipies that one should follow in order to "bake a success" in a new setting, we would of course not expect success to follow if some of the ingredients were left out. However, the recipe metaphor is not a very suitable one, since it again directs our attention to the origin of the model, whereas I have shown above that prototypes are formed and transformed as they are circulated.

Røvik's study of consultants who worked with public organizations in Norway provides another illustration of a similar kind (Røvik, 1992a). These consultants introduced market-like or enterprise-like models into the public organizations. Røvik asked the consultants about the sources of their suggested models. Only a few times did the consultants relate to their own experiences. Those consultants had in fact very few possibilities to learn about how the proposed models worked in practice, since they left the organizations too early to be able to know what the effects of their efforts were. They had also had very few contacts with other consultants or other organization reformers. One service company was repeatedly mentioned as a success and an example to follow – Scandinavian Airline System (SAS). Interestingly enough, these consultants did not refer to personal experience with the reformation of SAS, but rather to a published success story of this company, written by its CEO, Mr. Jan Carlzon.

A third example where a model was reformulated in the course of imitation comes from a state debt-collection authority. The authority is now presented, in policy documents, information folders, and internal meetings, in what can be described as a business or enterprise-inspired terminology. Concepts such as market, competitors and market share, which have traditionally been associated not with public authorities but with private enterprise, are now frequently heard at meetings. The authority has defined its "customers"; they are neither the debtors nor the creditors, but the public. In the state authorities' public documents, policy statements, etc., the importance of customer orientation is described in terms of the democratic ideal, people's governance. The customers are defined as those who pay for the authorities' operations − not directly, but via taxes. It turns out that this is the group traditionally called "citizens," a concept which, however, seems to be of less rhetorical value in the recent change processes.

The terms "customer" and "customer orientation" were frequently used by the personnel as well. They saw as their "customers" the persons they met every day: debtors. What "customer orientation" meant to them was that they had to be nice to the debtors, inform them about the ways the authority worked, and so on. What is more, this was accompanied by a concern that the debtors' cases should be handled as quickly, smoothly and easily as possible. The personnel emphasized, for example, that it was important for the debtors to be able to reach them by phone. The fact that the switchboard did not always work satisfactorily caused a lot of irritation among the personnel − especially in relation to the rhetoric of customer orientation. Even the head of the department sometimes used the term "customer" this way, although she used the term by its other meaning when talking about general policies. One should add that the authority is partly financed by fees from private creditors. These private creditors were never described as the authority's customers. While those parts of the market model which did not seem to fit the public agencies were not given attention, other parts were pulled out of their context and given a new meaning.

Westney (1987) showed that the common distinction between innovation and imitation, where it is often implied that imitation is less pioneering than innovation (innovation is then often assumed to originate in an idea that a certain person came up with), is a false one. The creation of new forms and innovative elements are part of the imitation process since there are no ready-made models which remain unchanged as they spread. Rather, the spreading models are continuously shaped and reshaped in the process (see also Sevón, this volume).

Edelman (1988) reminded us that it is followers who make leaders rather than vice-versa. Bourdieu (1977) demonstrated how impossible it is to explain the value of something by asking about its origin, its producer. His recommendation was to abandon the logic which leads one to seek the origin of a creation, and to look instead for the system of relations in the field where the value is generated. Thus, in order to explain which patterns of action are being imitated and defined as successes, we need to see how the imitation process proceeds.

According to Latour (1986) all knowledge acquired at a distance involves elements of translation. The follower interprets and translates experiences presented by others. Such translations, in turn, enrich the source of the knowledge with new ways of interpreting their experiences. It is a process in which the story of what has happened is constantly rewritten as it spreads. The imitating organization and the imitated prototype are continuously reinterpreted and reformulated. A success story cannot be explained by its origin, as the success is produced in the process of translation.

The Editing of Success

The circulation of certain prototypes can be described as a continuous editing[8] process in which, in each new setting, a history of earlier experiences is reformulated in the light of present circumstances and visions of the future. An exemplary story is edited relative to the circumstances under which the new venture is being designed. Certain practicies and forms are generalized, circulated and re-edited. Various contingencies, limitations and obstacles affect the story. Meanings ascribed to and derived from protypes are edited contingent upon changing situational and institutional circumstances and constraints. This is why, for instance, the story about how Silicon Valley developed often varies considerably depending on where and when it is told. After all, it is easier to change exemplary stories than the circumstances under which a prototype is to be realized.

Why call this "an editing process"? To some extent, the term is used literally. Models are often spread in written form − in books, journals, at seminars and in lectures. Czarniawska and Joerges note in this volume that ideas are often materialized through being written down. Organizational imitation processes tend to involve distribution of written material.

However, the term is used here in a more metaphorical way too. By using the term "editing," I want to emphasize that the models are told and retold in various situations and told differently in each situation. In this sense, the concept of editing approaches the same connotation as the model of translation that Latour (1986) has described. Some of my illustrations describe a process that seems to leave room for creative reformulations. Prototypes are presented in so many reformulations that they become almost unrecognizable. However, it is just as clear that it is a process characterized by social control. Unlike Latour's concept of translation, editing is also a process of social control, conformism and traditionalism. Just as numerous rules − explicit and implicit − are applied to various publications, so are various rules applied to success stories.

---

8   The term was suggested by John Meyer during a seminar in Stockholm in 1990.

Not only the concept of translation, but also several other concepts, have been used to emphasize the processual character of the spreading of ideas. In his article about how a Sudanese community came to terms with the external world − a world in great part infused with Western society − Rottenburg (1989) demonstrated how cultures change via nonlinear development. It is not simply a case of one culture being rejected and another adopted thus substituting for the earlier culture. Several aspects − old and new, local and alien − are combined in a process of accretion. Just as I claim here that the imitating organization is no passive adopter, Rottenburg says that the adopting culture is no passive receiver of new cultural aspects. New forms are invented or created as aspects and parts of local and alien cultures are combined.

The concept of accretion, as well as similar concepts such as amalgamation, aggregation, accumulation, absorption, fusion etc., give the image of various elements being combined. Rottenburg chose the term accretion because in his opinion this term showed, better than others, that a synthesis was formed. However, Rottenburg focused on how one community dealt with the external world, being only interested as he was in the adoption phase of models and ideas. The focus in this paper is different: the whole process of transformation, rather than strictly adoption. Thus, in using the term editing, I want to emphasize that the origins of a prototype, as well as its introduction into a new environment, are constructed and reconstructed in the telling and retelling of exemplary stories. Synthesis strived for and achieved in the adoption phase is only one of several forms of transformation.

Editors

Talking about an editing process leads one to ask who the editors are. There are several agencies in modern societies whose main task it is to edit and mediate success stories circulating between organizations. In the examples given in this chapter, researchers, professionals, leaders, consultants and planners comprised such agencies.

The consultants, planners and authors who circulated the stories about successful research parks formulated stories about these parks: stories that took the form of recipies, with a set of necessary ingredients, that it was possible to copy elsewhere. Some aspects of the described research parks were left out while others were reinforced. The editors pointed to certain persons − heroes − who came up with the ideas about the research parks and who then realized these ideas, thereby initiating a prosperous development of certain regions.

The consultants that Røvik (1992a) studied related and reformulated the success stories of the private service companies. We find more examples of such editors in studies of organizational reformations. During the last years, local governments have in great numbers been reorganized into a more business- or enterprise-like form (Brunsson, 1994). Instead of having designed the policy units as well as the administration in functional terms, as was done before — each unit responsible for a certain set of policy issues (such as schooling, social welfare, culture, leisure, environmental issues, etc.) — several local governments were now formed into purchaser and provider units. The expressed idea was that these units were to develop in response to a market. The reformers hoped that a market would be created as the buying units looked for and compared alternative providers. In some municipalities, the politicians formed purchaser units and the administrators acted as providers; in other local governments, we find politicians playing both purchaser and supplier roles. These reforms were pursued with the argument that competition would make local government more efficient. Consultants introducing purchaser and provider models into local governments as usual did not refer to their own experiences, but rather to stories about others' experiences and to ideal models — for example, about how a perfect enterprise should work on the market.

There is also a growing number of international editing organizations. One such editor is the OECD. One part of the OECD, named PUMA, collects data from the OECD countries concerning public management reforms. These presentations are then (literally) edited and summarized in reports which are spread around the world. One idea with such reports is that one should be able to compare the OECD countries in terms of how and to what extent they were reforming their public sectors. In this editing, in order to facilitate such a comparison, certain aspects of each country and certain aspects of the various change processes are omitted while others are elaborated upon.

A model may also be edited in the process of its adoption into the imitating organization, where the model usually has to be combined with local practices and other adopted models. The consultant who introduced the new organizational design into the debt-collection authority was one such editor who circulated translated experiences and protypes. He related others' experiences and used them to illustrate the points he wanted to make, and to support his suggestions regarding how to change the authority. With the help of a few models taken from basic textbooks of organization theory, he translated and generalized the present situation in the authority as well as the experiences of other organizations. The head of the authority, as well as its personnel, edited the customer concept as they applied it to their client relations. In this process, they ascribed new meanings to the term so that it captured both old and new ways of understanding client relationships and the societal function of the authority.

In these examples, we have seen how actors circulate stories about certain practices, events, pattern of actions, and organization models. What is more, they reformulate the stories as they circulate them. As is the case for all editors, they try to affect the way in which the message was presented. They cannot, however, disregard the context in which the editing is made, the text which is being edited, and the recipient of the edited text. We can identify a number of editing rules which restrict the editors' work.

Editing Rules

The editing rules for a publication evolve in specific contexts. Such rules are often implicit and not subject to choices or discussions. They can often be deduced only indirectly − from the way the published article is written − and they are taken for granted by the editors, if not always by the authors. Similarly, in the circulation of prototypes, it is hard to find a set of clear critera, or rules according to which the success stories must be constructed. These editing rules are not explicit and subject to discussion, and can only be observed indirectly from the way the prototypes are portrayed. The editors translate the story relative to the situation to which the prototype is to apply. They also translate their stories in terms of those prescriptions given by the greater institutional context. Editing rules restrict and direct the translation in each phase of the process, and are re-created in each such phase.

I use the term "rule" without implying that there exist written instructions of some kind that are applied in the telling and retelling of stories. Instead, by using the term, I want to imply that the restrictions visible in the ways experiences and models are translated, although created and re-created in the process of translation itself, seem to be rule-like. Thus, although there are no "rules to follow," each edited story seems to reveal the "rules which have been followed." As the ethnomethodologists tell us, social control is mostly self-applied. Let us then have a look at circulating success stories to see what rules can be deduced.

Editing Rules Concerning Context

A first set of rules concerns the context. When models are applied in a setting different from that of the prototype, time- and space-bounded features are excluded. Specific local prerequisites are de-emphasized or omitted. Thus the prototype is disembedded − distanced or decoupled from time and space (Giddens, 1990). This also means that scale is not treated as an important characteristic of models. But, when a model is adopted in a new setting, it may again be contextualized – reembedded – so that time, space and scale are added to the model as important characteristics.

In the success-stories about the famous research parks, neither scale nor the institutional context in which the park grew were put forward as important characteristics or central explanations as to the development of the parks or the regions in which the parks were situated. However, when referring to these success-models, the planners in Stockholm did refer to some aspects of time, space and scale. They claimed, with reference to the international examples, that the close location of the high-tech firms to each other and to the university hospital were of great importance, while the university in northern Stockholm was too far away to be important for the companies in the southern part of the region. At other times, however, frequent references were made to Silicon Valley – where the distances between different places are much greater than in Stockholm if we measure them in terms of kilometers or minutes – as a good exampel of how important it is that many high-tech companies and universities be located close to each other. As the example referred to in the process of editing was decontextualized and then again recontextualized in the new setting, the scale of the whole setting was adjusted to the context in which the example was related.

When the consultant in the collection authority made references to customer relations, and to theoretical models of competitive strategies, he said that it didn't matter whether the authority had any competitors or not; the model still applied. Here we see another example of how one part of a setting is disconnected from its context and then again applied in a new setting where it is edited so that the prototype is ascribed new meanings.

In the adoption of a model in a setting, several prototypes may be mixed, or at least adjusted, so that they do not seem to contradict (Rottenburg, 1989). Thus, the editors' translation may be affected and restricted by local tradition, or, in other words, the history of the local setting may restrict the translating. Another possibility when potentially contradictory models are adopted is that they are decoupled from each other. In such cases, one can expect each single model not to be edited as much in the local setting, but to remain decontexualized (see for example Brunsson, 1989).

Again the collection authority may serve as an example. In their presentation and management of relations with whom came to be termed their customers, they combined old and new, and local and alien models. When these models seemed contradictory, they divided their clients into on the one hand those who were cooperative and thus could be treated as customers who could be given good service, and on the other hand those who were not cooperative and whom they had to force themselves upon and threaten with far-reaching sanctions. Thus, what the inspectors working in the authority did was to mix the old models with the new terminology and the new ideals they implied to as great an extent as as possible. When the old model and the new ideals seemed contradictory, they decoupled old and new models by applying them to different situations.

Editing Rules Concerning Formulation

A second set of editing rules concerns the formulation and labeling of a prototype. Models that attract attention are circulated more often. Studies of policy-making, decision-making, agenda-setting, etc. show that issues formulated in dramatized ways attract more attention than others (Edelman, 1988; Hilgartner and Bosk, 1988). Issues that are perceived as new and extraordinary, but not too different from what is generally accepted — issues that thus fit societal genres — attract attention. On a more general level of rules, one can speak of the rules of telling a good story, or of rules governing the metanarratives mentioned by Czarniawska and Joerges in this volume.

An initial interpretation of a certain development is sometimes formulated by a person who considers himself or herself to be the hero of the story and who writes the story to be circulated and thus become well-known. It is also common that politicians, officials and managers who are planning a new project of some kind travel around to collect ideas, impressions and experiences from elsewhere. During such visits some prominent persons are usually asked to tell the story about how it all came about. Important as it is for the speaker to tell a good story and to be polite to the listeners, he or she tells an edited version of what had happened, but this version may be understood by the listeners as the only true description of the development of the project they wanted to get information about. He or she may for example overemphasize certain events; dramatize the story or include a few jokes so that the audience's attention is kept.

Stories about a certain development can also be formulated by some observers — researchers or consultants — who become impressed by a certain development, write about it and circulate it as an example of good practice or as just a good story. Such editing may include elements of generalizing where, for example, too unique elements of the story are to be disregarded. It is in this phase that explanations of why the model is a success — or promises to be a success — are often added. What is more, the model is ordered in a logic of causes and effects so that it turns out as a planable process. This points to a third set of editing rules.

Editing Rules Concerning Logic

A third set of editing rules concerns the plot of the stories. The dominant model of presentation when it comes to organizational settings is that of formal logic, that is, of rationality (Brunsson, 1989). In the editing of a prototype, practices and solutions tend to be described according to such a rationalistic logic. Causes and effects are clarified. Effects are presented as resulting from identifiable activities. Prototypes follow a problem-solving logic. One or a few actors are usually identified as those who initiated and controlled a certain development. In such a way the model takes the form of a recipe which it is possible to transform into an implementation plan.

In terms of a background: explanations are given as to why a certain development has taken place. References are often made to scientific concepts and findings. The role of scientific references is not only to provide an explanation of why a development came about and a guarantee that it will come, but also to legitimate the model as serious and true.

The Construction of a New Identity

In some of the examples given in this chapter, the actors who translated and circulated the prototypes referred to a specific event which was seen as the origin of the model to follow. In other cases the actors did not refer to a concrete event but instead to a concept or a more or less theoretical model such as "customer orientation" or the "purchaser and supplier model." In the imitation of specific organizations or specific processes, such ideals existing in each field form editing rules or frames through which the examples are interpreted.

The term "customer orientation" emphasizes similarities between the state agency and the private business company. This was also the way it was used by the consultant in the collecting authority, who emphasized similarities between the state agency and private enterprises. However, the terminology was ascribed different meanings by people who worked in different parts of the agency, and also by the same persons in different situations. The ambiguity characterizing such terminology may provide room for various actors who want to pursue different purposes and interests. Thus, when emphasizing the importance of a customer-oriented agency, some may want to stress the importance of the agency's meeting the needs and wants of every one. Customer orientation is then related to the democratic ideal and equated with consumer or citizen orientation. With the same terminology, others see the possibility of getting the privatization issue on the agenda. Thus the discussion about customer orientation is seen as the first step towards adopting a whole market-model.

The ambiguity which evolves as various meanings are ascribed to the same terminology, makes it easy to get the new planning strategy on the agenda (Sahlin-Andersson, 1992). This ambiguity may, however, cause problems in terms of implementation, since it gives few directions about how exactly to act in a specific situation (Baier et al., 1986). The ambiguous change strategy may be well suited to reflecting various interests and claims put to the organizations, but less well suited for guiding action (Brunsson, 1985; 1989).

The reforms pursued in the public sector during the last decade, where parts of the market-model have been adopted (for example decentralization, new forms of resource allocation based on output-control and output measures, various kinds of MBO) have been launched with the promise of far-reaching results, but in retrospect they seem to have had little effect on the daily operations of the organizations. Both when the models are seen as recipes which are to be copied and when one looks at how the reforms are implemented there are obvious reasons to be disappointed. The reforms do not seem to be based on others' experiences, and they do not seem to give the promised results. However, if we view these reforms from an institutional perspective, the conclusion that nothing results from the reforms seems too short-sighted. If we view these reforms not as ways to copy other organizations but as ways to enter a new field and to construct a new identity, the reforms may have greater effects.

Even though an observer can easily identify contradictory and changing uses of terms, in the organizational settings I studied, the concepts' relative meanings were not discussed. Just as Berger (1966) described how the "world is apprehended as 'objective reality', that is, as reality that is shared with others and that exists irrespective of the individual's own preferences in the matter" (p. 108) so were the concepts treated as if they had the same meaning and content in all different settings. This also means that the use of concepts such as "customer" to describe a relationship between a client and the agency may lead to the person being defined as a customer interpreting the concept in a way more in accordance with the ideal model, and starting in fact to try to act as a customer, assuming for example the right to exit the transaction. Such expectations can be formed because the term "customer" is part of the larger terminology implied by the enterprise model. In that context, a customer is one who can turn to other producers, and thus various producers compete on the market to attract customers.

When agencies are perceived in terms taken from the enterprise model – or from a generalized organization model – agencies and business companies are described in similar terms, and differences between them are not put forward as being relevant or critical for the operations of the organizations. A new environment for the state agencies has been produced, not only consisting of new categories of actors – customers, and possibly competitors – but also of ideals, references and models. Thus, as a result of entering a new field, using a new terminology, acting in a new environment, developing new expectations and meeting new expectations from those with whom they interact, the organizations develop a new identity. The models, language and reforms stemming from such references produce new expectations, new interests, new relations and thus a new identity.

Once similarities between the agency and the ideal enterprise model have been emphasized, irrespective of what the intentions of such a comparison were in the first place, we can expect further changes of the public agencies which build on and strengthen the changed identity. The field is under structuration and the homogenizing process may continue (Giddens, 1984; DiMaggio, 1983). Further reforms may be designed by organizational actors, based on problems being defined as the agencies are compared with models and examples. Also, actors in the environment may expect the agency to be as businesslike as the terminology and models seem to imply. For example, citizens being defined as customers may in fact start acting as such. They may start to choose between services, they may start to treat the received service as merchandise and thus place certain demands on the agency.

In the study of a hospital and a collection authority I found that this development was taking place in the hospital, but less so in the collection authority. A possible explanation of the differences in reaction to the changed terminology may be that the clients have a stronger position in relation to the hospital than the collection authority. Alternatives to public health care have after all existed for a long time, even though these alternatives have been viewed as marginal phenomena in Swedish health care. Such alternatives are totally absent for the collection authorities' debtors. Even more important may be the fact that health care is designed to help patients, while the collection authority's task is to control its debtors.[9] The development might have been different if the authority had defined not only the debtors but also the creditors as their customers.

If we look at the public sector as a whole, we can see that the transformed identity of the public agencies has meant that further reforms have been pursued aimed at making the agencies more business like. In the 1980s, decentralization reforms were introduced into Swedish county and city administrations, often modeled on private companies. From observations of these reforms one could conclude that nothing much happened, if effects are evaluated according to what was promised as the reforms were introduced. This conclusion is based both on evaluations done by the organizations themselves and from independent studies (for example Brunsson et al., 1989).

The subsequent reform of state, city and county administrations in the late 1980s and early 1990s was more resource-oriented and aimed in many cases at forming internal markets. For example, in some cities and counties

---

9   The importance of such definitions of the organizations' activity is further elaborated by Forssell and Jansson in this volume.

each hospital or each department in a hospital now forms profit centers which are to buy and sell services from each other. Several agencies, hospitals or departments in hospitals have also to a greater extent than before started to market their services, both to other departments and to the public, now treated as and partly functioning as customers. These later reforms seem to have had a great impact on the daily operations of the organizations.

Of course, there are still important features distinguishing hospitals as well as for example many public agencies from the market model: Ownership is still public; there is not much competition; prices are set not in markets but rather in administrative processes. However, the organization field will continue to homogenize, and the public organizations are still in the periphery modeling themselves after the more successful and more legitimate private companies, factors preventing the public organizations from working as the ideal private business enterprise will still be what define problems in public organizations. The current emphasis on internal markets is a product of the earlier reforms that grew out of comparisons between public organizations and private companies. The current reforms are some of the first products of this new identity. At the same time as these reforms are designed and carried out, similarities with private companies are further emphasized in the public sector. Information exchanges with private companies are strengthened, interaction is increased, and the field structured.

Thus, we may predict that this is only the beginning of a strong homogenizing process which will make organizations even more similar. The special characteristics for the public organizations are being decreasingly emphasized as far as the design of such organizations is concerned, and increasingly seen as disturbing factors hindering the public agencies from functioning as ideal profit-oriented companies. So naturally, claims are put on public organizations to reduce political control and strengthen economic control. The changes in identity precede and form the basis for further changes, forming as adaptations to the new organization field. Reforms which at first seem disconnected or decoupled from the operations of the organization change its institutional identity, which in turn forms the basis for further reforms more coupled to and with greater effect on daily operations.

Institutional Isomorphism and Organizational Heterogeneity

The institutional perspective is one of the main perspectives in which the diffusion of models among the population of organizations has been studied. It has been criticized for giving an impression of organizations as passive and over-socialized. Diffusion is then seen as an almost automatic process (Powell and DiMaggio, 1991). In reaction to this view Friedland and Alford (1991) showed that each organization is simultaneously influenced and shaped by several partly-contradictory orders. Their conclusion was that this allows the individual organization to choose. Therefore, the individual organization is no passive adopter of trends. Galaskiewicz also emphasized that one should not "underestimate the interpretative and creative capacities of actors" (Galaskiewicz, 1991, p. 295). This essay is both a confirmation of and a reaction to these points.

In this chapter, I intended to show that the "imitating organization" is not a passive adopter of concepts and models defined and spread at the macro-level. However, the ability to maintain and form local practices is not mainly found in the choice between institutions but rather in the editing of models and concepts. New meanings are ascribed to the imitated models so they can be combined with previous working models.

One may, however, question what possibilities local actors have to control the process of translation. I have given examples of editing rules that restrict the translation of earlier experiences and models. What is more, with the strong emphasis given in this paper on the mutual influence of organizations and the importance of organizational identities and comparisons, one may conclude that imitating part of a model will bring with it further comparisons and further modeling of the same models.

Hence, the process does not seem to be reversible, but may on the other hand foster reactions. For example, subordinating a field under another may start a reaction in which the subordinated field will again try to conquer the boundaries of the field. New local identities may form where the specifics of one's local situation are emphasized as a reaction to concepts that stress common characteristics. We can see in the recent debate in the Swedish public sector that many organizational actors have emphasized that their organizations are authorities which cannot be defined and organized as service companies. However, no common definition of what is an authority and what distinguishes authorities from other public agencies has as yet been formulated among these organizations.

Quite recently a public discussion has intensified in Sweden about how to define different types of organizations within the public sector. The discussion appears in official reports as well as in local responses to the popular purchaser-provider models. In these debates it is emphasized that there are public organizations which cannot possibly be defined in business terms. Thus, one possible development is then that a new identity for the authorities be formed in reaction to the enterprisation trend. Whether this reaction results in a changed identity and changed ideals for the public authorities will perhaps be known after years of further studies of public organizations' continued search for new identities.

The Logic of Organizational Transformation: On the Conversion of Non-Business Organizations

Anders Forssell and David Jansson

Organizational Transformation and Corporatization

Organizations, it is sometimes argued, constantly change. There are, however, different kinds of organizational changes. Some changes are small and partial, involving, e. g. the introduction of an additional department or new budget system. Other changes are much more thorough and permeat the whole of the organization. In this chapter we will deal with a certain kind of thorough change. What we have in mind are those cases where an organization exchanges its old organization form for a new one. We call this general type of change *organizational transformation*. To further specify, this chapter does not deal so much with organizational transformation in general, but rather with a particular kind of transformation. It deals with the kind of organizational transformation that occurs whenever an organization which has generally been conceived of as a non-business organization is converted into a business organization. We will refer to this particular kind of of organizational transformation as *corporatization*. Our impression is that corporatization is quite a common process in contemporary societies of at least the West European kind.

In this chapter, the purpose is to reveal the intra-organizational logic at play whenever an organization is corporatized. The argument we will present is based on field studies of three cases of corporatization. The argument heavily emphasizes the importance of how the task of the organization is defined in the ongoing organizational discourse. We claim that there is a social stock of organizational knowledge that produces a basic consensus among organizational actors on how to organize − given that there is agreement on how the task of the organization is defined. Certain redefinitions of the task of the organization lead to a de-legitimation of the prevailing organization form at the same time that they bring about a legitimation of another.

A Social Stock of Organizational Knowledge

The perspective we will apply has its roots in the phenomenology of Alfred Schütz (1899−1959) and his analyses of the knowledge that is used in everyday life. Schütz stressed that only a tiny part of the knowledge that people use can be traced back to their personal experiences. The greater part of a human being's knowledge is on the contrary social in its origin in the sense that it consists of substance one has been provided with by others, e. g. by parents, teachers, friends and colleagues. One's stock of knowledge at hand is not built up in social isolation, but is instead the product of background, training, socializing with friends, interactions in working life, and so on. From childhood on, the individual is involved in what Schütz called a "stockpiling" of typifications of the world. Language is a typifying medium of utmost importance in the transmission of knowledge (Schütz, 1973).

Without doubt, there are differences in the knowledge people have due to differences in their biographies, e. g. differences in their backgrounds and training. For instance, some people obviously "know more" about "the same thing" than other people do. Nevertheless, there is a stock of knowledge that many people share, despite their different biographies. There is a common stock of knowledge, made up of typifications, that produces agreement among people in their interpretations of experiences as well as conformity in their orientation towards the future, e. g. in their actions and in their anticipations of what is going to happen (Schütz and Luckmann, 1973).

The common stock of knowledge contains layers of knowledge that is not questioned or doubted but simply taken for granted. Unless we are confronted with what we conceive of as counter-evidence, we take for granted that what we know to be valid knowledge. Furthermore, the knowledge on which we capitalize in everyday life is incomplete or limited in its scope. We rely heavily on what Schütz called "recipe knowledge" − a kind of knowledge that provides us with types of means for types of ends, or types of solutions to types of problems. Since our everyday life is to a large extent governed by our practical motives, we normally are content with knowing that we can achieve what we aim for by behaving in a certain way or using a certain tool. We are not worried about or motivated to learn about all the complexity that may be involved in how those effects virtually are brought about (Schütz, 1971).

Although the work of Schütz never has been part of mainstream social theoretical thinking, his ideas have been quite influential. For instance, they were heavily used by Peter Berger and Thomas Luckmann in their prominent argument for a sociology of knowledge that did not focus on intellectuals and the history of their theories and ideas but instead on a phenomenon of much greater importance for social life, namely the social construction of reality (Berger and Luckmann, 1966). In the realm of organizational analysis, we feel that Schütz' work is at the very roots of so-called neoinstitutionalism, a line of thought the birth of which has been dated back to the end of the 1970s, when the sociologist John Meyer published several papers that proved to be very influential (Powell and DiMaggio, 1991, p. 11).

The concept of neoinstitutionalism indicates that there is another, older institutionalism in organizational analysis, and that there are some important differences between them. Some of the important differences concern the conceived object, meaning and context of institutionalization. The old institutionalism, very much associated with Philip Selznick and his work at the end of the 1940s and in the 1950s, argues that specific organizations sometimes are institutionalized in their local contexts in the sense that they are infused with value and therefore cease to be mere instruments designed to attain given goals, since their survival has become more important than goal-attainment (Selznick, 1957).

Neoinstitutionalism, on the other hand, claims that organizational models sometimes are institutionalized in non-local contexts in the sense that they become commonly known and accepted. These ideas have been very influential in accounting for similarities between organizations, a subject awkwardly dealt with by competing schools of thought.

In our attempt to answer the question of why a prevailing organizational logic is rejected and a new one celebrated by organizational actors, we too will claim the existence of organizational models that are widely known and accepted. However, we will direct attention to institutionalized organizational models that differ from those with which neoinstitutionalism has mainly been occupied. Neoinstitutionalism has mostly focused on models that are quite restricted in the sense that they concern specific elements of organizational structures and procedures, e. g. models of budgeting and accounting (see e. g. Røvik, 1992b). We will argue that the social stock of organizational knowledge contains models that not only are more abstract, but probably also more widely known and enduring.

Institutionalized Forms of Organization

Institutionalized forms of organization constitute an important part among those models. Institutionalized forms of organization are abstract typifications that can be used to distinguish among different types of organizations.

By claiming that forms of organization are institutionalized we mean that they are to be understood as phenomena that, at least approximately, describe a general or common knowledge about widely acknowledged forms of organization. By describing what "everyone knows," different forms of organization and their characteristics are used by people in general in their interpretation of organizational experiences as well as in their orientation towards the future, e. g. when they predict what will happen or deliberate on their own actions.

The extent to which a form of organisation is institutionalized or not depends on whether its typification is widely acknowledged by organizational actors in the field. Therefore, institutionalized forms of organization should be kept apart from the analytical constructions of forms of organization used by some theorists (e. g. Mintzberg, 1979; Morgan, 1986 or Scott, 1987a). In cases like these, the constructions used should be considered ideal types, constructed by the analysts as tools for their analytical purposes, rather than attempts at describing "what everybody knows."

Attempts at describing institutionalized forms of organization in the literature often differ somewhat, but most list the business enterprise, the public agency and the association among institutionalized forms of organization, and most attribute a common core of features for each of these forms (see e. g. Forssell, 1992; Sjöstrand, 1993; Brunsson, 1994; and Ahrne, 1994). However, it must be said that it is sometimes difficult to draw an absolute line between institutionalized forms of organization and more analytical constructions since the phenomenon of institutionalization is relative; it is a matter of more or less. The more widely acknowledged, the more institutionalized. Thus, if an analytical construction became an accepted description in the field, we would refer to it as an institutionalized model.

Specifying forms of organization is problematic. The more elaborate specifications, the more it is likely that the specifications will be contested. Only some core knowledge of forms of organization is common, part of a social stock of organizational knowledge. Many actors know only, and perhaps even vaguely, of that core knowledge, while others have much more detailed knowledge on what characterizes different forms of organization. Still we suggest that most actors would agree that organizations can be classified according to form of organization, as business enterprises, public agencies or associations, and that there are important differences between types of organizations, as regards e. g. the conception of organizational environment, the relations between an organization and its environment, and the internal organizational tasks, principles and means of control.

Since this chapter deals with the type of organizational transformation we call corporatization, we will focus on the institutionalized form of the business organization: the business company or enterprise. Starting with the conception of the environment, we claim that in the organizational life of modern societies it is taken for granted that business companies act in markets; that the relevant environment of a business enterprise is considered to be the market. The market is often defined in geographic terms and the business enterprise is supposed to be mobile; it is able to move, or to expand, from one market to another, whereas for instance, a public administration is perceived as being part of a larger political administrative organization that is tied to a particular geographic territory.

Different environments are considered to be "inhabited" by different kinds of actors, and the relationships between the organizations and these inhabitants are different. Organizations of different forms interact with different kinds of actors and the relationships are of different kinds. Thus, the business enterprise interact with suppliers and customers, and itself acts as both of these. Organizations and individuals are interacting in the market, and their exchanges are supposed to be temporary and voluntary, since the actors are always supposed to be looking for the best deal. Related to this is the idea of competition which is supposed to prevail in the market. This characterization can be compared to the public agency and the association, for whom other types of actors are crucial, and for whom the relationships with these actors are more lasting. For the public agency, the citizen is the "natural" actor and for the association the member plays the crucial role. In both cases the concept of competition is less relevant.

Another important feature of forms of organization is the mode of financing. The business company is, at least in the longer run, dependent on sales revenues for its survival. The public agency and the association on the other hand obtain their financial resources differently: the public agency is typically financed by taxes and the association by the members' contributions.

Other important points concern the internal logic. For instance, for the business enterprise one or several owners constitute the legal principals, who are in possession of the ultimate authority over the organization. The owners normally expect the business enterprise to generate profits. To control the achievement of its main task, the business company typically is subjected to demands for returns on allocated resources. This is very different compared to the public agency, which is considered to be an instrument for political intentions. To control the public agency its principal – a political assembly – decides on rules and directives for its operations. The members of an association, on the other hand, typically share some kind of interest. The shared ideas among members often serve as the main mode of control of the association. These ideas ensure that the organization in its operations continues to further the interests of the members.

From the dominant task and means of control of an organization a governing principle can be deduced. For the business company the principle of efficiency is of utmost importance since an inefficient organization is thought to be unable to compete and therefore not able to generate expected profits. This can be contrasted with the public agency, for which political effectiveness, i. e. its ability to implement politically decided rules and directives, constitutes the governing principle.

Features of the form of organization of the business company are listed in the table. To avoid misunderstanding, it must be said that not all existing organizations can be considered "pure" business companies or, for that matter, "pure" public agencies or associations. Many contain features of several institutionalized forms of organization or are in transition from one

Table 1: Common features of the institutionalized form of the business enterprise

Concept of environment	Market
Environmental actors	Customers/suppliers, competitors
Kind of relationships	Voluntary/temporary; Competition
Mode of finance	Sales revenues
Principals	Owner(s)
Task	To generate profits
Means of control	Return on investments
Governing principle	Efficiency

form to another — as we shall see later. But even in the cases of "mixed" organizations we would claim that most often one form dominates over the other.

It should also be added that the three institutionalized forms of organization mentioned above — the business company/enterprise, the public agency/ authority, the association — are not the only forms of organization referred to in the literature. For instance, Brunsson (1994) counts the political assembly, Sjöstrand (1985) the clan, and together with Ahrne (1994) the family as other examples of institutionalized forms of organization. But among formal hierarchical (Sjöstrand, 1985) and action-oriented (Brunsson, 1994) forms of organization the three forms referred to above are the most commonly mentioned.

Institutionalized Forms of Activity

In analyzing processes in which some organizations changed their form of organization and became more similar to the model of the business enterprise, we reached the conclusion that there are not only institutionalized forms of organization, but also institutionalized forms of activity: in addition to knowledge about different forms of organization, the social stock of knowledge consists of knowledge about how types of activity and types of forms are combined.

Using the term "type of activity" we refer to those abstract and well known, i. e. institutionalized, labels like teaching, entertaining, manufacturing, serving or farming, but also to their more specific subcategories like high school teaching, piano playing, production of cars, serving lunches, cultivating grain. However, we do not refer to those specific manual operations performed by the actors involved, i. e. the teacher, the piano-player, the assembly line worker, the waiter or the farmer, since these operations are hardly known to outsiders, either as linguistic or practical/manual knowledge.

In everyday life we do not typically experience organizations as consisting of form only. We do not experience them only as e. g. business enterprises, public agencies or associations, but also as entities that are engaged in some kind of activity. In other words, we conceive of organizations as entities combining activity and form. We live in a world in which there are numerous restaurants, industrial companies, schools, employment agencies, football clubs, trade unions, hospitals, et cetera. Not for all, but for some types of activities there is a general knowledge about their form of organization. The activity form is, in other words, institutionalized, meaning that "everyone" has some abstract knowledge about how the activity is organized. Its typical features, such as mode of financing, relation to environment, principals, et cetera, are elements of a social stock of knowledge.

Of course, the repertoire of institutionalized activity forms may vary over time and space. Activity forms are subjected to institutionalization as well as deinstitutionalization. The form of organization of one type of activity may in one period in time be unknown to almost everyone; later, its form of organization may be generally known; and later still it may be common knowledge that the type of activity is carried out not only in that form of organization but also in other forms of organization.

Furthermore, the repertoire of institutionalized activity forms may differ in space, e. g. between countries. For example, in one country the telephone system may be considered by everyone as an activity run by a public agency, while in another country it may be commonly known that the activity is conducted by several private telephone companies. Nevertheless, in analyzing organizational changes in a given context in time and space, we claim that the notion of institutionalized activity forms may be useful.

Organizations as Instruments

One reason why the notion of institutionalized activity forms may be useful in analyzing organizational changes has to do with what we claim to be yet another element in the social stock of organizational knowledge, namely that organizations should be instruments or tools for carrying out certain tasks or activities. This is contrary to how organizations are often described by organizational researchers. Careful observations on how organizations actually work have led organizational researchers to reach for metaphors that firmly reject the notion of organizations as instruments. Consider e. g.

the often-used metaphors of organizations as organisms, as anarchies or as political systems (Morgan, 1986).

But discourses in organizations on how to organize are not descriptive, but prescriptive, and thus governed by notions not of how things are, but how they ought to be (Brunsson and Olsen, 1993). Relying on our field studies, we claim that the idea that the organization should be an instrument is typically not questioned but instead celebrated or simply taken for granted by participants in discourses on how to organize. Consequently, definitions of the activities to be carried out by the organization are not only conceived of as obvious and natural elements of the discourse, but also elements of crucial importance for how competing ways of organizing are appraised in the discourse.

Our argument may be interpreted as contradictory to what is often claimed in research on organizational change, namely that definitions of the future task of the organization do not govern the way organizations change, while e. g. parochial interests (Pfeffer, 1981) or a propensity to adapt to external norms (Meyer and Scott, 1983) do. Therefore, we would like to stress that the question of local motives is beyond the scope of our argument. However, we have no reason to exclude the possibility that organizational actors participate strategically in the ongoing discourse. For instance, they can promote or simply not oppose definitions of the future activity of the organizations that they consider beneficial in their attempts to bring about outcomes which they value for other reasons; that are more obscure and controversial than the idea that the organization should be an instrument for carrying out certain activities.

A Logic of Organizational Transformation

Our analysis of processes in which the prevailing form of organization is rejected and a new one celebrated shows that it is of crucial importance how the future activities of the organization are defined in the ongoing organizational discourse. It is obvious that processes in which activities are defined are far from an insignificant play with words, but can have far-reaching consequences since different definitions of the organization's activity may imply completely different ways of organizing. Due to the existence of institutionalized activity forms, some definitions of activities legitimate one form of organization while simultaneously delegitimating alternative ones.

Obviously, organizational transformation is not likely to be brought about by any definition of the future activities of the organization. But if a new definition manages to push aside competing ones, and if this definition of the organization's activity indicates an institutionalized activity form that includes another form of organization than the one previously adhered to by the organization, the way is paved for transformation, i. e. change of form of organization. Given the definition, and provided that it is accepted, neither the need for a thorough change nor the nature of that change will be questioned or disputed, but rather collectively conceived of as quite obvious and natural.

In order to illustrate the logic of organizational transformation outlined above, three empirical examples of processes of corporatization will be presented. These descriptions show that in an on-going organizational discourse, features of the institutionalized form of organization of the business company that previously were not referred to, or played a rather insignificant role in the organizations involved, were introduced. At the core of the discourse was the organizational activity: What kind of activity was the organization supposed to be involved in? As has been shown many times, the relationship between talk, decision and action is problematic (March, 1984; Baier et al., 1986; Brunsson, 1989). Still, the illustrations show that the organizational discourse affected organizational practice, at least to some degree.

First Case: The Savings Banks

When this story begins − in the 1950s − many Swedish savings banks already had been in existence for more than one hundred years. These banks, sometimes described as charity organizations, were founded as popular savings associations, and throughout the history of the savings banks the main activity was always saving and the promotion of savings. In some rural areas the savings bank's role as a credit institute for local farmers was emphasized more, but lending was mostly just considered to be the other side of the coin, and the only purpose of the loans was to be able to invest the savings in the most secure way. For that reason, most credits were mortgage loans.

All savings banks used to be local banks, although some were very small, restricting their activity to one parish, while others were larger, spreading their activities across a city or a county. The legal form of savings banks resembled that of a foundation or trust; there existed no owner(s) and no demands for profits except for the need to secure the bank's existence. During this period, a common formal structure evolved which was encoded in the Savings Banks Act. According to this Act, a savings bank was put under some surveillance by its local government, which elected half of its trustees. The trustees elected the board, which was the most important governing body. The board decided on all major loans and employed the managing director.

During the 1930s, 1940s and the 1950s, the savings banks and their national organizations intensified their promotional activities in a variety of ways. They engaged elementary school teachers to teach the children to regularly save a small sum in the schools; in offices and factories they helped to organize savings clubs; infants were given money-boxes and an account were opened for them; weekly savings campaigns were organized by the local savings banks; the savings banks' union produced various papers, brochures, films and other promotional materials that were distributed throughout the country.

The many activities that the savings banks conducted during the 1930s, 1940s and 1950s for the purpose of promoting savings can be interpreted as an organizational response to, or part of, a wider societal change that carried Sweden through a phase of rapid modernization. The Social Democrats came into power in the 1930s and became a hegemonic political force for several decades thereafter. Their main mission became the construction of the welfare state. An important aspect of this project, that was not only political but also social and cultural, was the need to further educate and reform people, since modern society required modern people. Evidence of this effort can be found in many areas of social life. One was the activities of the savings banks. By promoting savings, the savings banks tried to teach people to rationally plan their economic future. In this way, the savings banks played their role in the task of modernizing society.

After the Second World War, big changes took place in Swedish society. Accelerating industrialization and trade increased prosperity among new strata of the population and turned these strata into interesting new customers for many business enterprises. For the savings banks this meant that their many savers became attractive potential customers for the commercial banks. This was a new situation, and for a group of young "progressive" managers it meant a challenge. For them it was obvious that the old project had to be replaced by a new one. At this time it was not at all clear what the new project should be, but for the "progressives" it was obvious that the savings banks had to adjust to the new situation by changing into more ordinary banks. From the 1950s onwards, they repeatedly stated this view in internal debates on strategy. The argument they used combined threat and hope, and the essence of it was:

> Competition is certainly going to be harder in the future, but if we change our way of doing things we will not only survive, but also be successful.

In this debate the concepts of competition and customers were, for the first time, seriously introduced into the discourse of the savings banks.

Actual competition between commercial banks and savings banks became evident for the first time when, in the late 1950s, companies started to pay wages to their employees via bank accounts instead of by direct payment of cash. For this payment, the employers used their own (commercial) bank. By doing this, they connected the employees to their own bank and thereby, intentionally or not, disturbed the link between the employees and their savings bank. For progressive savings banks managers, this was considered a threat; they saw the risk of losing many of their savers and thus their position as the major bank of the people. The response of the savings banks was not obvious however. Conservative managers and board members were hesitant to let savings banks introduce wage accounts themselves. They considered such a measure both risky and costly. But the progressive managers were eager to compete with the commercial banks, and they soon responded to the challenge by introducing wage accounts in the savings banks under their control.

This debate between conservatives and progressives in the savings banks was a crucial one for a number of reasons. On this specific issue it meant that although the competition between different banks for wage accounts continued for a long time, in the end the savings banks became the leaders in this race, and by this they reaffirmed their position as the major household banks. On a more general level, the outcome of this debate, where an internal progressive opinion won out over a conservative one, determined the strategic direction for years to come.

During this process, when savings banks became competitors to other banks, and savers were converted to customers, other measures were taken to make savings banks and other banks conform to one single bank model. This process started with the products and activities of the banks, but it was halted by the legislation regulating banks and bank operations. There existed different Bank Acts, each defining a specific bank institute, and for each institute a specific set of rules. Beside savings banks and commercial banks, co-operative farmers' credit societies were also defined as a specific type of bank.

In the beginning of the 1960s, a committee appointed by the government was given the task of proposing a new bank legislation. Among the members of the committee were representatives of the different bank institutes. The crucial issue for the committee soon became whether to maintain the traditional division of banking activities by keeping different rules of operation for each type of bank. The alternative was to open the whole banking sector to all types of banks, constraining all to one set of rules. That is, continued division of, or competition among, different kinds of banks. The representative of the savings banks was the executive of the Savings Banks Association, who at the same time was the most prominent "progressive" in the savings banks' camp. His position was clear: the savings banks ought to operate in all parts of banking. Thus he strongly argued for an end to the traditional division. This position eventually became the position of the whole committee. A proposal was written and finally decided on by the parliament at the end of the 1960s.

At the time it was probably difficult to see the importance of these decisions and actions. In retrospect though, it seems obvious that they paved the way for future actions and decisions. In the savings banks the long ideological campaign of the "progressives" had changed people's ideas of what activities savings banks ought to carry out and how they should go about doing them, and what their environment looked like. That is, new definitions replaced old ones.

During the 1960s, 1970s and 1980s, most savings banks continued their process of change. In order to become more competitive, a large number of mergers took place, reducing the number of savings banks from over 400 in 1960 to about 100 at the end of the 1980s. Most of these savings banks gradually started to offer the most common bank services. This process of change was never completed, however. Some savings banks refused to take part in mergers, but changed other aspects of their activity and organization. A few small savings banks, situated in rural areas, have remained "old-fashioned" in almost all respects.

The process of redefinition did not only occur in the savings banks. Since new legislation redefined the situation for the whole of the bank sector, providing banks with new rules and new environments, similar processes of redefinition happened in other types of banks with the result that all kinds of banks appeared increasingly more similar. But some differences remained; the commercial banks still had the big companies as customers, the farmers' banks still were the most important banks for the agricultural sector, and the savings banks still were the most important banks for the households.

In 1989, the savings banks decided on the largest merger thus far. The argument was the same that was used many times before: Competition was going to be harder in the future and in order to survive and be successful the savings banks had to adjust to this situation. The intention this time was to merge the twelve largest savings banks into one single banking group. This decision was made in the last days of the boom that had characterised the financial sector during the 1980s. However, in the beginning of the 1990s the real estate market collapsed and a crash in the financial sector followed. For the large savings banks this meant giant losses in 1991 and 1992. The losses made a complete merger seem urgent and necessary, and in 1992 a consolidated Savings Bank of Sweden was formed, being the largest of all Swedish banks. Legally it was constructed as a joint stock company, thereby definitively abandoning the old legal form of savings banks.

The boom in the financial sector in the late 1980s and the following crash in the early 1990s hit all types of banks in similar ways. First, they made big profits and then enormous losses. In this situation only the state has saved many banks from going bankrupt. The only banks that escaped this situation were those who kept a more conservative policy on loans during the boom. Among this group of banks was only one of the major commercial banks, but most of the small and local savings banks. Ironically, the savings bank which was the most eager to change also experienced the heaviest losses, and was one of the first banks to become bankrupt.

A process parallel to the one in the savings banks took place in the farmers' banks. After big losses the regional banks were merged into a joint Farmers' Bank which, similar to the Savings Bank of Sweden, was constructed as a joint stock company. By these events the isomorphic process of the Swedish banking sector had proceeded even further; after making products, services, ideas, and operations similar, all kinds of banks also adopted the same legal form of organization.

Conclusion

We have tried to show how the organizational discourse changed during the modernization of savings banks. First, the activity of savings banks was redefined from saving to banking and the production of bank services. Consequently the local community as a relevant conception of environment was replaced by the concept of the market, and the concept of savers were replaced by the concept of customers. Competition was introduced, and an emphasis on market-shares and profits replaced an emphasis on solvency. All these changes in discourse paved the way for those changes in practices, organization, and activities that converted most savings banks into organizations where a business logic prevailed.

Obviously, the activity form of banking contained another form of organization than the activity form of savings (banking). Thus, when the activity of saving banks was redefined, the logic of transformation came into play, making corporatization seem a natural and unavoidable outcome for most relevant actors.

Second Case: The Swedish Railways

Ever since its foundation in the middle of the 19th century the Swedish State Railways (SSR) had been a state-owned business agency. This specific form of organization, partly a business organization and partly a public agency was, and is, common in Sweden. Such organizations are financed partly by the state and partly by revenues from their businesses, i. e. from selling products and services to customers. The state appoints the board and the general director of the business agency and sets the regulatory framework, within which the board and management are supposed to run the organization. The capital of the agency is owned by the state, however, and the most important requirement of the agency is that it is supposed to generate a certain return on this capital. Other important organizations, apart from the Swedish State Railways, that have been organized as business agencies are the national organizations handling telephone and postal services.

The business agency is, as the term implies, a mix of the business enterprise and the public agency, but because of the many political restrictions, these organizations have been viewed mainly as public agencies. In the 1990s this is changing. Several of the business agencies are in the process of being privatized, which, in the first stage, means that they are being transformed into state-owned joint stock companies. In a later stage the plans are to sell at least parts of the stock to private interests and to open the monopolies to competitors.

The task of the SSR was historically to administer the railways and to provide the country with railway transport within the organizational boundaries of one single organization. In this respect the parliament's decision on the the railways policy in 1987 meant a dramatic change. The decision was to divide this single organization into two: one, called the Swedish National Rail Administration (SNRA), was to administer the railways, i. e. the infrastructure. This organization was legally constructed as a regular public agency. The other organization, which kept the name of the Swedish State Railways, was to actually run the trains, i. e. the railway transportation business. The SSR was still constructed as a business agency, but the intention was to explicitly run the organization in a more businesslike manner and to make the railways business profitable. The government was also preparing for the transformation of this organization into a joint stock company and for simultaneously revoking its monopoly on railway transport.

The arguments for the parliamentary decision in 1987 can be found in the debate on the railways issue that had been going on for decades. In this debate the main problem had increasingly been defined as economic. The specific problem was that the SSR was almost never able to generate the returns on the state capital that it was supposed to. A widely-spread opinion attributed this to the competition from other means of transportation, first road transport and then air transport, that had continually become more severe. Already before the second world war and accelerating ever since, road and air transportation seemed superior to the train in all respects. For many people, often including officials in the Ministry of Communication and in the SSR itself, the railways seemed doomed; railways transportation was considered outdated and belonging to the 19th century, while road and air transportation belonged to the future. The railways simply could not compete. This gloomy view was at its peak in the 1960s.

During the seventies a new interest in the railways could be seen, however. The Oil Crisis and a new public interest in environmental issues brought the railways into a more favorable light. A new management of the SSR launched a strategy that, at least initially, brought new customers to the railways. But the economic problem remained: losses continued and calculations in the mid 80s revealed that they threatened to reach new depths by the end of the decade.

At this time it seems that readiness for a more radical solution among politicians was growing. On several occasions the parliament had decided to depreciate the invested capital in the railways, thereby alleviating the financial burden of the Swedish State Railways, but nevertheless the losses continued and there seemed to be no way out of the economic problems. Mistrust of the organization's management rose among politicians and officials at the Ministry. Many of them considered the management and the organization ineffective and bureaucratic.

In 1986, an organizational consulting company engaged by the general director diagnosed the problems in organizational terms. Dividing the organization into two parts, where the infrastructure would be the responsibility of a new agency, would enable the SSR to compete on equal terms with road and air transportation. According to this line of argument, subsidies provided as compensation for losses, were to be replaced by payments from the government for running unprofitable railway lines. The consultants in their report promised that a restructuring into a more business like organization would turn the losses into profits in a few years' time.

The ministry and the political representatives of all major parties found this solution very attractive, and they incorporated it into the above-mentioned proposal that the parliament decided on in 1987. The restructuring of the SSR could then move from idea to action. As a result of the discussions on new organization and strategy and of the mistrust shown towards the old management, most of the top managers resigned. A new management group was recruited from the business world. They then took on the task of making the organization more businesslike. Up to the present, they have been rather successful; the Swedish State Railways is at present a profitable business. The Swedish National Rails Administration, on the other hand, does not have the economic problems of its predecessor. Since it is organized as a public agency, it is financed through the state budget, and since it possesses no capital, it does not need to generate returns.[1]

---

[1]   Many of these apparent improvements may seem to the observer to be due to changes in accounting practices. Whether the government actually pays more or less for the railway is hard to say.

The economic problems during the 1980s that seemed to become all the more acute despite several attempts to solve them made politicians and others more ready for new and previously untried solutions. One potentially attractive alternative was chosen for the SNRA. The old SSR could have been transformed into a conventional public agency. But one important factor directed the search for solutions in another direction. Competing means of transportation, i. e. road, air and water transport, all were organized differently from the railways. They all had a public agency that administered the infrastructure, i. e. the roads, airports, waterways and ports etc; but transport was considered a business operation and was handled by business enterprises. By defining railways as a means of transportation, the chosen solution therefore seemed logical.

Conclusion

Compared to the savings banks, the corporatization of the Swedish State Railways was less dramatic. The SSR used to be a mixed organization where features of both the public agency and the business company coexisted. However, the public agency form had precedence over the business form. This was obvious e. g. in the particular legal regulation of the Swedish railways, where certain "duties" heavily restricted the SSR's ability to act in a business-like way. The radical and innovative solution to this dilemma was to divide the old organization into two separate and independent parts; one public agency, the Swedish National Rails Administration, which was to run the railroads, and one business organization, the Swedish Railways, which was supposed to transport people and goods and to operate as a business organization.

The change was made possible when the activity of the SSR was defined in the same manner as that of the traffic on the roads or in the air, i. e. as means of transportation, and not as railways per se. The institutionalized activity form of transportation contained the form of organization of the business company. Thus the redefinition of the Swedish State Railways' activities triggered the logic of organizational transformation, and paved the way for the corporatization of the SSR and, correspondingly, the transformation into a "pure" public agency of the SNRA.

Third Case: A Local Government

In the beginning of 1984, a project promoting a concentration on service was launched in the local government, where the Social Democrats had long been in office. The attention paid to the notion of service was by no means an isolated phenomenon. The newly appointed national government

had repeatedly emphazised the importance of improving the service provided by public authorities. The national association of local authorities
supported the government by arranging seminars and producing printed
material about service. The success stories of service companies were told
to public sector managers by journalists and consultants. In 1984, a service
project was underway in a large number of Swedish local governments.

According to project managers in the local government, the improvement of the service provided by the administration called for a large-scale
internal marketing of a neglected way of thinking in the organization,
namely a way of thinking framed by a precise notion of the organization's
activity as service. Project management also promoted training of all personnel whose work involved direct interaction with the organization's "customers," as they were now called, in how to improve service, and the specification of measurable goals concerning the production of service in every
single administration in the organization. Responsibility for planning and
carrying out activities was delegated to the management of the various administrations.

The service project met with a mixed reception on the administrative level.
Some administrations gave no priority to the project and were quite inactive.
Doubt concerning the whole idea, approaching replacements of high officials,
implementation in progress of previously decided organizational changes,
and claims that the project was unnecessary since the administration was already oriented toward service as well as toward customers, were some of the
arguments given by managers in these administrations to project management for the absence of action. In other administrations there was strong support for the service project. In talk and internal documents the notion of the
administration's activity as service, oriented towards customers, was celebrated. Many employees participated in seminars on service and service-
training programs, and serious efforts were made to specify goals for the future production of service. One of the most active administrations was the
biggest by far: the administration for social affairs.

In a memorandum on the service project's implication for the administration for social affairs, the top manager of the administration claimed
that the following maxims, allegedly celebrated in some business firm in the
beginning of the century, undoubtly qualified as governing values for a
municipal administration as well:

> A customer is the most important person in this firm, whether he visits us person-
> ally or writes to us. A customer is not dependent on us, we are dependent on
> him. A customer does not interfere with our work, he gives rise to it. We do not
> do him a favor by serving him, he does us a favor by giving us an opportunity
> to satisfy his wishes. A customer is not a stranger in our business.

The service project was commonly understood as an attempt to change the
way of thinking in the organization and the behavior of front-line person-

nel, not the organization itself, but the manager concluded his memo by arguing that if the new ideas were to be taken seriously, some organizational changes would have to follow.

In the autumn of 1987 several such changes were put on the agenda in the administration for social affairs, when a memorandum entitled "Social welfare on the eve of the nineties – from authority culture to service culture," written by the assistent top manager, became the subject of continuous discussions on the managerial level. Prominent in the changes proposed was the confidence put in management by objectives, decentralization and output control. It was suggested that governing by rules and politicians' occupation with details should be replaced by a management that relied on specification of unambiguous goals and the following-up of performance, and that authority and responsibility should be decentralized to the so-called "front-level," where all the action was. Allowing front-line personnel far more autonomy, while at the same time holding them responsible not only for action, but also financially, would stimulate, it was argued, both service orientation and efficiency considerations.

The introduction of competition was yet another recommendation. Competition was described as giving rise to cost consciousness and incentives to change and adapt to needs of the customers. Internal competition would arise, it was argued, in the new organization, since management by objectives and decentralization allowed for different solutions on the operational level. In addition, the introduction of tendering procedures was suggested, but only in peripheral activites of a "technical" nature. The matter of competition was the only one that caused some controversy among politicians. When the social welfare committee in the summer of 1988 approved of the changes proposed, and decided to initiate an implementation of them, the politician who represented Moderaterna, the dominant party of the right wing, emphasized the usefulness of external competition, for instance from private firms, and argued that tendering procedures should be used not only in peripheral activities, but also in the core activities of the administration.

At the end of 1988, top officials and politicians initiated a reorganization of the central administration in the organization. One of the reasons given was that the administration, with more than 200 employees, was involved in far too many different types of activities. Issues of a conceived strategic nature – for instance, how to stimulate trade and industry in the region – were mingled with more operational ones, such as how to run the telephone switchboard in the town hall. Another reason given was that the administration suffered from an unfortunate mixture of roles, exemplified for instance by complaints from officials in the various administrations, formally subordinate to the central administration, that persons working for that administration sometimes acted as consultants, offering them various services, and sometimes not only monitored them, but also in an authoritarian way decided what they were to do. The state of affairs, it was claimed, caused uncertainty, bewilderment and, as a result, inefficiency.

The solution put forward, described as aiming toward increased efficiency, involved the establishment of different organizations for different types of activities. Planning, coordinating and controlling activities were to be carried out by a staff organization, while activities whose essence was defined as service were to be carried out by a separate service organization, called *Konsult & Service*. The service organization, it was proposed, was to be provided with a business strategy declaring that the task of the organization was to sell services, not only internally to different municipal units, but also, if possible, to external customers, in competition with other suppliers. But, it was pointed out that the organization would also face competition on the internal, intraorganizational market, since internal units would not have any obligation to buy the services they demanded from the municipal service organization. Structurally, the organization was to be divided into numerous profit centers, expected to finance the costs of their activities with sales revenues. If they failed, measures would be taken. Units that did not manage would not survive.

The provision of services on businesslike terms was proclaimed to be a non-political activity, and it was suggested that the service organization therefore was to be headed by a board, appointed by the local council but without any politicians as members of the board. Only managers from internal administrations, supposed to be significant customers, and experienced managers from private businesses, were to be appointed to the board by the local council. This was the only suggestion concerning the thorough reorganization of the central administration that gave rise to some disagreements among the political parties. Even though the notion of the non-political nature of the activity of the service organization was not challenged, there was some left-wing as well as some right-wing opposition to the idea of a board without politicians. In addition, there was some right-wing criticism of making internal customers members of the board. In fact, the ruling Social Democratic Party was the only one fully supporting the solution put forward. In the autumn of 1989, the proposed reorganization was formally decided.

Some months later, in the beginning of 1990, the newly founded staff organization played a significant role in initiating a project involving a reorganization of the various administrations responsible for social welfare, schooling, recreational and cultural activities. Other definitions of the activities than those were, however, crucial for the organizational changes proposed by project management, composed of top officials, in the spring of 1991. The proposal put forward, which heavily stressed the importance of improving efficiency, only made a distinction between two types of activities, namely production of service and exercise of authority. For activities defined as service, radical changes were suggested. They were to be oriented to customers and exposed to competition, and they were to be organized in autonomous profit centers whose financing depended on their performances. Politicians were not to interfere with operations, and governing by rules was to be replaced by management by objectives and output control. For activities involving exercise of authority, different solutions, it was emphasized, were necessary. The proposal did not present any solutions, but proclaimed that the only acceptable solutions were those that guaranteed political influence as well as legal security.

Given that the notions of service and efficiency were accepted, the ideals celebrated in the proposal were not challenged by anyone − either politicians or officials. There was, however, some strong opposition to the proposed reorganization. The organizational model for service activities put forward by project management involved a split of the municipal organization into two parts: one politically-governed, devoted to purchasing and ordering activities, and one non-political, devoted to the production of the services ordered. Some right-wing politicians found this model of purchasing and production confusing and ineffective, and promoted an alternative model involving the introduction of vouchers to be distributed to the inhabitants of the municipality. Not only the model as such, but also the local application of the model as suggested by project management, caused resistance; for instance, the suggestion of establishing the new political committees in the ordering part of the organization was questioned.

In addition, some critics, in particular left-wing politicians, argued that the proposal neglected democratic values, while at the same time claiming that the lack of democratic process was the problem that really needed to be solved. The validity of the definitons of activities used by project management was challenged as well, above all by the manager of the school administration, who strongly regretted that project management had not done any proper analysis of the true nature of the different administrations' activities, and firmly objected to the notion of the school administration's activity as service, arguing that the essence of that activity was education of pupils not of customers − an activity that, in addition, involved some exercise of authority. Left-wing politicians and the manager of the school administration were commonly recognized as the most ruthless criticis of the proposed reorganization. In any case, supported by the Social Democrats and Liberals, the reorganization was formally authorized in the summer of 1991.

Conclusion

From this example it should be clear that those parts of the local governmental organization that were described as producers of service, i. e. whose activity was defined as the production of service, were conceived of as business organizations. For these parts the whole array of business concepts were introduced into the organizational discourse: competition, revenues, efficiency, customers, suppliers, profit centers, etc. It is likewise clear that those parts of the organization that were described as being involved in the exercise of authority, i. e. whose activity was defined as the exercise of authority, were not conceived of as business organizations. Instead, in these cases, the "normal" form of organization of the public agency seemed to fit well.

Thus, two different and separate activity forms seemed to be involved in the transformation processes of the local government. One activity form combined the activity of service with the form of organization of the business company, and the other one combined the activity of exercising authority with the form of organization of the public agency. Before the transformation, the whole of the local government organization was considered to be a public agency, but when many influential organizational actors started to describe some of the organizational activities as service, the logic of transformation came into play, resulting in decisions to change, at least, parts of the organization according to business models.

Summary: An Institutional Logic in Play

Two observations regarding the processes described are crucial for our conclusions. First, in all three cases, a redefinition of the activity of the organization preceded proposals for making the organization more like a business organization. In the savings banks, the definition of their activity as savings was replaced by that of banking; in the Swedish State Railways, the conception of the organization's activity as railway transport *per se* was replaced by one as transport in general; and, in the local government, the transformation process was preceded by the stressing of efficient service, at the expense of exercising authority, as the true nature of the activities of the organization. However, activities defined as something other than efficient service, e. g. exercise of authority, were not subjected to the transformation. Second, not one of the transformation processes was characterized by anxiety, uncertainty or conflict, at least not regarding the need for organizational change or the general direction of that change, provided that the new definition of the organization's activity was accepted. Given the new definition, the need for change as well as the general nature of that change was collectively conceived of as quite obvious and natural.

These observations, we argue, may be explained by the existence of the phenomenon we have called institutionalized forms of activity. The existence of the phenomenon explains, in each case, the collectively conceived need for organizational change as well as the collective agreement on the nature of that change when the activity of the organization was redefined – that is, when the activity of the savings banks was redefined as banking, when the activity of the Swedish State Railways was redefined as transportation, and when the activity of the local government was defined as efficient service. The institutionalized activity forms for banking, transportation and efficient service, all involved the form of organization of the business organization. Therefore, a future state of affairs involving customers, competitors, sales, revenues, output control, etc., was celebrated in the savings banks, in the Swedish State Railways, and in local government, while, simultaneously, elements of form and conceptions of the environment that were not part of the form of organization of the business company lost their meaning and value, or, put differently, lost their legitimacy.

The studies of corporatization processes emphasize the importance of how activities are defined in the ongoing organizational discourse. Due to the existence of a social stock of knowledge that not only consists of knowledge about different forms of organization, but also knowledge about what an organization is supposed to be and how types of activity and types of form are combined, some definitions of activities play a crucial role in legitimizing and delegitimizing different forms of organization. By doing so, they may when applied pave the way for organizational transformation. Our analysis is based on studies of processes in which only one type of organizational transformation occured, namely corporatization, i. e. the introduction into non-business organizations of a coherent set of features of the institutionalized form of organization of the business enterprise. However, we see no reason to exclude the possibility that our analysis may prove itself useful when analyzing other types of organizational transformation as well.

Although the logic of organizational transformation may seem to be the prototypical organizational mechanism, it must be emphasized that it is not. Neither is it a natural law. Instead it can be more accurately described as a social tendency. It has been derived from observations of organizational processes – not from observations of natural or mechanical phenomena. Thus it can be questioned and, perhaps, even changed by actors involved. In our field studies we observed, as mentioned above, little resistance or conflict, and in neither case the opponents succeeded in preventing change. Reasons for this are inherent in the argument presented in this chapter: Since the logic of organizational transformation is derived from such heavily institutionalized constructions, it is very difficult for individual organizational actors to resist the organizational consequences once a new definition of organizational activity is generally accepted. Therefore, in order for opponents to succeed in preventing the logic of organizational transformation from being set in operation, they must be able to stop other definitions of activities than their own from becoming hegemonical. Obviously, the opponents of corporatization in the savings banks, in the railways and in the local government did not manage to do this.

A Note on Ideas that Travel

It has been suggested that the business model is an idea that has been travelling around, particularly during the 80s and afterwards. The idea of privatization could be another related idea on tour. Interpreting corporatization that way, the idea of the business model should be considered contagious, infecting the organizations that it finds in its travels.

As the observant reader has noticed, our argument contradicts such an interpretation. What we have claimed is rather that the business model is not an idea that travels. It is part of a social stock of organizational knowledge and for that reason, it already permeats Western society, and there is thus simply no need for it to travel.

So the question we have to ask is another: what is it that activates the latent idea of the business model in an organization where it was previously not considered? Based on our studies the answer is: it is the definition of organizational activity that, under certain circumstances, starts the logic of organizational transformation and thus makes the business model seem the natural organizational solution.

In all our cases, a distinctive organizational activity or set of activities was redefined into a new, broader and more abstract category. Saving was redefined into the broader concept of banking, railways were redefined into the category of transportation, and the local government's distinctive activities like social welfare and education were redefined into the single broad category of service. In these cases the new ideas of what kind of activity the organization was involved in triggered the process of organizational transformation, since they made a new activity form seem logical.

These ideas were not invented within these organizations. The savings banks did not invent the concept of banking, the Swedish State Railways did not invent the concept of transportation and local government did not invent the concept of service. So, when investigating travelling ideas that affect processes of organizational transformation, one should look for ideas about organizational activities, because they are potential triggers of organizational transformation. However, the investigation of these ideas, their origins and journeys, is beyond the scope of our current project.

Technical and Aesthetic Fashion

Eric Abrahamson

Modes, vogues, fads, fashions, rages, and crazes frequently revolutionize many aspects of cultural life. Theories of fashion, however, focus narrowly on fashions in forms that gratify our senses and emotional well being. This focus on *aesthetic* forms confines the study of fashion to forms considered trivial − such as popular music (Hirsch, 1972) or men's beards (Robinson, 1976) − or to forms traditionally associated with women or children − not only dresses (Barthes, 1983; Richardson and Kroeber, 1940), but also interior design, cuisine, or childrens' names and toys (Lauer and Lauer, 1981). Few scholars examine fashions in forms valued according to primarily *technical* criteria − forms evaluated according to how well they provide the means to certain ends in what are traditionally labeled as more important areas of endeavor: war, science, technology, politics, and management.

I suggest, in this article, that technical forms are open to the swings of fashion. My primary thesis is that aesthetic and technical fashions differ markedly, although they bear certain surface similarities. Fashion swings in technical forms, far for being cosmetic and trivial are in fact deadly serious matters. This is because, contrary to Blumer's (1968; 1969) seminal theory of fashion, technical fashions are not in demand because technicians consider them to be modern, or find them to be congruent with their aesthetic sensitivities or tastes. Fashionable techniques are in demand because technicians consider them to be both *rational* and *progressive* − that is, both new as well as improved rational means to technical ends.[1] Therefore, in this article, I define fashion setting in technical realms as a social process that repeatedly redefines technicians' collective conceptions of what constitutes rational progress. These collective conceptions can not remain stable for too long, otherwise progress will not appear to be progressing. I define a

---

[1]   I use the term "progress" or "progressive" rather than the "modern" advisedly. The term "modern," such as is used when we speak of "modern art," does not carry with it any connotations that modern art is better, or improved relative to classical, traditional, or primitive art. Only that modern art is new and current. To the contrary, the term progress, as when we speak of "technological progress," denotes both novelty and improvement by some technical criteria. Of course, these criteria are subjective and change along with technical fashions.

technical fashion, therefore, as a relatively transient collective conception of what constitutes progress in rational techniques, at one point in history.

I am a scholar in the field of management and I will, therefore, illustrate my thesis by discussing fashion in only one realm of technical activity with which I am familiar: management practice. I believe, however, that the argument has general applicability to many technical forms, as long as some ambiguity surrounds conceptions of their utility. I begin this article by considering why management fashion has received so little attention.

What Explains the Unfashionability of Managerial Fashion?

The fashionability of management techniques has remained a conspicuously unfashionable topic of scholarly interest.[2] This inattention to management fashions should surprise us, considering that many popular and academic writers have for a long time now used the term "management fashion" to describe swings in the popularity of management techniques (Dunnette and Bass, 1963; Woodward, 1965; Lawler, 1971; Rumelt, 1974; Mintzberg, 1979; Nystrom and Starbuck, 1984). Moreover, transitory swings in management fashions reveal themselves quite readily in various types of quantitative data that are often used by fashion setters themselves to declare what is, and what is not in fashion. Surveys indicate, for instance, that Quality Circles (QCs) underwent a rapid swing in popularity. Nearly a third of US organizations with more than 500 employees reported adopting QCs between 1980 and 1982 (*New York Stock Exchange*, 1982). Lawler and Mohrman (1985) estimated that 90% of the "Fortune 500" companies had adopted QCs during this period. At the same time, they also predicted an impending decline in their use. A survey by Castorina and Wood (1988) indicated that more than 80% of "Fortune 500" companies adopting QCs in the 1980s had abandoned them by 1987.

Another source of evidence on the QC fashion comes from looking at the attention that QCs have received in various print media. The International Association of Quality Circles (IAQC), an association of practitioners and consultants, meets yearly and publishes proceedings of these meetings. Figure 1 graphs the thickness, in decimeters, of the yearly proceedings volumes.

Figure 1 also indicates, that the number of articles on QCs listed yearly in the *Business Periodicals Index* grew rapidly in the early 1980s, yet this trend reversed itself after 1983. By 1986, this measure returned to its pre-

---

2   See articles by Czarniawska and Joerges and Røvik in this volume.

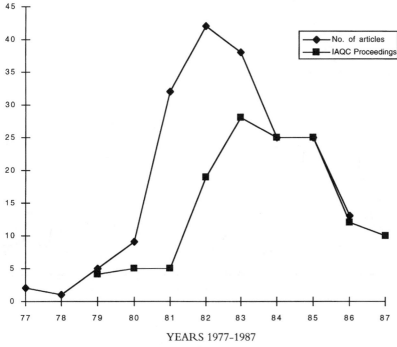

YEARS 1977-1987

Width of IAQC Proceedings is measured in decimeters

Figure 1: Shifting Attention to Quality Circles

popularity level, reflecting the swing in QCs popularity. Print media evidence also indicates that certain management techniques can repeatedly gain and lose popularity. Figure 2, for example, graphs recurrent swings in the number of articles about employee stock ownership published between 1914 and 1986 (Abrahamson, 1989).

At least two obstacles forestall interest in technical fashions, generally, and management fashions, particularly. First and foremost, sustained inattention to management fashions occurs because organizational stakeholders — employees, suppliers, clients, regulators, and the like — assume that rational thinking governs the realm of management, just as they believe it governs in other realms such as technology, war, or science. For organizations to appear correctly managed, and for managers to manage as managers should, managers must project an appearance of rationality. They do so, organizational scholars have argued, by adopting or appearing to adopt management techniques that are collectively believed, in specific contexts,

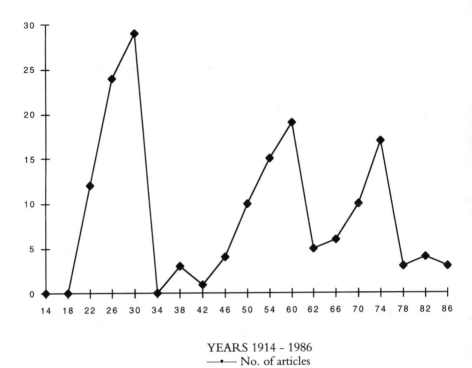

YEARS 1914 - 1986
—•— No. of articles

Figure 2: Prevalence in the Number of Articles on Employee-Stock-Ownership Programmes

to be rational ways of managing organizations (Meyer and Rowan, 1977; Rottenburg, in this volume).

This focus on rationality, however, may suggest that managers cannot adopt management techniques for an apparently technically-irrational motive such as appearing fashionable. The danger of conflating aesthetic and technical fashion becomes apparent. What such a conflation misses is that management fashion is primarily about technical rationality, and only peripherally about aesthetic sensitivities and tastes. Management fashion defines managers' ends, be they quality, flexibility, profits, speed, client satisfaction or risk reduction, as well as the best means to these ends: particular management techniques, such as Quality Circles, for example. Moreover, what this conflation obscures is that whereas we do not expect aesthetic forms to improve (sartorial fashion do not constitute closer approximation of some aesthetic ideal), norms of technical progress create the expectation that management must progress towards some ultimate end, much like science, technology, and military tactics. Old management problems, therefore, must appear to be solved and new management problems appear to be addressed. Old management techniques must, therefore, be replaced by newer and better ones. Managers, consequently, must appear to use not only rational management techniques, but also innovative, improved and then also rational management techniques. I believe that it is the management fashion setting process that fosters this continuous impression of managerial progress, even when this progress is only an illusion. It is for this reason that I define management-fashion-setting as the social process that repeatedly redefines managers' collective conceptions of what constitutes progress in techniques for managing organizations and their employees. As noted above, these collective conceptions of technical progress can not remain stable for too long, otherwise progress will not appear to be progressing. A management fashion, therefore, is a relatively transient collective conception of what constitutes progress in rational management techniques, at one point in history.

A second obstacle, however, stands in the way of careful theorizing about fashion. We implicitly believe that management fashion holds sway only in relatively trivial management matters. This implicit belief exists because words like "fashion" and "fad," due to their previous use in primarily aesthetic realms, connote unimportant and trivial when they are used in technical realms. As a result, we feel at ease using the term fashion to describe a popularity swing in something as potentially harmless as Quality Circles. Why spend time theorizing and studying a phenomenon that can exact only little harm on organizations?

Consider now that in the 1970s, many US banks rushed to adopt an innovative strategy consisting of making large, "Jumbo" loans to lesser-developed Countries (LDCs). By the early 1980s it was clear that many LDCs would face great trouble in repaying these loans, prompting an international debt crisis whose effects is still being felt today. Why not call this the Jumbo-loan fashion? Why not talk of a merger fashion in the 1980s in the US involving in excess of one trillion dollars in assets? More generally, why not remain open to the possibility that not only management, but also every area of technical endeavor is open to the swings of fashion? Why not attempt, then, to develop a theory of fashion that explain when fashion will hold sway, instead of assuming outright that it will hold sway only in either aesthetic matters or in trivial technical matters?

My argument in the remainder of the paper rests on certain assumptions that flow from the preceding discussion. First, management fashion, far from being about aesthetics, is about technical rationality and technical progress. Second, aesthetic and technical fashions differ markedly and, therefore, we need a theory of technical fashions.

The remainder of this article falls into four parts. First, I discuss the norms of rationality and progress that create the context for management fashion. Second, I examine the functioning of the management-fashion-setting community which *supplies* management fashions. Third, I consider the nature of management fashion demand. Fourth, I discuss when technical fashion holds sway.

Norms of Rationality and Progress

Scholars postulate that general norms of rationality shape organizational structures and processes (Parsons, 1958; Crozier, 1964; Child, 1968; Meyer and Rowan, 1977). These general norms become specified in much more precise and powerful ways in specific organizational contexts − to appear rationally managed, for instance, a U.S organization in 1981 had to use Quality Circles. For organizations to appear in conformity with these specific norms of rationality their managers must use a particular management discourse − a stylized spoken and written language about managerial ends (product quality, for instance) and labels denoting technical means to these ends (Quality Circles, for example) (Meyer and Rowan, 1977). As Rottenburg highlights in this volume, these appearances are frequently nothing but facades behind which managers ply their trade.

Organizations that deviate from these legitimate appearances lose stakeholder support − their facade collapses exposing managerial irrationalities. Case studies indicate that organizations experience great difficulties when it appears to stakeholders that these organizations are being run irrationally. Starbuck and Nystrom (1981) tell the story of a small company that made,

> expensive chemical instruments which is sold by mail order at prices well below its competitors'. This company doubled its revenues and profits every six months for a dozen years, eventually attaining a net worth of $ 40 million (in 1981 dollars). This success attracted the attention of several large firms, one of which bought the company. The new owners were horrified to discover that their subsidiary had only rudimentary paper-work procedures, no cost accounting system, and no sales staff. No modern firm could operate in this fashion! They installed paper procedures and cost accounting, and they hired sales staff. Costs rose, so prices were raised. Demand fell, revenue fell, and profits became losses (Starbuck and Nystrom, 1981, p. 9).

In this instance, the stakeholders rejected the company's radically new practice − eliminating cost-accounting techniques and salesmen in order to cut sales costs − as soon as they were brought to their attention.

Organizations may also reject their more radical inventions without the intervention of stakeholders. Managers may reason that the mere fact that stakeholders may learn of a radical invention and evaluate it negatively warrants not implementing it. Perrow (1970) tells of a pharmaceutical firm that could efficiently and reliably train pigeons to pick out defective pills traveling on a conveyor belt towards the packaging section. This new technology represented a notable improvement over the prior technology that utilized humans. However, the organizations never utilized pigeons in order to avoid criticism by its stakeholders.

In both anecdotes, organizations had to reject radical innovations in production screening or in formal structure because these did not and would not conform to specific norms of rational management. In the second example, stakeholders considered the innovation deviant, and bizarre, and decided to return the organization to a more rational, legitimate appearance.

Management fashion is somewhat of a mystery because it involves the apparent use and spread of management techniques vaunted as being radically innovative. Yet, the apparent use of these techniques, unlike those just examined, raises rather than lowers legitimacy. Why is this the case?

There is a two-part answer to this question. First, organizations that adopt fashionable management techniques do not appear illegitimate because they conform to general norms of management progress. That is, norms calling for new, more rational management techniques. Total Quality Management (TQM), for instance, replaced Quality Circles as the latest expression of rational management progress. Until recently, organizations that did not appear to be using TQM appeared outdated and poorly managed – now they must be "reengineered" in order to avoid this fate. Second, if new management techniques do not result in charges of deviance against organizations when their stakeholders learn about them, then norms of rationality must have changed, as well as the management discourse with which managers demonstrate conformity to these new norm. How do these new discourses evolve? This article's answer to this question is that there exists a management fashion-setting community, populated by management fashion-setting organizations dedicated to launching certain management techniques into fashion.

Fashion-Setting Communities

The terms used to describe the social process which animates fashion both help explain and obscure this process. The language used to describe fashion, as a social process, indicates rightly that fashion requires two types of actors. First, are what the vernacular calls "fashion leaders" or "fashion setters" – actors who fashion the discourses that make new fashions appear fashionable and their user appear legitimate. Second, are what the vernacular calls "fashion followers" – actors who translate the fashionable techniques into practice when the legitimating discourse becomes fashionable. This distinction between fashion leaders and followers helps because it suggests that those who appear to use innovative management techniques cannot always produce the discourse necessary to legitimate these techniques on their own.

Terms such as fashion leader and follower can, however, also obscure our understanding of technical fashions. The term fashion leader, in particular, can suggest that there are leaders exerting power over fashion followers. Yet, the careful observer of fashion in technical realms will recognize many instances in which fashion setters attempt to render a form fashionable, but the form never gains popularity. Fashion leaders attempt to lead, but followers do not follow. Moreover, the term "fashion follower" tends to connote that these followers are led like sheep in a flock. The term "herding behavior" is sometimes used synonymously with the term "fashion." Yet the careful observer of technical fashion will recognize that those who adhere to fashions early are nothing like sheep. On the contrary, they are often extremely discriminating.

It may not be so much the term fashion leader that obscures fashion phenomena in technical realms, but rather how we understand what leadership means in these realms. Indeed, the term "fashion leader" only obscures the phenomena if leadership is conceptualized as some inherent capacity − creativity, taste, reputation − that allows fashion setters to push a social form into fashion, despite the adherence of followers to past fashions.

Fashion leadership may be more like market leadership in a competitive arena. Most market leaders do not lead because they have the monopolistic power necessary to force customers to buy their product. Rather, they lead because they can sense, before their competition, customer *demand*. They can also *supply* products that satiate this demand before their competitors can, and market these products successfully. Those organizations do not satisfy customer demand, lose their market leadership. Moreover, when market leaders satiate customer demand they create new demands. Market leaders must discover and satiate these new demands to retain market leadership.

It is not entirely incorrect, then, to think of management discourse as a commodity open to fashion swings. Fashion setters, like any other market leader, lead because they can sense a demand for ideas that could legitimate the use of management techniques. They can *procure* these ideas, like they would a raw material, and *fashion* a legitimating discourse with which they can *market* these ideas back to managers who translate them into practice or into practical facades. This suggests the model depicted in Figure 3.

This conceptualization raises two questions. First, who supplies management fashions? Second, how do these fashion suppliers procure raw ideas, fashion legitimating discourses, and market ideas back to managers?

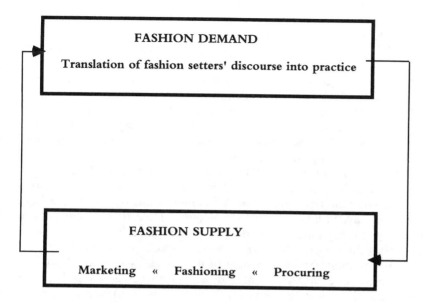

Figure 3: Fashion Supply and Demand

The Supply of Management Fashion

Empirical research has gone a long way towards dispelling the notion that radical innovations become mass fashions by direct popular demand (Blumer, 1969; Hirsch, 1972; Peterson and Berger, 1975). Intermediaries often stand between innovators and the mass public that adopts fashionable translations of their innovations. These intermediaries attempt to make the innovations legitimate. Hirsch (1972), in particular, focused on organizations in the publishing, record, and motion picture industries that stand between the creators and consumers of cultural innovations. These fashion-setting organizations use talent scouts to penetrate artistic, musical, or literary circles in order to discover new talents. They select a small set of manuscripts, scores, or scripts from the vast array of literary and artistic innovations. These organizations then package and attempt to launch the cultural product that they have selected. They attempt to co-opt mass media gatekeepers (critics, editors, etc.) in order to bring their new prodigy's cultural innovations to the public's attention. As a result, mass audiences get exposed through mass media to a limited number of cultural innovations. These innovations may or may not, depending on the reactions of fashion followers, become fashions.

With some notable differences, the analysis of the setting of organizational fashion in technical realms, such as management, can follow the outlines of Hirsch's (1972) model for fashion setting in aesthetic realms. There are probably a variety of organizations that participate in setting management fashion. I call the network of these fashion-setting organizations "the management fashion setting community." I use the term community because it suggests interdependent industries that jointly produce fashionable management discourse. In the United States, for example, various scholars have claimed that management consultants, business schools and business-press organizations comprise such a community (see my review of the literature, Abrahamson, 1991).

For the purpose of simplicity, this article considers only these fashion-setters. In truth, however, very little is known about such management fashion-setting communities. What types of organizations populate them? Do all countries have at least one such community? Do certain countries have many? How do they differ across different technical realms?

The article distinguishes between three types of actions carried out by fashion-setting communities: procurement of new ideas, fashioning of rational and progressive discourse about these ideas, and marketing of this discourse to managers. I assume that innovative variations in management ideas abound among fashion followers. Moreover, there exist many old and forgotten management ideas that fashion setters can bring back to managers' collective attention. Thus the procurement of new ideas is largely the selection of a few management ideas from a vast array of potential candidates. Management fashion setters must then fashion discourse to present the ideas they have procured. Finally, such discourse is marketed back to organizational communities where it may be translated into new discourse and practices by managers in organizations; that is, where the management technique goes from being only management discourse, to being translated into both new discourse and practice. This translation process transform management ideas: they are tailored to particular contexts and identities; they are distorted through interorganizational transmission; they may appear to succeed or to fail, or to have become irrelevant (Sevón, in this volume). All this may require new cycles of translations. The fashion-setting community re-procures these ideas, re-fashion a modified discourse about them, and re-market this discourse back to managers. Repeated translation cycles generate fashion trends — such as the addition of the Quality Circles discourse, to the broader Total Quality Management discourse, followed by the challenge to this discourse presented by the current Reengineering fashion.

Procurement

As Figure 4 indicates, the procurement process can be broken down into two stages for analytical purposes. In a first stage, like the talent scouts of the music industry, management fashion setters scout out management

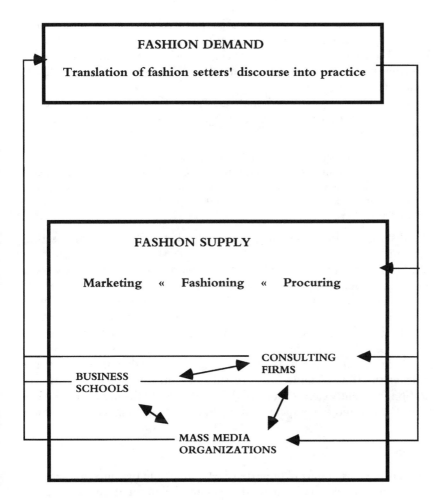

Figure 4: The Fashion-setting Process

ideas that could be brought into fashion. These ideas may represent real inventions, or old defunct management ideas waiting for a breath of new life. In a second stage, the discovery of a management technique by a member of the fashion-setting community may lead to the spread of this technique across fashion-setters.

Who scouts out management ideas and how they spread across fashion-setters may differ across fashion-setting communities. The model of scouting out and spread that appears below should only serve to indicate one possible chain of translations.

In this model, a management idea could be scouted out by either business schools academics, consulting firm management consultants, or business-press journalists. Academics frequently come into contact with managers during the course of their research or are called upon by journalists and consultants.

Mintzberg (1979) suggested that consulting firms also play a decisive role in the scouting out of ideas that become fashionable. Mintzberg observed that

> Paris has its salons of haute couture; likewise New York has its offices of 'haute structure', the consulting firms that bring the latest in high structural fashion to their clients — long-range planning (LRP), management information systems (MIS), management by objective (MBO), organizational development (OD) (Mintzberg, 1979, p. 293).

Journalists may also scout out management ideas for the fashion-setting community.

As I will discuss below, fashion-setters advertize the fashions they try to launch. Consequently, they can be easily imitated by other fashion setters. In a rare study of its kind, Barley, Meyer, and Gash (1988), for example, studied how the academic and popular management-press influence each other. Their study suggests that the conceptualization of the Corporate Culture fashion, developed in the popular management-press, influenced its conceptualization in the academic business-press, rather than vice versa. Whatever the flow of imitation between different types of fashion setters, imitation frequently causes multiple different types of fashion-setters to imitate each other and to compete in marketing the same management fashion.

Fashioning

Although Barthes (1983) wrote extensively about the discourse of aesthetic fashions, not much has been written about the rational and progressive discourse fashioned by management fashion setters. An interesting question is: what are the editing rules that make this discourse progressive? (Sahlin-Andersson, this volume). First, progressive discourse describes older techniques as retrogressive. Quality circles had to be described as failed and outdated for Total Quality Management (TQM) to appear as progress and as state of the art. This de-legitimation sometimes takes the form of demonizing. The demons of the day, in the US, are always a few currently poorly performing firms. Their sin is that they are inflexible, mired in what the current academic jargon calls competency traps, and unresponsive to market changes. Against this background, currently successful firms shine like nimble, market-driven angels. Occasionally, of course, angels heralded by current management best-seller perform poorly and have to be demonized.

The articulation of progressive discourse about management techniques has at least four components: 1) the statement of ends, 2) the claim that these ends are currently un-attained 3) the revelation of the means to attain these ends and 4) the justification as to why these means will lead to these ends.

Discourse stating ends and claiming that ends are un-attained — problem discourse — follows certain editing rules. The discourse generally reveals the problems as new, universal, abstract, unidimensional, and important. These problems are portrayed as new. There can be little mention that problems of centralization/decentralization, employee motivation/control, flexibility/efficiency, quality/cost and other tradeoffs, have perplexed managers since their rise as an occupational category at the turn of the century. In managerial progressive discourse, however, progress is linear. Past problems have emerged and have been resolved and only new problems loom on the horizon. There are no cycles of attention to problems, no new wine in old bottles, no managers forgetting the past and being condemned to relive it.

The problems are also universal in this progressive discourse. All but a few firms, or a rapidly growing number of firms, suffer from them. These problems are generally abstract and vague — quality, flexibility, speed, competence, cooperation — and unifaceted. The problems, if they are too concrete and precise, might actually be solved rapidly or be shown, all too clearly, not to be solvable by the current fashion. Finally, and obviously, discourse about problems highlights their extreme importance. It threatens with hellish promises of managerial demise and sublime opportunities for stardom.

Discourse describing and justifying managerial means to managerial ends — solution discourse — has characteristics that parallel problem discourse. Solutions are new and embody progress, as are the stylized arguments invoked to justify their efficacy. Solutions are also universal and unaffected by context. Quality circles produced the Japanese miracle one solution discourse suggests, implant them in any and all US firms, and then watch the US miracle. Solution discourse is also magical. A byline for a *Harvard Business Review* article provides the flavor. "With workers defining their own job standards, quality and productivity at the Fremont plant went from worst to best." These solutions are powerful, infallible and perfect. They are frequently portrayed as simple and described in equally simple, moving terms. The discourse is more like evangelism than theology and it frequently appeals to values other than profit. TQM gives the customer fair value and hostile takeovers displace lazy, greedy managers (Hirsch, 1986). But solution discourse is not all emotion. Scientific grounding, usually provided by citations or miss-citations of the legitimating discourse of business schools, often gives solution discourse a patina of rationality.

Marketing

Little has been written about the marketing of the progressive discourse from the management fashion-setting community to managers. Hirsch (1972, p. 643) argued that in the realm of aesthetic fashions, we should view "the mass media in their gatekeeping role as a primary institutional regulator of innovation" and that "the diffusion of particular fads and fashions is either blocked or facilitated at this strategic checkpoint" (Hirsch, 1972, p. 649). But the mass media may not play as pivotal role in the emergence of management fashions. In many cases, consulting firms, rather than the mass media may set management fashion (Ginsberg and Abrahamson, 1992). The mass appeal of recent popular management books written by consultants and academic entrepreneurs may indicate the ascendancy of this type of fashion-setter (Kanter, 1983; Peters and Waterman, 1982). It might also indicate the growing importance of the publishing industry in selecting and promoting management books. Mass media and their critiques may also play an important role in popularizing both these management books and the reports of management techniques that these books contain.

The Demand for Management Fashion

At least two divergent types of explanations have been advanced to explain fashion demand. The first socio-psychological type of explanation of fashion suggests that profit maximizing fashion-setters take advantage of the psychological weaknesses of gullible managers. The metaphor is that managers, like spoiled children, are easily frustrated and bored. Thus, they have an insatiable and fickle appetite for modern, flashy management techniques to play with. In this type of explanation, the management fashion-setting industry, like the toy industry for children, is there to capitalize on the insatiable demand of managers for modern, glitzy management techniques.

A second type of technico-economic explanation suggests that a variety of technical and economic forces open gaps between organizations' actual and desired performances. It is the management-fashion process that brings these performance gaps to collective awareness and that articulates new, progressive, and collectively-acceptable techniques for narrowing these gaps. The remainder of this section reviews socio-psychological and technico-economic explanations in turn.

Socio-Psychological Explanations of Fashion Demand

These explanations are both the oldest (Hurlock, 1929; Flugel, 1930; Bergler, 1953; Blumer, 1968; 1969) and the ones most recently found reflected in current treatments of management fashion aimed at non-academic audiences (e. g. *Business Week*, 1986; Eccles and Nohria, 1992; Nohria and Berkley, 1994). The fundamental assumption undergirding most socio-psychological explanations is that fashion-followers are rendered vulnerable to fashion by one of four social-psychological states: 1) collective frustration, 2) collective boredom and striving for novelty, 3) collective striving for status differentiation, or 4) collective striving for the gratification of collective taste. These four explanations are examined in turn.

The collective frustration explanation. The first type of socio-psychological explanation suggests that frustration and despair across a collectivity of individuals renders them vulnerable to unrealistic hopes that a quasi-magical solution will relieve their source of frustration (Klapp, 1969; Smelser, 1962). An unrealistic hope, in time, can only give way to a new round of frustration and despair, and a receptivity for a new hope-inducing fashion. Versions of this argument abound in treatments of management fashion aimed at non-academic audiences (*Business Week*, 1986; Eccles and Nohria, 1992; Nohria and Berkley, 1994; *Wall Street Journal,* 1993). In these accounts, the Japanese competitive challenge, as well as the relative decline of US and European businesses generates a powerful source of collective frustration for US and European managers. In the words of Mitroff and Mohrman (1987, p. 69):

> It is not surprising that in this environment U.S. business easily fell prey to every new management fad promising a painless solution, especially when it was presented in a neat, bright package. But all simple formulas are eventually bound to fail.

The collective boredom explanation. A second type of socio-psychological explanation suggests that new management techniques relieve boredom or satiate individual needs for appearing different and novel. A classic article by Sapir (1937) provides a dated, yet outstanding and succinct treatment of this explanation. Applying this explanation to the realm of management fashion suggests that organizational life is drab and routine, and that new management techniques break this routine and generate excitement. In time, however, these fashions become the new routine, regenerate boredom, and, as such, regenerate receptivity for a new exciting fashion. Additionally, fashionable management techniques gratify competing psychological drives for individuality and novelty, on the one hand, and conformity and traditionalism, on the other. Managers appear individualistic and novel, relative to the mass of managers who are out of fashion. They maintain some measure of conformity and traditionalism, however, by using techniques used by other managers who are in fashion. But what is new and individualistic ineluctably become old and common with the passage of time and with the growing number of adherents to a fashion. This explanation suggests, therefore, that "new innovations" will always be in demand to feed managers' insatiable appetite for individuality and novelty.

The collective status seeking explanation. Still a third type of socio-psychological explanation suggests that fashionable management techniques serve not only to symbolize management individuality and innovativeness, but also to symbolize those managers and organizations that are progressing and those that not (Simmel, 1904/1973). This explanation, when extended to management fashion, suggests what can be called a trickle-down fashion processes (Abrahamson and Fombrun, 1994); reputedly more innovative organizations adopt management fashions to distinguish themselves from reputedly less innovative ones. The more that organizations with lower reputations adopt fashionable techniques to look like organizations with high reputations, however, the more both high and low reputation organizations look similar. Hence, the greater the pressure on higher-reputation organizations to adopt a new fashion that will re-distinguish them from lower-reputation organizations.

The collective frustration, boredom and status-seeking explanations suggest that cunning management fashion-setters lead psychologically vulnerable and gullible management fashion-followers. The popular-management press is usually most strident in denouncing how management fashion-setters exploit these vulnerabilities and harm large numbers of business firms. They suggest that, to stay in business, fashion setters make sure that management discourse about one fashion does not last too long, or there will be nor room for a new fashion. Consequently, fashions setters launch fashions with little attention, or even with active disinterest in there staying power (*Wall Street Journal*, 1993). Their discourse generates unrealistic hopes with the consequence that these hopes are easily dashed (*Business Week*, 1986). Or, they present very complex problems and solutions in very simple terms, with the consequence that complex problems are never resolved (Mitroff and Mohrman, 1987; Morgan, 1986, p. 16). Fashion setters, moreover, are accused of actively discrediting old fashions in order to make room for new ones.

The most pessimistic accounts of management fashion suggest that, as a result, of fashion-setters' opportunism, the vast majority of fashionable management techniques are technically inefficient and fail to solve all or most problems for all or most organizations. Therefore, these techniques lose popularity, creating receptivity to new, equally useless streams of fashionable management techniques. A passage from a *Harvard Business Review* article (Nohria and Berkley, 1994, pp. 128−129) is illustrative:

> The 1980 witnessed the spectacular rise of management schools, consultants, media and gurus who fed on the insecurities of American managers fearful of foreign competition and economic decline. Mistrustful of their own judgment, many managers latched on to these self appointed pundits, really adopting their last panaceas. Off-the-shelf programs addressing quality, customer satisfaction, time-to-market, strategic focus, core competencies, alliances, global competitiveness,

organizational culture, and empowerment swept through U.S. corporations with alarming speed. (...) For some businesses, the new ideas worked. (...) But in the majority of cases, research shows, the management fads of the last 15 years rarely produced the promised results.

Another pessimistic line suggests that fashion processes animate changes in the popularity of both discourse about performance-gaps and solutions. Performance gaps, such as gaps in desired product or service quality, can therefore remain in fashion, whereas solutions for narrowing these performance gaps go in and out of fashion. Therefore, if the performance gap is defined broadly and vaguely enough, a long series of useless new management fashions may be applied to it over time. Total Quality Management, for instance, has gradually come to serve as an umbrella term for a growing number of management techniques.

Such trajectories of discourse development may, however, spell their own demise. First, there may be nothing left to add. The appearance of progress may reach a dead end. Second, and more probably, the discourse may become over-saturated with solutions to the point of becoming meaningless. In a recent presentation about Total Quality Management (TQM), for instance, a manager argued that TQM made up 100% of what his managers did. In other words, TQM was everything and, therefore, nothing. Fashions may go through punctuated equilibria in which discourse evolves incrementally up to a point of over-saturation at which time a radically new path of fashion development becomes necessary.

The collective taste explanation. Blumer's (1968; 1969) collective taste theory of fashion provides a fourth, and more optimistic, socio-psychological explanation of fashion. He defines the demand for fashion as guided by managers' collective taste. Blumer (1968, p. 344) defined collective taste as "an organic sensitivity to objects of social experience as when we say, for example, that 'vulgar comedy does not suit our taste'..." Collective taste "is like an appetite in seeking positive satisfaction; it operates as a sensitive selector, giving a basis for acceptance or rejection; and it is a formative agent, guiding the development of lines of action and shaping objects to meet its demand" (1968, p. 344).

Unfortunately, Blumer remained vague about what shapes collective taste other than the action of fashion-setters. At one point he declares that "taste is initially a loose fusion of vague inclinations and dissatisfactions that are aroused by new experiences in the field of fashion and in the larger surrounding world." What are these new experiences in the surrounding world that shape incipient collective tastes for technical fashion? Whereas Blumer's theory is a model of clarity in other respects, this question remains unanswered. As a result, the notion of collective tastes and its determinants remains too vague to serve as an explanation of the demand of technical fashions such as management.

Technico-Economic Explanations of Fashion Demand

It is my sense that socio-psychological explanation of fashion highlight the aesthetic dimensions of fashion demand in primarily technical forms, such as management. It seems clear, particularly in our more cynical moments, that like fashions in clothing or in toys, management fashion is driven by status seeking (Abrahamson, 1991), or by childlike excitement (Mitroff and Mohrman, 1987), or even by something approaching mass-hysteria (Eccles and Nohria, 1992). To capitalize on these intuitions, a theory of management fashion must build upon theories developed to explain fashion in primarily aesthetic realms. Such a theory must, however, be complemented by technico-economic explanations of fashion in order to understand the technical determinants of fashion in primarily technical forms.

A good starting point in building a theory of fashion demand in technical forms, such as management, is provided by Blumer's (1968; 1969) notion of collective taste − "collective preferences" would be a better term in the realm of technical fashion. Technico-economic explanations can cast light on influences emanating from outside the management fashion setting community that shape managers' collective preferences for certain types of progressive management discourses. What I have in mind, here, is not a narrow technical determinism whereby management techniques that solve technico-economic threats or capitalized on technico-economic opportunities inscribe themselves automatically into these discourses. What I suggests instead is that fashion sense incipient technico-economic threats and opportunities and scout out ideas that managers facing these threats and opportunities will tend to be responsive to. Having clarified this important point, I turn now to reviewing extant technico-economic explanations of fashion demand.

Macro-economic explanations. Technico-economic explanations of fashion demand come in various flavors. The first flavor points to long-term macro-economic fluctuations that could create sudden surges of demand for certain types of management ideas. Barley and Kunda (1992) hypothesize that long-term, 50 year cycles of economic expansion and contraction parallel broad changes in managers' preferences for different types of management discourses (Kondratieff, 1935; Schumpeter, 1935). Their review of historians' works supports the hypotheses that because profits hinge on capital investment and automation during expansionary periods, managers gain interest in discourse about management techniques that stress the efficient use of structures and technologies as a means of increasing labor productivity. During periods of contraction, however, both the supply and returns on capital investment decline, and managers gain interest in labor as a factor of production and in discourse about employee-management techniques that stress employee relations as a means of increasing labor productivity.

My own quantitative analysis of 33,000 business-press articles between 1913 and 1993 supports Barley and Kunda's thesis (Abrahamson, in print). Results indicate that the emergence of new forms of management discourse are related to the onset of macroeconomic longwaves' expansionary and contractionary stages. I find, however, that yearly variations in the voluntary-turnover rate and the frequency of strikes affected the post-emergence prevalence of these types of discourses.

The political-contradiction explanation. A second class of technico-economic explanation stress the existence of contradiction in the structure of organizations that cause changes in the demand for management fashions. Neo-Marxist accounts stress the inherent, irreconcilable, structural conflict between management and worker strata in organizations. In this approach, management fashions are seen as so many forms of control that emerge to suppress this conflict. This conflict is unsolvable, however, as long as these techniques do not change the underlying structure that generates the conflict. Therefore, all management fashions eventually fail, and new fashions must emerge to re-suppress the conflict. As Edwards put it, transformations in management fashions

> occurred as a resolution of intensifying conflict and contradiction in the firm's operations. The period of increasing tension was followed by a relatively rapid process of discovery, experimentation, and implementation, in which new systems of control were substituted for the older, more primitive ones. Once instituted, these new relations tend to persist until they no longer effectively counter worker resistance (Edwards, 1979, p. 18).

The technical-contradiction explanation. Another technico-economic explanation suggests that unsolvable contradictions of a technical, rather than political nature, cause changes in fashion demand (Blau, 1971). Centralization, for instance, allows for centralized control but stifles the autonomy of parts. Decentralization allows for such autonomy, but causes loss of centralized control. Fashions cause organizations to centralize, lose autonomy, and become receptive to new fashions causing them to gain autonomy, lose control, and become receptive to a new fashion that swings the pendulum back again. Likewise, fashions for flexibility cause organizations to lose efficiency causing receptivity for fashions that increase efficiency but reduce flexibility. Similar tradeoffs, may cause pendulum swings in managers' preferences for techniques stressing employee motivation and control, product cost and quality, in-sourcing and out-sourcing, to name a few.

A slightly more optimistic version of this technical-contradiction explanation of fashion demand sees technical or political contradictions as the many syntheses and antitheses of a dialectic. This dialectic generates receptivity to fashionable syntheses of these contradiction. These syntheses, in turn, give rise to their antitheses, and to new dialectical movements in the demand for management fashions.

What Is the Scope of Management Fashion

Are all technical realms open to fashion swings? The answer must be no, otherwise the term technical fashion now becomes synonymous with the term technical change. Technical realms where unambiguous standards guide the evaluation of techniques may not be open to the swings of fashion.

In the case of management techniques, their utility is unambiguous when technique are well institutionalized. An institutionalized management technique is one that has become taken-for-granted − its use is beyond question. The technique of giving employees vacations, for instance, after its inception around the turn of this century, ceased going in and out of fashion. Management techniques can also become institutionalized when their continued use and development is sustained and regulated by powerful social actors, professional groups or government regulators (DiMaggio and Powell, 1983). The use of certain cost-accounting management techniques in the US, for instance, are not open to the sway of fashion because they are mandated by General Accepted Accounting Standards, defined by the accounting profession and enforced by regulators such as the Securities and Exchange Commission.

When certain realms of management are not institutionalized, however, ambiguity surrounds the utility of management techniques in this realm, and fashion swings can take hold. Ambiguity is opaqueness or lack of clarity surrounding assessments of an innovation's utility (March and Olsen, 1976, p. 12). A variety of ambiguities can be distinguished depending on what it is that is not clear. Three types of ambiguity concern us: 1) Ambiguity of goals − goals in this realm of management are relatively unclear, 2) Ambiguity of means-ends relations − what is unclear is both the range of possible outcomes of means in this realm of management, and the probability that these means will produce certain outcomes, and 3) Ambiguity of environments − both the range and probability of occurrences of future environmental states pertaining to this realm of management are unclear.

Ambiguity opens up social forms to the sway of fashion. The popularity of these forms is no longer a function of their utility, whether it be taken-for-granted, or defined, or sustained and enforced by powerful social actors. Utility becomes instead a matter determined by the reciprocal relation between fashion demand and supply.

Conclusion

I suggested, in this article, that not only primarily aesthetic forms, but also primarily technical forms are open to the swings of fashions. My primary thesis was that aesthetic and technical fashions, although they bear certain surface similarities, are characterized by marked differences. I illustrated this thesis by considering how norms of rationality and progress generate a market for an unending series of management fashions. I focused on how this market is supplied by a fashion-setting community, populated by fashion-setting organizations – management consultants, business schools, business mass-media organizations – dedicated to procuring management ideas, fashioning management discourses that cast these ideas as the embodiment of rational management progress, and marketing these fashionable discourses back to managers. I also reviewed a variety of socio-psychological and technico-economic explanations for fashion demand.

This article did not attempt to assess the value added of fashions or of the management fashion setting system I described. This is an important question and one that will continue to be hotly debated.

The opponents of fashion will no doubt argue that fashions facilitate the spread of technically-inefficient techniques. They will claim that fashions spread techniques that are of little utility and cause the rejection of techniques that could have helped had they been used carefully and persistently. Others will argue more charitably that fashions fulfill symbolic and emotional functions, such as symbolizing progress and instilling hope. Still others will argue that while single fashionable techniques cause little harm, the repeated failure of fashionable techniques undermines the credibility of any innovative technique in this realm.

This article suggests that this treatment of technical fashions as irrational, trivial or dysfunctional is a result of uncritically extending explanations of fashion in aesthetic realms to fashion in technical realms. This approach is not entirely wrongheaded, because since all technical forms have certain aesthetic dimensions, theories of fashion in aesthetic realms highlight the non-technical dimensions of technical fashions. They do so, however, at the cost of obscuring how aesthetic and technical fashions differ. In particular, this approach obscures how technical fashion brings to collective attention technical and economic changes and offers up collectively acceptable means to cope with them.

Deinstitutionalization and the Logic of Fashion

Kjell Arne Røvik

Institutionalized standards are widespread, up-to-date prescriptions for how to organize successfully, prescriptions that nowadays "travel" quickly and with little resistance among people, organizations, countries and global regions. This concept links together much work on the new institutional paradigm in organizational theory. Diffusion and adoption studies help us understand how institutionalized standards travel *into* organizations. However, we know considerably less about whether, how and possibly when they travel *out* again. This article is an attempt to explain why institutionalized standards are usually deinstitutionalized after a while; i. e. why they lose their appeal and fade away.

Initially two traditional approaches to this phenomenon are presented. Thereafter, an alternative theory is developed based on insights into the logic of fashion. It is hypothesized that fashion is a genuine social mechanism with a fairly broad explanatory potential in organizational analyses, but at the same time it is both overlooked and frowned upon by most organization theorists. This article, on the other hand, is an attempt to take fashion seriously in organizational analysis.

An Observed Phenomenon

Consider the following empirically documented observations from Norway, the USA and Sweden respectively:

1. For over a hundred years the local political control in Norwegian municipalities was partly organized through an intricate system of many specialized committees established to handle various policy areas. However, during the period of 1981–1986, a full 91 percent of all Norwegian municipalities replaced the old committee system with so-called *principal standing committees*. In each municipality the number of committees was drastically reduced from 20–30 to 3–4. The intention was to achieve greater efficiency and a greater concentration on political matters of principle. The introduction of the principal standing committee model (PSC model) has been characterized as one of the most extensive reforms in the Norwegian public sector in the 1980s (Stava, 1990, p. 156), a reform that was awaited with great expectations (the KT Report, 1977). In 1987 the Norwegian Associa-

tion of Local Authorities investigated the individual municipalities' experiences with the PSC model. A full 92 percent reported at that time that they were generally satisfied with the reform and that it had improved their efficiency (Stava, 1990, p. 165). However, only four years later, in 1991, the attitude had changed markedly. In a new study a great many municipalities now report that they are generally dissatisfied with the PSC model (Røvik, 1992c). Many of these municipalities have also abandoned this model and have already adopted other models (e. g. the area model and the function model).

2. In the period 1980−1982 about 1/3 of all American companies with more than 500 employees adopted *Quality Circles* (QCs) (Lawler and Mohrman, 1985). QCs were regarded by many as a long term basic strategy in the task of improving American companies' competitive power, especially in relation to Japanese companies (Yager, 1981). However, only a few years later survey studies reveal that about 80 percent of the organizations that adopted QCs in the 1980s no longer make use of them (Pascale, 1990).

3. In the latter half of the 1980s, most Swedish municipalities tried to employ *management by objectives* (MBO) as an administrative technique to help achieve a more efficient utilization of available resources. In 1990 a group of researchers visited a number of these municipalities and surveyed their experiences with MBO. Their main impression was that the municipalities were very satisfied with the results so far. In nearly all of the municipalities, plans were being made at that time to spend five to ten years adapting established routines to this technique (Hansson and Knutsson, 1991). However, in 1991 the researchers recorded a rather dramatic change in the attitude to MBO in these municipalities: among the municipalities that one year earlier had reported in an inquiry that they were employing MBO and were very enthusiastic about the technique, there were many that were no longer willing to acknowledge their previous statements (Isacsson and Knutsson, 1992, p. 115). Many municipalities that were once engaged in MBO have focused their attention on new reforms, such as the utilization of the so-called "purchaser-supplier" model. The researchers found it rather puzzling that attitudes had changed so quickly and drastically. One year earlier MBO had been widely regarded as the most important tool for improving efficiency, whereas now it seemed to be a technique that many municipal workers had completely forgotten. The researchers did not attempt to explain this change, but closed as follows: "It cannot be denied that we wonder what has happened" (Isacsson and Knutsson, 1992, p. 115, translated from Swedish by KAR).

In all of the above-mentioned cases whole groups of organizations almost simultaneously either "forget," verbally dissociate themselves from, stop using, or try to get rid of institutionalized standards, i. e. prescriptions for organizing successfully (the PSC-model, Quality Circles, MBO), that they had adopted some time ago. I shall call this phenomenon *deinstitutionalization*. More specifically, deinstitutionalization refers to the process whereby a prescription for organizing successfully, which for a while has enjoyed the status of a legitimate model or prototype that many organizations have attempted to adopt, gradually loses this status. Deinstitutionalization processes can express themselves in many ways, e. g. the rate at which these prescriptions spread may decline and perhaps even come to a halt (Abrahamson, 1991; Oliver, 1992), or organizations that have already adopted a prescription may abandon it, or perhaps "store" it in the organization in some form or other without making use of it in carrying out their daily work (Røvik, 1992b).

Even though deinstitutionalization can be easily observed by practitioners as well as researchers, there has been little research on this phenomenon, nor is it completely understood. This is one reason why I, in this article, will try to identify characteristic features of the development and outcome of deinstitutionalization processes. The aim is to develop a more comprehensive theory about this phenomenon.

Institutionalized Standards Travel in Time and Space

This article was inspired by the basic insights from the new institutional paradigm in organization theory. The idea is that modern organizations exist in institutional environments where there are socially defined and legitimized norms for how an up-to-date and efficient organization should appear, e. g. as regards structural arrangements, procedures, routines and ideology (Meyer and Rowan, 1977; Scott, 1987a; DiMaggio and Powell, 1983; 1991). Organizations are judged on the basis of how well they comply with whatever is defined − according to prevailing social conventions − as reasonable, efficient and modern at any given time (Zucker, 1987; Forssell, 1992). Organizations usually experience these conventions as "rule-like social facts" (Zucker, 1983; 1987). These rule-like social facts can be called *institutionalized standards*. By that I mean a socially constructed and widely accepted prescription for how part of an organization should be organized, e. g. how personnel should be recruited, which principles should apply in the formulation of budgeting and accounting systems, what the "correct" principles should be for formal coordination and specialization, etc. (Røvik, 1992b). These are prescriptions that become prototypes for many organizations, hence the "standard" concept. The PSC-model, MBO and Quality Circles − which were mentioned in the introduction − are good examples of institutionalized standards. They are organizational prescriptions that have undergone a kind of social transformation process (institutionalization) and that have thereby become a meaningful form or practice — gradually taken for granted — that many organizations have tried to adopt.

Institutionalized standards are prescriptions, but the extent to which they give detailed practical specifications for organizing varies considerably. Some are vague ideas that allow a lot of room for each individual organization to give them its own interpretation. Other institutionalized standards, however, provide more detailed prescriptions for how organizational activities should be carried out, e. g. prescriptions for how corporate planning should be implemented in Norwegian government departments, and for how quality control should be carried out in Norwegian fishing companies (Johansen, 1994; Strand, 1994).

Institutionalized standards are not prescriptions for building a whole complex organization. On the contrary, they apply to small parts of the organization and may therefore be regarded as institutionalized "building blocks." Thus, an organization is often also a *multistandard* organization because it has usually adopted many institutionalized standards over a period of time from various institutional environments (Røvik, 1992b).

The idea that institutionalized standards have limited dissemination in space and time is (often) implicit in the new institutional literature. Each standard has a realm of validity that is limited to certain groups of organizations (e. g. the PSC model is primarily a standard for Norwegian municipalities). Hence, it is important that institutionalized standards are also assumed to have limited duration, in the sense that they "have their day": they arise, spread, last for a while and then deteriorate and are forgotten (for a while, at any rate). Given this fact, one should strive for a better understanding of the "life cycles" of institutionalized standards (Scott and Meyer, 1991; Røvik, 1992a; 1992b).

The literature pertaining to the ways in which standards travel in time and space tends to describe the process, for analytical purposes, as one that consists of three important phases. The first is the actual *institutionalization phase*. In this phase a concept is developed into a socially legitimized and meaningful prescription, a prototype that many organizations wish to adopt. The second phase is the *spreading phase*. Here the focus is on the speed and direction of the spread of an institutionalized standard within a group of organizations. The third phase is the *handling phase*, which focuses on what organizations do with institutionalized standards after they are adopted, e. g. how and to what extent they are tied in with the other prescriptions for success that the organization has previously adopted.

I would like to add a fourth phase which this article will focus on, namely *deinstitutionalization*. As mentioned previously, I will try to answer several questions here, such as to what extent, when and how an institutionalized standard loses its status as a prototype within a group of organizations.

New Institutionalism and Deinstitutionalization

New institutionalists have only occasionally been interested in the phenomenon of deinstitutionalization. One gets an impression of this by looking at which of the above-mentioned phases in an institutionalized standard's "life cycle" the new institutional literature has concentrated on. Attention has primarily been devoted to the spreading phase: most empirical research within this tradition is concerned with describing the speed, direction and extent of the spread of institutionalized standards, such as the spread of matrix organization (Burns and Wholey, 1990), multidivisionalized structure (Fligstein, 1990; 1991), autonomous work groups (Cole, 1985), municipal governing arrangements (Tolbert and Zucker, 1983; Singh et al., et 1986; Tolbert, 1988), training programs (Scott and Meyer, 1991), and financial reporting and accounting systems (Kamens, 1977; Meyer, 1986b; Mezias, 1990). Very few studies within this theoretical tradition attempt to explain the origins of institutionalized prescriptions. Even fewer studies, if there have been any at all, deal with deinstitutionalization. However, if we stick to the presumption that institutionalized standards are ideas that travel and that "have their day," the research effort must not be limited to merely explaining how they travel into organizations − as the diffusion and adoption studies attempt. One must also keep in mind and develop analytical tools to explain that they also travel out of, i. e. leave organizations. Thus, the deinstitutionalization of "old" prescriptions is probably a phenomenon that occurs just as frequently as the institutionalization and travelling of "new" prescriptions into organizations. Yet no explicit theory has been developed that captures this clearly dynamic aspect of institutionalized standards − i. e. the fact that they are generated and then subsequently deteriorate.

The lack of interest in deinstitutionalization clearly reflects a well-known bias in institutional theory. Researchers working in this field are generally more interested in − and have better developed analytical tools for understanding − stability than change. The implicit assumption appears to be that when a prescription has first been institutionalized and has become a meaningful arrangement, it is permanent and can, almost by definition, not deteriorate and fade away.

However, we need a theory that accounts for a phenomenon that can be easily observed, i. e. that institutionalized prescriptions only serve as *temporary* imperatives within a group of organizations. It would be challenging to establish a theory that explains how these prescriptions, as socially constructed rule-like "facts," can be reinterpreted and suffer a decline. This may be expressed by roughly paraphrasing one of the basic arguments of institutional theory: just as our conception of reality is socially constructed, it can also be de-constructed through a social process of reinterpretation.

Within other schools of organization theory, however, researchers have both observed and acknowledged that organizational forms occasionally deteriorate. In the field of population ecology, for example, we find ideas about continuous selection of forms where new ones arise and are perpetuated while others die out because environments – usually meaning markets – change and thereby have a crucial effect on the life and death of organizations (Hannan and Freeman, 1977; Carroll, 1988). There are also theories relating to this phenomenon based on the idea that organizations make rational calculations and decisions regarding which forms are most efficient. When organizational prescriptions are exchanged and replaced with new ones, it is taken to mean that organizations learn and unlearn from their experiences with different prescriptions and adapt their organizational arrangements accordingly (Hedberg, 1981; Levitt and March, 1988).

In the few cases where new institutionalists are interested in the decline of organizational forms, explanations have usually been borrowed from the above-mentioned established research traditions, e. g. from population ecology (Powell, 1991; Brint and Karabel, 1991). However, these well-established explanations are based on mechanisms that are not usually associated with institutional explanations (e. g. natural selection and rational calculation).

Deinstitutionalization, however, is a complex phenomenon, and in order to understand it one must obviously make use of insights that have been developed in other schools of organization theory. I shall argue nonetheless that there is a more specific *institutional* explanation for why institutionalized prescriptions can relatively quickly go from being collectively acclaimed to being collectively rejected and apparently forgotten within an organization field. There is a well-known social phenomenon that can form the basis for the development of this kind of institutional explanation, namely fashion. This is a social mechanism that accounts for the origin, the distribution and, last but not least, the decline and "fall" of a variety of ideas, forms and practices. I shall argue that fashion is a genuine institutional mechanism, and I shall try to clarify its importance for the task of understanding why ideas about how to organize travel not only into, but also out of organizations.

Competing Theoretical Explanations of Deinstitutionalization

Deinstitutionalization of an institutionalized standard is a process, and a theory should help us to understand why these processes are triggered, how these processes typically develop and what sort of outcome they are likely to have, and how organizations will be most likely to deal with deinstitutionalized standards. Let us take a closer look at these three main questions:

What triggers the process? Deinstitutionalization processes have an origin, and a theory should help us to identify and understand the circumstances that typically trigger these processes.

The development of deinstitutionalization processes: Theories about deinstitutionalization must also help us identify and scrutinize the typical sequence of events that follow in the development of deinstitutionalization processes. We need to know what characterizes the processes that cause a prescription for organizational success to lose its status as an institutionalized standard. Secondly, whereas institutionalization involves the spread of a standard to several organizations, deinstitutionalization involves the opposite: a *roll-back process*. This statement is based on observations that deinstitutionalization is a collective phenomenon, in the sense that over a period of time a standard loses its status as a prototype for − and may also be replaced in − most organizations within an organization field. Important questions that must be answered include: In what way and in what order will organizations within a field alter their opinion of an institutionalized prescription? Does it occur as a consequence of a "contagious spread" of opinions among organizations, or does each and every organization learn through its own experiences and almost simultaneously come to the same conclusion? What characterizes organizations that change their opinions about an institutionalized standard early as opposed to those that do so later?

The organizational handling of deinstitutionalized standards: What happens to a prescription that has lost its status as a prototype within a group of organizations? How are deinstitutionalized standards handled internally within the organization, i. e. what is done with particular structural arrangements, routines and ideologies that have "had their day"? This question is an important one, partly because organizational inertia makes it more difficult as a rule to get rid of "old," faded standards than it is to adopt new ones. Thus, the question is whether organizations alter, replace or perhaps "store" deinstitutionalized standards in one form or another. A good theory on deinstitutionalization must also be able to account for this aspect.

In the following section the two most common explanations in organization theory of why institutionalized standards decline as organizational prototypes are briefly summarized. These arise from two theoretical perspectives, which I shall call the "adaptation and selection" (A&S) perspective and the "natural rejection" perspective. The emphasis in this article, however, will be on the development of an alternative theory (in contrast to the two just mentioned) about why and how organizational forms often deteriorate and fade away. I shall call this the "fashion" perspective.

Deinstitutionalization as Adaptation and Selection

Two schools of organization theory can be distinguished from the others because they have been particularly interested in explaining the origin and decline of organizational forms. These two schools are often called the resource dependency perspective and the population ecology perspective. Although they are often presented as contrasting theories in organization theory textbooks (Hall, 1982; Perrow, 1986; Scott, 1987b), they give such similar explanations of why and how organizational forms deteriorate and fade away that I shall merge them into a single perspective, i. e. the adaptation and selection perspective.

The key argument in this school of thought is the simple idea that an organization's structural arrangements are mainly determined by features of the technical environments with which it must deal at any given time. Technical environments are often defined as the counterpart of institutional environments. Important actors in the technical environments are suppliers, receivers of the organization's output, political authorities and competitors (Dill, 1958; Thompson, 1967).

From these actors in the technical environments come demands that the organization must be efficient: the products must be produced at the lowest possible price and the best possible quality. This requires the most appropriate and up-to-date structural arrangements, technical equipment, routines, procedures and personnel. Thus, changes in technical environments require subsequent organizational adaptations in order to maintain structural isomorphism in response to these changes. At the organizational level, these adaptation and selection processes may be detected as a continuous "throughput" of institutionalized standards: old, poorly adapted ones are discarded and new ones are adopted.

Consequently, in this theoretical tradition an institutionalized standard will be an administrative technique that has proven superior to other possible techniques at a given period of time and in a particular context as regards adapting to the demands of technical environments.

What Triggers the Process

From the adaptation and selection perspective there are primarily two situations that can activate deinstitutionalization processes. The first occurs when technical environments change and thereby reduce or completely erase a standard's comparative advantages. This is no doubt the simplest, and also the most frequently cited, explanation in the literature for why organizations may find it necessary to replace "old" organizational forms with new ones (Thompson, 1967; Lawrence and Lorsch, 1967). This is also the explanation that is most frequently used by practicians to justify reforms in organizations. (It is argued, for example, that when so many Norwegian municipalities now want to get rid of the PSC-model, it is because this administrative model is poorly suited to deal with the worsening in the municipalities' economic constraints, which occurred at the close of the 1980s). According to this school of thought, the other situation that can trigger deinstitutionalization occurs when new and better administrative techniques arise, which the organization becomes aware of (Bernas, 1981), and which lead to the realization that an established institutionalized standard has lost its comparative advantages.

The Development of the Deinstitutionalization Process

Resource dependency theoreticians and population ecologists agree that organizational forms disappear and about why these processes are triggered (i. e. in response to changes in technical environments). They differ, however, about how this occurs, i. e. about the development of these processes.

Resource dependency theoreticians assume that organizations are not captives of their environments, but are relatively free to choose alternative structural arrangements (Lawrence and Lorsch, 1967; Pfeffer and Salancik, 1978). The basic mechanism that governs the development of the deinstitutionalization process is rational adaptation. The simple idea here is that changes in technical environments that require new organizational forms will usually be discovered by the leadership of the organization, which then acts to replace old, inappropriate forms with new ones that are better adapted to the requirements of the altered environments.

The population ecologists, on the other hand, argue that natural selection is the most important mechanism for explaining the decline of organizational forms. Organizations are limited in their ability to adapt their forms to changing environments. The faster the environments change, the greater the chance that they will be unable to cope with these changes, and the more likely it becomes that organizations with poorly adapted forms will "die" and that a group of organizations with better adapted forms will see the light of day (Hawley, 1968; Hannan and Freeman, 1977; 1984; 1989; Carroll, 1988). Common to both schools of thought, however, is the notion that the "fall" of an institutionalized standard is brought about by loss of comparative technical or economic advantages.

In what order and in what way then will the realization that an institutionalized standard has lost its comparative technical or economic advantages be spread among organizations within a field? These questions concern the roll-back process. One can obtain some help in answering them from the very extensive literature that deals with what is called the spread of innovations (Rogers, 1962; Rogers and Shoemaker, 1971; Kimberly, 1981). In this literature, adopting a new, more efficient technical solution is regarded as synonymous with also getting rid of old, comparatively less efficient solutions (Bernas, 1981). Consequently, the roll-back process takes place simultaneously and in the same order as the spread of the innovation.

Much of the research effort in this school of thought has been focused on discovering what distinguishes those who get rid of the old and adopt new, more efficient solutions relatively early from those who do so later. Despite a considerable research effort, there are few indications so far of a clear pattern (Kervasdoue and Kimberly, 1978). To some extent, there is data to support a hypothesis that the biggest and financially strongest organizations are the first ones to get rid of old, inefficient solutions (Mytinger, 1968; Mohr, 1969).

In this perspective the realization that an institutionalized standard has lost its comparative technical or economic advantages spreads "contagiously" to the other organizations within a field. This "contagion" does not stem from any social pressure to conform, however. It is more a process driven by rational calculation and learning, a process where the advantages and disadvantages of a solution are evaluated in light of experiences gained previously by others (Rogers, 1962).

Handling of Technically Inefficient Solutions

Rational adaptation entails that organizations are able to rapidly get rid of inefficient organizational forms. Structural inertia, in the sense of a tendency to wait too long to get rid of inefficient forms, is regarded in this theoretical tradition as one of the greatest threats to an organization's chances of surviving (Hannan and Freeman, 1989).

Deinstitutionalization as Unlearning and Natural Rejection

The natural rejection perspective combines important insights from "old" and "new" institutionalism in organization theory. Institutions are regarded as "value-infused" organizations, each with its own distinct character and capable of solving extremely complex tasks on a routine basis (Hughes, 1939; Selznick, 1949; 1957; March and Olsen, 1989). Institutionalized standards, on the other hand, are usually described as vague, simple, popular reform ideas that come from "outside," penetrate and sometimes even threaten "real" institutions (Meyer and Rowan, 1977; Brunsson, 1989; 1994; Brunsson and Olsen, 1993). Institutions are subjected to pressure from institutional environments to adopt institutionalized prescriptions. If an institution tries to make use of these prescriptions, however, they will often find that the new "solution" either conflicts with their basic values and norms or that it is too simple and thus cannot be utilized to coordinate complex organizational activities (Brunsson et al., 1989; Andersen et al., 1990).

For organizational actors this will often take the form of a process of *unlearning* (Hedberg, 1981). By gaining practical experience they generally loses the illusions that often motivate such an adoption, namely the belief that the prescription is especially well-suited for improving organizational efficiency. Moreover, unlearning can easily develop into deinstitutionalization: if an institutionalized standard has proven to be unusable for practical purposes, it can easily lose its status as a prototype within an organization field.

Thus, the dynamic element inherent in this perspective is the idea of simple and ever-travelling popular prescriptions for success that penetrate the complex, stable, value-based organization and are later discarded. Institutionalized standards, or reform ideas, are generally treated as abstract ideas dissociated from a complex reality (Meyer and Rowan, 1977; Covaleski and Dirsmith, 1988). Nevertheless, these standards often have their origin in a particular organizational context where they have been especially well-suited for improving efficiency (Thomas and Meyer, 1984; Røvik, 1992a). When they spread, however, they are usually disengaged from their original complex context and become simplified standard prescriptions for organizing successfully (Zucker, 1987). Thus, it is not the complex organizational practice in itself, but rather simplified, dematerialized, abstract *representations* of them that become institutionalized standards and travel in space and time.

Simple institutionalized prescriptions cannot be easily employed in complex institutions, partly because the complexity of the institutions' tasks requires complex solutions based on practical experience and partly because the popular institutionalized prescriptions that come from "outside" may challenge the institutions' basic values and norms and threaten their identities.

In a study of the Swedish State Railways, Brunsson and Winberg (1993) give the following description of the enormous complexity that one must confront and find practical solutions for in this business:

> There are close technical links between what the various units do: at any point in time there are thousands of engines and carriages in hundreds of terminals or on different parts of the railway network, and their locations at that point in time determine what can be done next. Customers use thousands of different combinations of routes along the lines for their trips or for transportation of goods;

less busy lines feed into busier ones which feed back into less busy ones again. Transport sold in one region gives rise to costs in others (Brunsson and Winberg, 1993, pp. 111–112).

Such complexity also makes specific demands on which solutions can be employed. Hence, the structures, procedures and routines that are actually used will usually also be intelligent solutions (as opposed to most popular institutionalized prescriptions) because they are perfected through a long period of trial and error. Statistically speaking, the vast majority of institutionalized prescriptions that are adopted will not have the qualities required for coordinating complex activities in an institution (Mitroff and Mohrman, 1987; Levitt and March, 1988). Organizational actors will discover this if they make whole-hearted attempts to make use of simple institutionalized prescriptions to coordinate established practices (Trist and Bamford, 1951).

However, externally generated popular standards can also clash with a particular institution's norms, values and identity. A reform idea, or institutionalized standard, that is not consistent with the institution's basic values and identity runs a great risk of being rejected (Olsen, 1988; 1992; March and Olsen, 1989). The difficulties encountered in implementing certain planned reforms in Norwegian courts in the 1980s, for example, have been interpreted as an indication that the reforms' focus on economic savings and organizational efficiency could not always be reconciled with the courts' historical role as the guardians of justice and legal protection (Andersen et al., 1990; Gjerde, 1991; Pedersen, 1992; Magnussen, 1992).

I call this way of thinking "the natural rejection perspective" because the deinstitutionalized prescription here has its obvious analogy in the concept of the foreign body that one tries to implant in an organism (the institution). The organism (institution), however, is a complete system with a finely attuned natural balance among its various sub-functions. The institutionalized standard, in the role of foreign body, will partly be too different and too simple in relation to the organism's complex logic, and it will partly be a threat because it can upset the system's natural balance. Thus, just as with biologists' concept of an immune system, processes can be activated in the organism that cause the foreign body to be rejected.

Let us take a closer look at the ways in which deinstitutionalization can be interpreted within this theoretical framework.

What Triggers the Process

Initially, actors who adopt institutionalized standards are usually convinced that they really are well-suited to their own institution (Johannessen, 1993). Consequently, most institutions will also try to make use of the standards to coordinate practical, routine activities (Røkenes, 1993). This will give them the first indication of how well the standards function in dealing with complex tasks. In this perspective it is precisely these first experiences with the new prescription that are thought to trigger the unlearning and later the deinstitutionalization processes because in most cases they clearly reveal the prescriptions' shortcomings to the organizational actors: partly by proving to be too simple to coordinate established complex practices and partly by revealing inconsistencies between the new technique and the institutions' basic norms and values (Tiller, 1990).

The Development of the Deinstitutionalization Process

In this perspective the basic mechanism and driving force in the deinstitutionalization process is *experiential learning*. It is assumed that organizations' attempts to make use of institutionalized standards will involve some trial and error. The process will most likely develop from simple, so-called "first-order learning" to more fundamental "second-order learning" (Argyris and Schön, 1978; Fiol and Lyles, 1985). Even if one finds in the early introductory phase that the popular prescriptions cannot be utilized at once to coordinate complex tasks, this will not necessarily be interpreted as a warning that something is wrong with the actual prescription. It will most likely be interpreted to mean that the prescription must be specified in greater detail and adapted to the organization, that the employees need more information about the technique, and that one must just be patient. Gradually, however, the process will take the form of more fundamental learning; sooner or later it will be recognized that the difficulties that confront an organization when it tries to implement a popular prescription indicate that it is just too simple or that it somehow conflicts with the fundamental values and norms in the organization (Van de Ven and Polley, 1990). Consequently, it cannot be employed. A side effect of this kind of learning process might be that the organizational actors themselves simultaneously discover the enormous complexity of the tasks they routinely handle and thereby become more aware of the fundamental characteristics of their institution (Trist and Bamford, 1951). This is unlearning in the sense that through practical experience an institution is able to discard superstitions it may have entertained about an institutionalized standard.

Unlearning currently takes place within the individual institution, whereas I have defined deinstitutionalization as a phenomenon than can be detected at the meso level, i. e. that the prescription loses its status as an institutionalized standard for *many* organizations during roughly the same period of time. This raises questions about the roll-back process, i. e. in what way and in what order do the individual organizations within a field arrive at this realization.

The point of departure for this school of thought is that each organization is a unique institution with its own distinctive core activities, values and identity. Each and every one of these institutions must therefore gain and learn from its own experiences, and the experiences of an individual organization can rarely be conveyed to other organizations. They may therefore reject the prescription independently of each other and hence in a random order. Consequently, the order of the roll-back process will be only slightly determined by the "contagious" spread among institutions of the belief that an institutionalized standard is inappropriate. If we nevertheless observe that organizations almost simultaneously arrive at the same conclusion, it suggests that uncoordinated but simultaneous unlearning processes have taken place, often because the prescriptions were adopted at roughly the same time as well.

Handling of Inappropriate Prescriptions

If the natural rejection perspective has explanatory power, one would expect organizations to make sure they get rid of deinstitutionalized prescriptions There are two reasons why. First, unsatisfactory experiences with prescriptions are in themselves an important incentive to replace them. Second, we recall that an important aspect of this perspective is the idea that an institutionalized standard is only a simple conceptual representation of a complex practice. Since institutionalized standards are so rarely materialized in a concrete organizational activity, there is usually very little to bind it to an organization after it has been deinstitutionalized. This makes it easy to get rid of because it is more a matter of "forgetting" an idea than of terminating an established activity.

The Fashion Perspective

Most attempts to explain why organizational forms deteriorate derive from one or both of the above-mentioned perspectives. Neither of these can be called a specific institutional explanation, however. One reason for this is that very little attempt has been made within these theoretical traditions to explain the decline of organizational forms with explicit reference to *social* mechanisms. Thus, the above-mentioned explanations both originate from ideas about how system defects can arise and be coped with in biological, ecological and mechanical systems. This borrowing of systems theory from other disciplines has been most clearly and deliberately practised by population ecologists, especially in their ideas about continuous natural selection of the best adapted forms at any given time (Hannan and Freeman, 1977).

I shall argue that there is a *human-made* phenomenon, familiar from social life (and hence not just mechanisms familiar from natural science) that can help us explain the decline of organizational forms. This is fashion.

There are three aspects of fashion that make it especially interesting for our purposes: i. e. that it is a *universal*, a *dynamic*, and a *social* phenomenon.

Although many regard fashion as something that only concerns certain kinds of human expression, e. g. cars and architectural designs, it is in reality a considerably more universal social phenomenon that can explain the distribution of a large number of ideas and forms in time and space (Blumer, 1969; Czarniawska and Joerges, in this volume). Therefore, I must initially leave the possibility open that it can also explain the distribution of institutionalized standards.

Fashion is dynamic. It explains how forms of human expression can achieve popularity, become widespread, and then later become unfashionable. Fashion's transient nature (which naturally interests me the most) is well-known: both individuals and organizations are constantly abandoning ideas, styles and forms that once had an imperative status while focusing their attention on new ones, not necessarily because the old ones have ceased to be useful, but simply because they are no longer considered to be up-to-date. I therefore ask: is it conceivable that in fashion's generally transient nature one can also find explanations for why institutionalized prescriptions fade after a while and "travel out" of organizations again?

Fashion is a social phenomenon: It basically deals with our ability as social creatures to construct and to deconstruct whatever we perceive to be authentic reality.

Let us begin by taking a closer look at precisely these aspects of fashion.

Fashion as a Socially Constructed Reality

One important reason why new institutionalists should take interest in the logic of fashion is that this phenomenon offers the best illustration of a key insight on which all institutional theory is based: that of the socially constructed reality. Berger and Luckmann succinctly formulated Schützian thought in 1966: through interaction and discourse people are able to create their own common standards of behavior, standards which are perceived by the individual, however, as an externally given objective reality (externalization and objectivation). Thus, these socially constructed standards confront the individual as rules of behavior that he or she gradually takes for granted (internalization).

These three processes (externalization, objectivation, internalization) are expressed in a particularly condensed and readily apparent form in the fashion phenomenon. This is what makes fashion a genuine social mechanism, and this is what clearly distinguishes it from the mechanical and biological mechanisms on which explanations of the decline of organizational forms have traditionally been based.

Fashion Is a Human Creation

Perhaps the fashion phenomenon was neglected for so many years because its theoretician, Herbert Blumer, refused to espouse the biologistic tendencies of the 1950s, stating bluntly that fashion is a human creation, not a natural product. Although fashion is often depicted and perceived as an expression of an objective Zeitgeist, it is, of course, primarily a social product. Blumer (1969) observed how Paris fashions are created as a result of the confluence of many buyers at the annual fashion shows who interact and influence each other and thereby jointly create the fashion. Here is his lively description of this process, which sharply depicts the social construction of fashion:

> Inquiry into the reasons for the similarity in the buyers' choices led me to an observation, namely, that the buyers were immersed in and preoccupied with a remarkably common world of intense stimulation. It was a world of lively discussion of what was happening in woman's fashion, of fervent reading of fashion publications, and, above all, it was a world of close concern with the woman's dress market, with the prevailing tastes and prospective tastes of consuming public in the area of dress. It became vividly clear to me that by virtue of their intense immersion in this world the buyers came to develop common sensitivities and similar appreciations (Blumer, 1969, p. 279).

Fashion Is Objectified

Even though fashion, as illustrated above, is a social product, it is perceived as an objective reality, a "given" on which one has little personal influence. This objectivation is expressed linguistically, for example, when fashion is treated as something that is externally dictated (e. g. "this year the color *will* be...," "the current trend *is*..."), i. e. more a product of the current Zeitgeist than a human creation.

Fashion Is Internalized

The Schützian school's concept − the internalization of socially constructed reality − has its parallel in the way prevailing fashions can leave their mark on a particular individual (or a particular organization). When the fashion is internalized, it affects both our values and habits. It affects our values in the sense that our perceptions of what is good, efficient and beautiful, for example, can actually be changed in step with the current fashion. However, fashion is also internalized because it establishes unconscious habits. It can take root in an individual as a rule-like "fact," a prescription for how things are and ought to be which is gradually taken-for-granted (Sellerberg, 1994). Fashion thereby influences actors' perceptions of what is authentic (Bell, 1976). Here again we can see a clear parallel to the assumption in new institutional theory that institutionalized standards are taken for granted and regarded as objective facts.

Taken together these tenets show why fashion is such an apt illustration of the basic insight on which all institutional theory is based, namely the social construction of reality.

The Dynamic Character of Fashion

I have argued that we need a theory that can capture the dynamic aspect of the rise and fall of institutionalized standards. Here the logic of fashion offers help: it is a stable social mechanism that continually produces change. Fashion's ability to change both collective and individual values and preferences is easy to illustrate with practical examples relating to clothing: when one buys new clothes in the fashionably correct colors and put away the old ones, it is not just because we have a conscious desire to appear fashionable. Fashion will often have also changed the buyer's perception of how a smart garment should look, so that he or she may begin to take a different view of his/her old garments as well! If you take a look in the closet reserved for all your discarded garments, you will often wonder what on earth could have made you once like all the monstrosities that are hanging there.

At the individual level (or the individual organizational level) changes in fashion are most easily expressed as described above: we adopt new fashions and discard and forget the old ones for a while. At the group level we can observe the fashion's origin, spread and decline over a period of time as a wavelike movement through a population of individuals (or a set of organizations). Let us take a closer look at this.

Fashion as a Mechanism of Change at the Individual Level

One explanation that has been offered for individuals' (and organizations') tendency to follow fashions is that they are an expression of generally operating cognitive-psychological mechanisms, e. g. based on a desire to attract attention (Flugel, 1973; Sapir, 1937). Another explanation of this fashion-following tendency is that it is an expression of the extent to which we are more or less helpless captives of the Zeitgeist, i. e. a kind of metaphysical phenomenon.

It is, however, considerably more fruitful to interpret the individual's attempts to keep up with the current fashion as a manifestation of a paradox, namely the tension between the motive of signalling that one belongs to a social community on the one hand, i. e. a desire *to be like the others*, and the motive of individuality, to stand out and attract attention on the other hand, i. e. a desire *to be unique*. These two motives obviously conflict with each other. Thus, fashion conveys the most essential dynamic element in social life in a condensed form, namely the tension between the individual and the collective (Simmel, 1973). Changes in fashion emerge from the contradiction between these two opposing motives and are expressed by the individuals in their actions as a continuous vacillation between *imitation of* and *differentiation from* the prevailing fashions. In other words, the core mechanism of change consists of imitation processes provoking differentiation processes and vice versa (Brenninkmeyer, 1963).

It is also important to pay attention to the many complex ways that imitation and differentiation processes can be intertwined. Sometimes actions that are primarily aimed at imitating a fashion will also lead to a certain amount of differentiation from it. Imitation does not necessarily involve copying every detail (Sevón, in this volume). A well-known point made by the classic imitation theorist, Gabriel Tarde (1903), is that those who imitate often manage to achieve a certain amount of personal expression within the prevailing fashion. On the other hand, actions that primarily aim at differentiation and contrast are often seen in retrospect to involve some imitation of things that were (actually) prevailing fashions. Sellerberg expresses this as follows:

> When we choose something fashionable, we often experience it as a highly personal aspiration. Later it turns out that our attempt at personal expression has taken place in safe company with a large number of others who act in the same way at the same time (Sellerberg, 1987, p. 129, translated from Swedish by KAR).

This clearly illustrates how the individual and the collective impulses wrestle with each other in the arena of fashion and thereby shape its dynamics.

Fashion as a Mechanism of Change at the Group Level

As mentioned above, changes in fashion can also be observed within a population where the units consist of individuals or organizations. A fashion will pass through the population in a wavelike movement over a certain period of time. This movement arises because the individual units in the population − or field − do not all reject an outmoded fashion (nor adopt a new one) at exactly the same time; each of these processes occurs sequentially (Abrahamson, in this volume). The wavelike movement at the population level becomes apparent if one plots the points in time when each individual unit adopts and discards the fashion. Such movements have been studied empirically (Young, 1937; Richardson and Kroeber, 1940; Robinson, 1958; Reynold, 1973).

The research challenge consists of identifying any patterns in these wavelike movements and then shaping them into a coherent theory. One possible summarizing explanation derives from what I shall call *the fade-out hypothesis*: here too the "driving force" giving rise to change is the paradoxical vacillation between social differentiation and imitation processes. A fashion has its greatest attention-getting potential when it is new and few people have yet adopted it. Thus, early adoption of a fashion is often motivated by a desire to differentiate – one distinguishes oneself from the rest of the population with a distinct feature. As the fashion gradually spreads, however, it loses its attention-getting capacity (to borrow an image from physics: it loses its "energy" and degenerates). However, it still remains to explain why the last units in the population – or field – that adopt the fashion want to do so when it is obviously in the process of losing – or has already lost – its attention-getting capacity. The answer is that at some point in the fashion's spread the motives among those who adopt it switch from differentiation, i. e. wanting to be unique, to imitation, i. e. wanting to be like those who have already adopted it. If one is among the last who have not adopted a fashion that has gained great acceptance, one risks being stigmatized as one of the few who are unfashionable and "out." Imitation will then usually be motivated by the desire to avoid negative responses. Bluntly stated, whereas the early adoption of a fashion is motivated by a desire to achieve a "snob effect," late adoption is partly motivated by the desire to avoid a "mob effect."

For those who first adopt the fashion, however, the fact that it has gradually become "common property" will mean that it has lost its distinguishing, attention-getting capacity. This will again trigger the search for a new distinguishing feature. From this perspective, fashion is subversive, in the sense that when it spreads it undermines itself (Sellerberg, 1987). In 1904 Georg Simmel described a variant of this phenomenon, which was subsequently called the "trickle down effect." Simmel's hypothesis was that fashion is a way of visualizing and reproducing class distinctions. A new fashion arises in the upper class and spreads downward through the class pyramid as a result of the lower classes' desire to resemble the well-heeled. Thereafter, the elite must find new distinguishing features, and the cycle is repeated (for further discussion of the "trickle down effect" see Nystrom, 1928; Barber and Lobel, 1952; Fallers, 1973; and King, 1973).

Fashion's Cyclical Nature

In the preceding discussion I have taken my point of departure in *one* fashion and described factors that affect its travel through a population. One can also expand the time perspective so that it becomes possible to study the characteristic features of the relationships among *several* fashions that continually succeed each other in a population. Most researchers who have studied this empirically have thereby discerned another important aspect of fashion as a mechanism of change: namely, its repetitive or cyclical nature. In other words, there is an obvious tendency for a fashion, which fades and becomes outmoded in one period, to later be revived so that it can again set the standards for what is to be regarded as "in."

It has been thoroughly documented, for example, that changes in various fashions (e. g. dress fashions), when observed chronologically over a couple of hundred years, have developed as slight modifications within a few (three, four) constantly recurring main cycles (Young, 1937; Richardson and Kroeber, 1940; Horn, 1968; Wills and Christopher, 1973; Carman, 1973). Thus, changes in fashion are not linear progressions, but rather, to use Agnes Young's expression, "evolution without destination" (Young, 1937, p. 109). A schism may easily arise when there are only a limited number of forms that circulate between being in and out of fashion, at the same time that continuous innovation and progress are both associated with and demanded of each new fashion. Roland Barthes (1973; 1983) shows that fashion creators and fashion journalists tackle this dilemma by constantly developing new linguistic categories with which to describe the same old forms, which have merely been revived. Hence, "the new" is primarily just a linguistic renewal.

Fashion cycles also obey certain rules. It looks as if a certain amount of time must elapse after a cycle has run its course before the fashion can be revived again. Any attempt to repeat a cycle with a fashion that has just recently become outmoded will usually be unsuccessful because the fashion is still remembered and identified with that which is regarded as passé (Barthes, 1973). Thus, fashions from the 1970s, which are clearly in evidence today, first became ripe for revival in the 1990s, not in the 1980s.

The essence of the above discussion is that fashion is a genuine social and autonomous, but also a paradoxical, mechanism of change. It is *eigendynamisch* (Nedelmann, 1987) in the sense that it is both self-renewing and self-destroying (subversive). The dynamic nature of fashion stems from the "energy" that arises when conflicting social forces, such as the desires for individuality (differentiation) and conformity (imitation) vie with each other. This leads to series of reactions to reactions that take the form of a self-generated, evolutionary circular movement.

Deinstitutionalization as a Process of Becoming Unfashionable

In this section I shall discuss fashion's potential for explaining deinstitutionalization, i. e. the process whereby popular prescriptions for organizing successfully lose their status as organizational prototypes. I argue that the logic of fashion can help us to understand what triggers deinstitution-alization, how the process is expected to develop and how organizations will deal with deinstitutionalized prescriptions.

What Triggers the Process

In the fashion perspective it is assumed that an institutionalized standard's attention-getting capacity decreases proportionally with its spread within a group of organizations (the fade-out hypothesis). The process whereby a fashionable organizational prescription becomes unfashionable is most likely to commence when, and because, it is about to be spread to most organizations within an organization field. The underlying tenet is that modern organizations, like individuals, are constrained in their actions by social norms, i. e. they are torn between the motive of signalling a common identity and sense of belonging to a group of organizations (organization field) and the motive of distinguishing themselves from the other organizations and attracting attention. This vacillation between actions that seek to imitate and differentiate respectively is also the driving force that triggers both institutionalization and deinstitutionalization processes. When an organizational prescription is spread and has become an institutionalized standard, it will cease to be able to function as a distinguishing, attention-getting feature. This might trigger the search for a new prescription. Thus, it is not sufficient to explain deinstitutionalization solely as a result of the advent of "something new" that attracts attention (Sellerberg, 1987). The "new" will only be perceived as such in a context where other forms of expression can simultaneously be defined as "old." It is primarily when an institutionalized standard is about to be adopted by all of the organizations within a field that some of these organizations (especially those who adopted it first) may be motivated to find something new.

In the other two perspectives that are discussed in this article, i. e. adaptation and selection, and natural rejection, it is emphasized that the decline of institutionalized standards is triggered when they cease to be technically or economically efficient. In the fashion perspective, on the other hand, it is primarily a *social* logic that triggers deinstitutionalization, i. e. the fact that an institutionalized standard has lost its socially differentiating and attention-getting power.

This sheds light on cases where researchers, and also practicians, have observed that organizations do not take the time to learn from a reform before they lose interest in it and focus their attention on a new one (March and Olsen, 1983a; Brunsson et al., 1989). In a study of Swedish municipalities' introduction of MBO, the researchers draw the following conclusion:

> During 1990 it was said [in the municipal administrations] ... and almost everyone we interviewed agreed that the implementation would take a long time and last for a five to ten year period. Today [1992] we know that the assessment of MBO is changing. Long before this administrative technique had been given the implementation time that was initially considered necessary, the power of this verbal magnet has declined (Isacsson and Knutsson, 1992, p. 117, translated from Swedish by KAR).

Evaluated on the basis of rationalistic efficiency criteria, actions of this sort might easily be judged irrational. In the logic of fashion, however, they can be interpreted as an indication that a social differentiation process is underway.

The Development of the Deinstitutionalization Process

How do processes in which an institutionalized standard loses its status as a prototype develop? In the fashion perspective deinstitutionalization is regarded as a process of becoming unfashionable. This process has two important characteristics: a reinterpretation of the prevailing institutionalized standards and a subsequent collective "amnesia" of sorts as regards the former institutionalized standards.

Just as an institutionalized standard can be said to be a kind of a socially constructed reality, deinstitutionalization, bluntly stated, can be regarded as the social "destruction" of reality, in the sense that an established perception of a prescription as an organizational prototype deteriorates. This occurs through a process of reinterpretation with the active use of linguistic labels which then create the impression that the previously so popular prescription for organizing successfully is now passé.

The process of becoming unfashionable has its own characteristic rhetoric: quite typically an organizational prescription appears to be obsolete because it is presented, for example, as too simple, unfruitful or uninteresting. Organizations act, however, under the influence of strict norms of rationality. Therefore, it is difficult to justify replacing a prescription through explicit use of linguistic labels like "outdated" and "old-fashioned." In formal organizations the rhetoric of becoming unfashionable is usually thoroughly interspersed with rationalistic terminology. This may give somewhat paradoxical results at times: e. g. the process whereby a prescription becomes unfashionable can accelerate precisely because it is said to be "just a passing fashion." At the same time, *new* prescriptions, which are just about to acquire fashion status, are usually defined as technical improvements, and any decisions to adopt these prescriptions are often interpreted and justified exclusively on technical or economic grounds. This phenomenon can be observed, for example, when Norwegian municipalities try to justify their declining interest in MBO at the same time as their interest in quality control is now − in 1996 − increasing rapidly.

Another way in which the process of becoming unfashionable may express itself as a process of social differentiation is when actors continuously and demonstratively specify what they are doing right now, as opposed to what they were doing earlier (Sellerberg, 1987; 1994). This process of specification usually involves small modifications and can be limited to the introduction of a new linguistic label (e. g. as when the managers of a large hospital argue that MBO is definitely not practised there any more, but rather "activity planning" (Bie, 1992). By making these specifications, organizations are constantly signalling which prescriptions are new, and, indirectly, which have become passé.

The process of becoming unfashionable is also reflected in the seemingly inexplicable decline of attention to and interest in an institutionalized prescription, which may occur quite rapidly. It is precisely this phenomenon that Isacsson and Knutsson (1992) have observed in Swedish municipalities:

> During 1991 we have noticed a changed attitude to the utilization of the concept of MBO. Through a round of calls to municipalities, which, according to the above-mentioned questionnaire, were in favor of MBO a year ago, we found that many would no longer stand by the answer they had given then so that in our sample of municipalities we had a difficult time finding any suitable objects for study (Isacsson and Knutsson, 1992, p. 118, translated from Swedish by KAR).

The process whereby an organizational form becomes unfashionable is also experienced by the actors themselves and may find expression in a perceptible loss of enthusiasm. It is also reflected in the practicians' language, e. g. "the air has gone out of the balloon" or "it used to be MBO, but now the latest craze is quality control."

The Roll-Back Process

The process of becoming unfashionable can also be studied as a meso-level phenomenon in the sense that the acceptance of a prescription as a prototype, which has spread through a number of organizations, abates again. In what order, however, and in what way? Based on the logic of fashion, it can be argued that the roll-back process will follow the same pattern as the process of spreading: when an institutionalized standard is spread, it is those who first adopted it that will feel most strongly that it has lost its socially differentiating capacity, and who will therefore have the greatest incentive to discard it and find some new prescription to adopt. In other words, one gets rid of standards in order to recover a "snob effect." Opinions about what has become outmoded, which one should perhaps discard, spread just as contagiously within a group of organizations as ideas about what is new and modern. Once again the driving force behind this spread is the tension between social differentiation and imitation processes.

Handling of Obsolete, Unfashionable Prescriptions

How will organizations deal with organizational prescriptions that have been adopted and then later lost their status as prototypes? We recall to begin with that both the adaptation and selection, and natural rejection perspectives led one to expect that organizations will get rid of deinstitutionalized prescriptions rather quickly.

The fashion perspective furnishes us with other expectations about how institutionalized standards that have become unfashionable will be dealt with by organizations. Modern organizations face a characteristic dilemma that will be especially apparent in questions of what to do with organizational prescriptions that have lost their status as fashionable prototypes: on the one hand norms of fashionableness dictate that they should adopt and get rid of prescriptions with as little resistance as possible in accordance with cyclical fluctuations in organizational fashions. On the other hand, organizations will also be affected by certain inertial factors because they are subject to norms of efficiency and rationality as well. The rationality norm dictates, for example, that an organization should not discard administrative techniques until it becomes evident that they no longer function efficiently or until better techniques are discovered − not just because they have "gone out of fashion." Replacement in step with rapid fashion swings is also hampered because prescriptions get firmly entrenched in the organization. This occurs, for example, when budgets are prepared and money is allocated, when meetings and seminars are held, when long term plans are made, and, last but not least when fashionable organizational prescriptions give rise to new jobs (and when educational programs are established at schools and universities to train people for these fashionable jobs). In practice, organizations have to deal with the dilemma that arises when norms of fashionableness dictate a rapid replacement of an obsolete organizational prescription, while norms of rationality keep that prescription entrenched. Many observations indicate that a compromise between replacement and incorporation often cause obsolete prescriptions to slowly fade away and lose their practical importance.

The fading process is partly reflected in a general decline in enthusiasm: the internal promoters of a formerly fashionable technique no longer attract attention (Christensen, 1991), fewer conferences and meetings are held, the technique is discussed less and less, and among those who still discuss it, it is usually the critical voices that dominate. In cases where the obsolete prescription has gotten more firmly entrenched in the organization, the fading may be detected as a declining frequency of use. We have observed, for instance, that the fading of the MBO prescription, which has gradually gone out of fashion in the Norwegian public sector is reflected in various ways; e. g. more and more time elapses between each attempt to revise MBO plans, the attempts become less and less enthusiastic, and fewer and fewer people are involved. Finally, the activity relating to MBO in the organization may have dwindled to such a small ritual performed so halfheartedly by so few participants that few will even notice when it is done away with entirely. At that point the fading is complete.

Prescriptions that have become obsolete may have become very entrenched in an organization, however, e. g. in cases where jobs have been established and personnel hired to carry out a particular function; but here too, we may observe fading processes, though they may develop somewhat slower. Fading and replacement can occur quite rapidly, if, for example, the implementation of a prescription has been organized as a short term project (this is also the reason why people with a lot of experience in the management of various short term projects are often very useful sources of information if one wishes to find out how organizational fashions have altered with time).

The process of becoming unfashionable may also take the form of a fading process in cases where more permanent jobs and departments have been established. When vacancies arise, for example, the content of those jobs can be redefined so that they again are more in line with the most fashionable techniques, at the same time as the prescriptions that have become obsolete will usually disappear. For example, Norwegian municipalities have been dominated in the postwar period by several planning and development ideologies, each of which can be regarded as an institutionalized standard. Toward the middle of the 1970s, "the general planning ideology," which strove for a strong coordination of geographic, economic and demographic factors through a comprehensive, long term municipal planning effort, and which had been the fashionable regional development philosophy of the 1960s, began to fall out of favor. Partly as a contrast to this ideology, "the local development ideology" emerged in the latter part of the 1970s − an ideology with less emphasis on bureaucratic planning and greater emphasis on a more active municipal marshalling for the establishment of economic activity and jobs (Røvik, 1982). In practice most municipalities handled this transition in such a way that the general planning ideology slowly and almost imperceptibly faded away while local development gained a more positive image. When general planning consultant jobs became vacant, they were often redefined so that they were advertized again as jobs for development or economic consultants. In the work with the general plans, an increasing number of municipalities in the latter half of the 1970s seemingly "forgot" their ambitions of achieving a comprehensive coordination of geographic, demographic and economic factors. Instead the planning work was refocused in the direction of economic development planning, which clearly reflected the new development ideology.

Storage

Although standards that have become obsolete can undergo fading processes, the fading will usually not be complete. In most cases the remains of obsolete standards are "stored" in the organization and institutionalized

practices become "sedimented." This kind of storage will partly occur because the obsolete prescriptions are incorporated and materialized in jobs
that cannot easily be phased out, and partly because the prescription may
have given rise to robust administrative units that strongly resist the process
of becoming unfashionable, and which therefore can remain as monuments
to the standard that was once so popular. Obsolete standards may also be
preserved in particular routines and procedures, and even if these should
fade away so that the standards no longer have a *structural* mooring in the
organization, they will still usually have a cognitive representation because
they are "stored" in employees memories and language.

Stored obsolete standards are also interesting in light of the concept of
the repetitive nature of organizational fashions; i. e. the fact that faded
forms often become fashionable again at a later date. The stored standards
may then undergo a "revival process" with the old standard returning perhaps in a new linguistic package. Since remains of the old standard are
already stored in organizational structures and/or language, i. e. as a cognitive representation, the members of the organization will usually have no
difficulty recalling the basic ideas and arguments. This may cause previous
institutionalized standards that are stored in particular jobs, organizational
units, programs and routines to be revitalized and presented to the environments as something to which the organization (again) gives high priority.
Thus, the storage of remains of obsolete standards makes it easier for organizations to deal with changing organizational fashions. This storage
gives them a certain preparedness, which enables them at little cost, and
above all rapidly, to appear fashionable again.

The concepts of the fading, storage and revival of obsolete standards
can be summarized in an image. Let us think of an organization as if it
were an elderly fashion-conscious person's closet, where the organizational
fashions from different periods have been stored away. They aren't used
any more, but can nevertheless be found in the closet. The experienced
researcher who takes a look inside (perhaps in the role of a fashion histo-
rian!) will be able to see which "garments" belong to which periods and will
be able to show how different organizational fashions have replaced each
other and how they have later been stored and preserved. If fashions of
bygone years should again become fashionable, it may even be possible to
a certain extent to take out some of the discarded clothes again.

Contrasting the Three Perspectives

An implicit assumption in new institutional theory is that institutionalized
standards (in the sense of widespread prescriptions that are taken for
granted) have their day. They are established as prototypes that attract

groups of organizations for a while, but later deteriorate and fade away. However, the phenomenon called deinstitutionalization in this article has neither been extensively theorized nor empirically investigated by new institutionalists.

The most frequently mentioned explanations of this phenomenon in organization theory are based on either the adaptation and selection perspective or the natural rejection perspective. In contrast to those two perspectives, I have attempted to develop an alternative theory to explain how and why institutionalized standards may gradually become passé and lose their status as organizational prototypes. This theory is based on insights into the logic of fashion. In Table 1 (p. 166–67), the main tenets of the fashion perspective and the other two perspectives are summarized and compared. This layout reveals the main distinctions between the adaptation and selection and natural rejection perspectives on the one hand and the fashion perspective on the other.

What about the relative explanatory power of each of these three perspectives? I shall argue for a certain amount of pluralism in models. The fact that institutionalized standards lose their attractiveness, "fade" and perhaps disappear is such a complex phenomenon that a comprehensive interpretation must obviously mobilize insights from all three perspectives. Nevertheless, there is reason to assume that the logic of fashion is acquiring an *increasing* potential to explain organizational phenomena, including deinstitutionalization.

Organizational Fashion: Sources for a Theory

Fashion probably has a great potential for explaining various phenomena in modern organizations, e. g. how popular ideas fade out as indicated above. However, as Abrahamson clearly points out (in this volume), a theory of organizational fashion has not yet emerged. An effort should therefore be made to develop such a theory, and there are at least three sources of potentially relevant literature that will have to be investigated: a) classic fashion theory, b) new institutional theory with implicit tenets from fashion, c) organization theory with sporadic references to fashion. Let us briefly consider each of these sources.

Classic Fashion Theory

Classic fashion theory will obviously be an important source for a theory about organizational fashions. It can be divided into an empirical variant and a sociological-analytical variant.

Table 1: Three Perspectives on Deinstitutionalization

	The Adaptation and Selection Perspective	The Natural Rejection Perspective	The Fashion Perspective
1. Basic Idea	An institutionalized standard is an administrative technique, which, in a given context, is better adapted than others to the demands of technical environments.	An institutionalized standard is a simple idea that one tries to "implant" into complex institutions	An institutionalized standard is an organizational fashion that has its day.
2. What triggers deinstitutionalization	It is triggered because: • changes in technical environments undermine the standard's comparative advantage, and/or • new and technically better techniques are developed that reduce the standard's comparative advantage.	It is triggered by experiences that are gained when the institutionalized standard is employed to coordinate complex activities within an institution	It is triggered when the standard is about to become widespread and has thereby lost its socially differentiating and attention-getting power (the subversion of fashion).
3. The Development of the Deinstitutionalization Process			
3A. Typical Process	*a) Adaptation:* Changes in technical environments are discovered, and old techniques are replaced with new ones that are better adapted technically.	*Unlearning:* Experiences gained when the standard is employed, lead to a gradual loss of belief in (the myth of) its comparative advantages.	*Obsolescence:* Through reinterpretation a socially constructed impression is established that the standard has become unfashionable and passé.

b) Selection:	Organizations with technically inappropriate forms "die." New organizations with better adapted techniques arise.		
3B. Characteristics of the Roll-back Process	• Roll-back as "rational contagion": spread of technical experiences within a field. • The innovators, i.e. the first to get rid of inefficient standards, are often the biggest and financially strongest organizations.	• No process of contagious spread: experiences gained in one organization are of little value for other organizations. • Each organization learns from its own experiences with the institutionalized standard so that each rejects it in a random order.	• Roll-back as "social contagion." • The trickle-down effect: the fashion-setters, i.e. those who first adopt the standards, will be the first to experience that the standard's differentiating potential is decreasing. They will be the first to begin searching for a new distinguishing feature. Those who adopt a standard later will then imitate the fashion-setters.
4. Organizations' Handling of Deinstitutionalized Standards	Organizations want to get rid of the inefficient deinstitutionalized standards as quickly as possible. If not, they run the risk of "dying."	Organizations will try to get rid of deinstitutionalized standards.	• Gradual fading of obsolete institutionalized standards as a compromise between norms of rationality and norms of fashionableness. • Organizations are like "clothes closets": storage of obsolete prescriptions.

The empirical variant is a quantitative research tradition that emerged just after the turn of the century. Almost all of these studies deal with the ways in which fashion is manifested through a particular form of human expression, namely clothing. One of the pioneers in this field, Agnes Brook Young, expressed an important common denominator for this research by postulating, "Fashion has its laws which should be discovered" (Young, 1937). The research concentrated to a marked extent on identifying and describing patterns in fashion cycles over long periods of time. A classic study of this sort is Kroeber's examination of how women's dress fashions evolved over a hundred years (Richardson and Kroeber, 1940). This also paved the way for a number of other studies where an attempt was made to describe fashions' cyclical nature with the use of modern statistical techniques (Nystrom, 1928; Young, 1937; Koplin and Schiffer, 1948; Carman, 1973). There are also a few studies in which the *spread* of fashions within one and the same cycle have been empirically mapped out. These studies also deal more or less exclusively with clothing fashions (Brenninkmeyer, 1963; King, 1973; Kønig, 1974).

In addition to this empirically oriented tradition with its emphasis on clothing fashions, there is also a classic analytical school of fashion theory. The best known contributors are sociologists who set out to develop general theories about the emergence of modern society in the period around and just after the turn of the century. They conceived of fashion as a universally operating mechanism that could make modern societies appear less complex and that might explain the distribution of ideas, tastes and forms in space and time. Thorstein Veblen (1899/1973) and later Georg Simmel (1904/1973) both formed schools of thought by hypothesizing that fashions are established by the non-laboring upper class in order to make apparent and reproduce class distinctions.

In what may so far be the most thorough theoretical analysis of fashion, Herbert Blumer (1969) indicates that it no longer belongs in the study of class distinctions. Fashion has become instead an important way of reducing complexity in a world with a steadily increasing number of stimuli and possible choices. Thus, with fashion, a temporary order (at least) is established because only a *few* ideas, tastes and forms achieve a brief imperative status as fashions. Fashion's ability to reduce complexity and thereby establish order is partly expressed by the tendency of different groups at different times to actually make the same choice from a number of different tastes, ideas and forms that they *could* have chosen.

Another feature that unifies the classic fashion sociologists is that they all describe fashion as a social phenomenon that encompasses many paradoxes, ambiguities and contradictions. Many of them have observed that in a fashion's success, i. e. its spread, also lies its demise (Simmel, 1904/

1973; Nystrom, 1928; Sellerberg, 1994). However, fashion also encompasses other contradictions, such as the continuous vacillations between imitation and differentiation, between conformity and deviation, and between tradition and change (Czarniawska and Joerges, in this volume). Although the classic fashion sociologists have shown no interest in organizational fashions, they describe fashion as a universal social phenomenon with a realm of validity that is by no means limited to people's manner of dress. They argue that one characteristic of our times is that the logic of fashion may be applied to more and more forms of human expression. If that is the case, then why shouldn't it account for the design of formal organizations which are just as much human creations as cars or buildings?

New Institutional Theory with Implicit Tenets from the Logic of Fashion

My interest in fashion as a potential explanatory factor has partly emerged through a reading of new institutionalists' contributions to organization theory during the last 10−15 years. In this literature there are many theoretical tenets and many empirical observations that may all be combined and synthesized by treating them as fashion phenomena. In spite of this, the new institutionalists themselves rarely if ever explicitly refer to fashion as a theoretical framework for interpretation. Let us take a brief look at some of the new institutionalist assumptions and observations that can be given a comprehensive interpretation in light of the logic of fashion.

In new institutional literature one finds the idea that institutional environments are constantly generating *new* institutionalized standards, which organizations must respond to and should preferably adopt (at any rate as an outwardly visible façade!) in order to gain legitimacy and recognition (Meyer and Rowan, 1977; Brunsson, 1989; 1994). It is easy to see that this idea has its clear parallel in fashion's basically dynamic nature and its ability to define the style of the moment, which individuals and groups must respond to.

New institutionalists and "real" fashion theoreticians have nearly identical interpretations of how and why ideas and forms are spread and adopted. New institutionalists argue that organizations' adoption of institutionalized prescriptions mainly serves to instill confidence in their environments, so that the organization is perceived as credible and legitimate. However, it has also been observed that these institutionalized prescriptions may very well be useless for improving efficiency (Tolbert and Zucker, 1983; Meyer, 1990a; Singh et al., 1986; DiMaggio and Powell, 1991; Boland, 1982). The parallel tenet that is often proposed by fashion theoreticians is that fashionable things are often useless, in a strictly technical or functional sense (Simmel, 1973; Sapir, 1937). They are primarily adopted to give a signal to others about how one wants to be perceived, i. e. a social motive rather than one aimed at improving efficiency (Brenninkmeyer, 1963).

New institutionalists have observed that institutionalized standards from former times can be reinstitutionalized and appear once again as the new and correct way of organizing. In a study of reforms in the Swedish State Railways over roughly a century, Brunsson, et al. (1989) have shown that certain reform ideas turn up and succeed each other in almost every other reform. This applies, for example, to ideas about decentralization and centralization. Brunsson (1993) refers to this cyclical pattern as a "process of oscillation." Hood and Jackson (1991) have identified a few so-called "administrative doctrines" that affect concrete organizational changes, and which alternate as the dominant doctrine in different periods. The parallel to the concept of fashions' repetitive or cyclical nature is striking and needs no further comment.

These examples all give the clear impression that the new institutional literature in organization theory, and especially many of the empirical observations that have been made by researchers working within this paradigm, are good indications of the usefulness and necessity of interpreting organizational phenomenon in light of fashion. At the same time, however, we may wonder why the new institutionalists themselves have not made use of fashion to help synthesize the numerous insights that exist within this paradigm.

Organization Theory with Sporadic References to Fashion

Even though only a few organization theorists have tried to develop a theory of organizational fashion, there are quite a few sporadic and casual references to fashion in organization theory. In many of these references, fashion is depicted as a threat to the organization. This often occurs, for example, in studies of the conditions for the diffusion and adoption of technological innovations. Fashion is usually perceived here as destructive in the sense that it can mislead leaders to adopt techniques that they *think* are innovations, but which in fact are merely fashions (Rumelt, 1974; Kogut, 1988; Porter, 1989; Mitroff and Mohrman, 1987). In many other cases fashion is referred to in an even more casual way, usually as a residual category when other explanations are inadequate (Dunnette and Bass, 1963; Woodward, 1965).

None of the contributions in this category proposes a comprehensive theory about fashion. Thus, the analyses are often superficial, and in most cases they are of rather limited value as a source with which to interpret fashion's effects on formal organizations.

Toward the Increasing Relevance of Fashion in Organizational Analysis

The preceding section provides a basis for arguing that fashion has been largely overlooked as an explanatory factor in organization theory. (This point is thoroughly discussed by Abrahamson in this volume.) There are several reasons for this. One is the widespread view that fashion only affects certain kinds of human expression, such as clothing, furniture, buildings and cars. Thus, it is difficult to imagine that fashion concerns anything as rational and serious as the design of formal organizations. Moreover, the logic of fashion is not just overlooked, but also generally frowned upon by organization theorists. On the one hand, fashion is regarded as a façade that is concerned with the extrinsic and aesthetic rather than the intrinsic and essential. It is as transitory as a mayfly; it is useless for practical purposes; and it is more likely to be adopted on a wave of collective hysteria than as a result of rational decisions. Arguments like these help partly explain why organization theorists find it difficult to imagine that organizations are influenced by fashion. It is also symptomatic that in many of the cases where fashions are referred to in organization theory, they are usually presented as a seductive and destructive mechanism that draws the managers' attention away from whatever they should be doing to improve efficiency and that causes resources to be wasted on useless measures (Rumelt, 1974; Mitroff and Mohrmann, 1987).

Although fashion has so far been both overlooked and frowned upon in organization theory, there are still good reasons to assume that its explanatory power with regard to various organizational phenomena is, in fact, generally increasing. Blumer stated in 1969 that modern society is characterized by a general extension of fashion's relevance to more and more kinds of human expression. Thus, he outlines a number of characteristics of the social spheres in which fashion is most likely to operate: it must be a sphere where change is highly regarded and where those who are most receptive to change are rewarded; there must be an ample supply of alternative ideas, forms and tastes, and the individual must be able to choose relatively freely among them; it should be difficult to judge by objective criteria and supplementary examination which of the forms are the most appropriate ones.

Although Blumer tries to develop a *general* theory relating to fashion's extension, there is little doubt that the above-mentioned characteristics are also highly pertinent to the conditions faced by modern organizations:

The imperative to change. The economic and political crises in western countries during the last 20 years have created an ideological climate where more and more attempts are made to improve the ability of organizations to change and innovate. Thus, the rhetoric and symbols of our time concur in the esteem they bestow on the organization that searches for "the new" and gets rid of "the old."

A multitude of prescriptions. There is an ample supply of alternative organizational prescriptions competing to become fashionable: various business schools, consulting firms, strong professions and influential and successful firms ensure a steady flow of organizational prescriptions that are communicated rapidly and with little resistance between various organization fields, over national boundaries and even between different global regions.

The objectivity problem. It is usually difficult, if not impossible, to determine on the basis of objective criteria and tests which of the prescriptions are best or worst for enhancing efficiency. If it were possible to measure and compare the effects of the various prescriptions on the basis of objective standards, (which, for example, is nearly possible in the field of medical science), then the logic of fashion would have considerably less scope. This is not possible, however, and so the climate in formal organizations is currently quite favorable for the logic of fashion.

The logic of fashion should be taken seriously in organization theory. It is symptomatic that when organizational researchers refer to fashion in their work, they often add an explicit disclaimer that this is "just a metaphor." The implication is that the organizational phenomenon that is being studied is not really a fashion phenomenon, but that, partly because of all the good points and punch lines it facilitates, one can try to present it as if it were one. Mintzberg's statement that "The swing between centralization and decentralization at the top of large American corporations has resembled the movement of women's hem lines" (Mintzberg, 1979, p. 294) is typical in this respect. However, this kind of metaphorical, "as-if-it-were" reference to fashion overlooks its indisputable explanatory potential in organizational analyses. Thus, it is my contention that many organizational phenomena are probably also *real* fashion phenomena.

Global Transformations

Tony Spybey

The rise of Western civilization involved the translation of ideas from other civilizations and their incorporation into Western culture. Equally, colonialism and the pursuit of trade ensured that Western institutions were carried to all parts of the world, implanted and thereby reproduced globally. Through this was created the difference between Western civilization and other civilizations. It was Western civilization that produced the world's first truly global culture.

In some cases the propagation of Western culture involved the return of technology in a translated form as when canon and gunpowder, which were Chinese inventions, were used in more developed forms and with devastating effect to enforce trade with a reluctant China. There was little doubt in the West at the time, morally or practically, about the superiority of Western civilization. It is an attitude which Gong (1984) has described as involving a notion of "the standard of civilization." He particularly refers to its systematic use during the early twentieth century in the establishment of a world order that was to transcend colonialism and provide today's global milieu. At the beginning of the twentieth century Sun Yat Sen acknowledged that the new republican China which replaced the old imperial order would have to fit in with the (Western) notion of a civilized nation in order to obtain the benefits of that status (Gong, 1984, p. 158). The pervasive extension of Western culture in time and space has not only resulted in the first truly global culture but also in a situation whereby when people participate in social interactions they do so with a frame of reference that routinely includes a global perspective. Once created the global culture is by definition there for all, particularly in contemporary conditions of virtually instantaneous communication. The translation of cultural inputs and the dissemination of culture by an all-powerful, all-pervasive Western civilization has determined the nature of global institutions. Yet once created the global culture was by definition subject to global participation and there was no guarantee that its Western creators would always control it. Although the West's cultural influence backed up with its political and economic power has ensured that Western countries continue to play powerful roles. But it is the process of global participation, I would argue, that has given rise to a number of explanations for change in the socio-economic structure of the West.

These explanations are not only to do with changes in Western societies but also are connected to the West's relationship with the rest of the world. These have been described variously as post-capitalism (cf. Dahrendorf 1957) or "the end of organized capitalism" (Lash and Urry, 1987); post-industrialism (Bell, 1973; Touraine, 1974); and postmodernity (Lyotard, 1985). Post-capitalism refers to the decomposition of the class relationship in the West but it needs to be taken in conjunction with the concept of a "new international division of labour" (Fröbel et al., 1980) and the employment in globalized industries of people in a variety of locations, especially in Asia and Latin America. Similarly, post-industrialism, as far as it exists at all, is a condition of the West but only a relative condition resulting from the transfer of certain industrial activities from the West to other parts of the world. This marks the end of organized capitalism in the sense that the West no longer acts as a workshop to the world and no longer has control of the global economy. In any case it is unsatisfactory to analyse global developments purely in terms of their economic content and post-modernism is one response to this. It refers to changes in a range of institutions in the course of which the West has lost those advantages which it originally acquired through becoming the first "modern culture." *Modernity* was a condition created by the West in which the West tautologically and ethno-centrically saw itself as supreme. As a result of this *progress* was regarded as a scientific/technological process in which people had seemingly boundless confidence. But in *late modernity* towards the end of the twentieth century that feeling no longer pertains and its premises are subject to question and doubt. These are the grounds for concepts of *postmodernity* which in my view are mistaken concepts because society is still very much in the grip of modernity whatever problems and doubts it has raised.

In orthodox sociological terms the pervasiveness of Western culture was described as a "drift to rationality." Weber wrote of *legal rational* forms of authority gaining precedence over *traditional* or *charismatic* forms. Talcott Parsons developed these ideas into concepts of the *universalization* of the *particularistic*, the triumph of *modernity* over *tradition*. But orthodox modernization theory failed to take adequately into account that the process of universalization is not a passive one. In order to adopt Western institutions people must actively reproduce them and in so doing a certain amount of translation is involved. In other words there are also reactions to the universalization process which may be termed as the *particularization* of the *universalistic*. Western institutions do not just materialize in different cultures. They have to be reproduced by active, thinking human beings who have something to contribute themselves.

Roland Robertson's recent work on globalization is clearly important here and the duality inherent to the globalization of culture he describes as the *interpenetration* of the two processes, *universalization* and *particulariza-*

tion (1992, p. 100). Universalistic Western institutions become assimilated into other cultures through particularistic processes of local translation. An example of this is the case of language use. When faced with English as a language of global communication, a virtual global language, other language users adapt it and extend it. What is today taken to be standard English is replete with inputs which are the legacy of centuries of international contact, particularly through colonialism, and this process of transformation continues.

In fact it is possible to examine the process of cultural assimilation outside of Western cultural imperialism altogether. Drawing from his work on belief systems, Robertson (1992, p. 94) provides a non-Western example of cultural exchange and adaptation in describing the import of Confucianism and Buddhism into Japan. These two very different forms of belief system, received in this case from China, gave rise to indigenously "discovered" religious forms and especially to "Shinto" which became a state-sponsored religion during the Meiji period of Japanese modernization. Of particular note is the fact that state-sponsored Shinto included the Confucian code of loyalty and more recently the legacy of this has been identified as "post-Confucianism," a major factor in Japanese industrial success according to writers such as Herman Kahn (1979). Other writers (e. g. Morishima, 1982) go further to argue that whilst the original Chinese version of Confucianism emphasizes benevolence the version assimilated into Japanese society emphasizes loyalty and so has fitted well into modernized Japan especially in terms of industrial relations.

The problem with Robertson's arguments about the interpenetration of Western universalized modernity and localized particularistic translation is his tendency to separate culture from economy and polity. This is reminiscent of the post-capitalist thesis and the claim to separate out capitalist dealings and "old-style capitalists" as undesirable elements in modernity – to be superseded by progressive "managerialism" as an inexorable part of the "logic of industrialism" in the continuing modernization process. In hindsight it has proven more realistic to accept that, in the modern world, capitalism has touched all culture and that we all in various ways enter into capitalist dealings.

The example of Japan can be taken up again, this time to illustrate the highly successful assimilation of Western institutions, their translation and their subsequent utilization independently in the global systems created by the West. Put simply Japan, having been unwillingly prised open to Western trade, began to participate in global institutions and made a success of it. Robertson describes the apparent contradiction of "globewide, universal supply" and "particularistic demand" (1992, p. 100) which has apparently been resolved by the Japanese innovation of flexible *post-Fordist* manufacturing. Japan has been described as the perfect example of the self-modernizing society. During the early twentieth century it underwent a process of modernization that involved state-building, social emancipation, at least in part, and above all rapid industrialization. As part of this, Japan took up Western manufacturing techniques and, drawing from some of its own cultural resources, it improved upon them. Now it dominates global manufacturing with a subsidiary production network that extends not only throughout East Asia but also into the West. But at the heart of this is Japan's own consumer culture, a translation of "the American dream," influenced by the US occupation after 1945. According to Ohmae (1985, pp. 143−144), as referred to by Esser (1992, p. 11), the Japanese way is the "combination of a 'Californization' of demand behaviour and a 'Toyotization' of the production process (as the successors to Fordism and Taylorism in the original Western model of industrialization)." During early modernity it was the West and especially the USA that built car plants all over the world but during late modernity it is the Japanese who are doing it.

All of these are broad examples of translation processes in social change. What I shall be arguing here is that all transformations of social organization, including the specific examples of formal organizations and work organizations, are during the late twentieth century accomplished almost exclusively in the global context. To all intents and purposes the term *globalization* refers to institutionalization in the contemporary period of *late modernity*. Robertson (1992, pp. 58−60) specifically refers to a "heightening of global consciousness" in the late 1960s as part of a final "uncertainty phase" in the "temporal-historical path to the present circumstances of a very high degree of global density and complexity." However, his reference to a "general autonomy and 'logic' to the globalization process" is reminiscent of Kerr et al.'s (1960) "logic of industrialism" and probably reveals that Robertson, too, is an inveterate modernization theorist. Although, his assertion that global systems are more complex than the outcomes of processes of merely an inter-societal origin, that the global culture is greater than the sum of its parts is I think correct and this certainly contradicts the work of other interpreters of late modernity such as Niklas Luhmann (1982b).

Social organization in all its forms consists of the institutionalization of patterns of social interaction and changes to this take place through processes of translation by human agents. At the same time this occurs against a background of influences external to immediate social interaction many of which are, in a globalized society, global institutions. This externality is what Giddens (1984, p. 181) has referred to as the *distanciation* of social institutions in time and space and globalization is the ultimate terrestrial expression of such distanciation. Social organization can only take place when human agents interact to reproduce institutionalized patterns and they bring to this the whole range of their experience of social institutions.

This represents the conditions for social interaction, which in the routine of daily life are mainly unacknowledged. However, in Western civilization and wherever its pervasive influence has spread, the individual's experience of social institutions has increasingly come to include global influences through what was earlier described as the interpenetration of universalistic and particularistic influences. Once people become aware of social institutions reproduced on an extended scale in time and space (through mass communications and the global information system) – once they have assimilated such knowledge into their experience (nowadays a continual process which is hard to avoid) – it is impossible for them to participate in social interaction without the global influence. We go about our day-to-day affairs with images of the world and its global institutions in our heads.

For social science there is one important question which must immediately arise. That is whether processes of globalization involve increased social emancipation and equality. The answer to this, I suggest, is that globalization is emancipatory but not necessarily a force for equality. The concept of globalization is not in itself meant to imply equality but there are grounds for arguing that it involves some changes in the structure of power. Arguably there is an implicit suggestion of an emancipatory tendency when people have increased access to knowledge through the global information system and to resources of a political, economic and legal nature through the globalization of these institutions too. The nation-state system, the global economy and the world (military) order all represent these forms of globalization. However, Giddens has in his recent work (1990; 1991; 1992) associated globalization with the development of what he describes as *life politics*. Through the media of movements for feminism, environmentalism and peace, particularly, new dimensions of human freedom have been both conceptualized and to some degree realized. According to Giddens these take the form of *late modern* additions to the *emancipatory politics* of *early modernity*.

> Life-politics – concerned with human self-actualization, both on the level of the individual and collectively – emerges from the shadow which 'emancipatory politics' has cast (Giddens, 1991, p. 9).

Liberal democracy was established as part of modernity and its inherent fragility came to be associated with human freedom itself, characterizing the very essence of *civilization* in the rise of the West. This principle also provided the rationale and justification for Western influence and domination throughout the world. But the history of the late twentieth century is one of a loss of hegemony by the West and an end to the traditions that were enshrined in the "pax Britannica" of the nineteenth century or the "pax Americana" of the twentieth. *Life-politics* is much more questioning of the parameters on which Western dominance was built and I shall now go on to outline the dimensions to globalization − the time-space dimensions from which it is argued *life-politics* have emerged.

Dimensions to Globalization

Consider, to begin with, human communication in itself. In tribal society this takes place almost wholly face to face in conditions of mutual presence, whereas one of the primary distinguishing features of other types of society is that means have been devised to increase the scale of communication. In the earliest city-states, which are generally recognized as the earliest examples of civilization, clay tablets have been discovered on which written records were kept. Writing enables a message to be communicated virtually indefinitely in time and space, especially when paper and printing are introduced to extend the effect. The distinctive contributions of Western civilization to the process of human communication were the printing press and the electric telegraph. The printing press was apparently another Chinese invention but the Chinese failed to develop a popular press and an emancipatory literature to match its technological potential. By contrast its development in Europe coincided with the Renaissance. The fifteenth century introduction of the printing press by pioneers such as Gutenberg was cumbersome and limited and hardly provided an advance on the considerable existing resources for the copying of illuminated manuscripts, especially in monastic *scriptoria*. But during the sixteenth century printing went through a widespread and speedy development in Europe to provide an outpouring of literature that was emancipatory for the arts, science and technology. During the nineteenth century the invention and development of the electric telegraph, which was entirely Western in origin, involved the crucial advantage of enabling messages to be transmitted not only over great distances without the accompaniment of a human messenger but also at much greater speed. From our present day standpoint we can readily see that a whole panoply of electronic devices and space technology has been added to the humble electric telegraph. These are now the commonplace media of mass communication with the great variety of applications of solid-state physics in the transistor and the micro-processor. In principle now, any human being can communicate instantaneously with all the other human beings on the planet. Thus global technology is potentially emancipatory and enabling but in practice access to it must be seen, as with other aspects of society, in terms of constraint through political and economic institutions. For instance, market principles largely determine the way in which mass communication and data-processing technology is used, whilst the politics of international relations govern the use of cables and airwaves. These two mechanisms are quite clearly global issues connected with the pervasiveness of Western inventions now used globally.

In the current period of late modernity the whole world is divided up territorially and politically into nation-states. The nation-state is virtually a universal entity and it is the institution which provides the arena for national politics. In global terms nation-states collectively form the nation-state system and the relationships between them make up the international politics of "world order", the subject of the specialized area of study known as "international relations". There are however almost as many variations to the nation-state model as there are nation-states. This is a primary example of a universalistic institution reproduced with particularistic features. Nevertheless, the model is recognized as an ideal in the modern world and it has emerged from the development of liberal democracy in the rise of the West. It has a variety of sources. The notion of the *polis* comes from ancient Greece upon which the West has always looked back as a classical and formative era. Indeed, the Renaissance was so described by Western historians precisely for its recourse to classical ideas and aspirations, especially in the Italian city-states which are seen as exemplars of Europe's early-modern cultural advancement. However, larger and more powerful states were created during the time of the "absolutist" monarchs between the fifteenth and the eighteenth centuries when larger and more effective forms of administrative and military organization were developed. These forms made it possible to amass greater amounts of wealth and reflexively they were enhanced by that greater wealth. More efficient centralized methods of revenue collection were combined with standing armed forces so that the control of larger amounts of territory took place on a more consistent basis than had been possible before. Part of the control process was the establishment of a singular national identity to coincide with the political sphere of influence of the state. This was usually derived from the amalgamation of regional cultural identities existing amongst subject populations. It is from this that the term nation-state emerges and the power of the state to withstand alternative national identities is part of its nature.

To provide a contrast to the European nation-state system, writers such as Mann (1986) have drawn attention to the tendency for the classical militarized empires to break up in a relatively short time. According to this argument the lines of communication in a singular hierarchical structure characteristically become over-extended and the continual pressures involved in the pacification of territory cause the power structure to fail. This obviously contributes to any explanation for the success of the European state system in the form of "a multiple acephalous federation" (Mann, 1986, p. 376) and as a model for the global nation-state system of modernity. There were no singular hierarchical lines of communication amongst the European states once Charlemagne's goal of a Holy Roman Empire had failed and the successors to this title proved to be only a part of the developing European state system. Instead, over the centuries, an increasingly regulated system of international relations was developed, punctuated of course by what might be seen as the various European "civil wars."

As part of the process of European development in general, Rosecrance (1986, p. 77) has identified the enhancement of the domestic infrastructure of society during the approach to the modern period and contrasted this with its neglect during the Middle Ages. This, surely, is explained largely in terms of state organization and is connected with the "surveillance" capabilities which enabled new categories of "civil servant" to administer populations in ways undreamed of even by the Chinese emperors with their Mandarin administrators. It was broad transformations across whole populations made possible by the widespread expansion of capitalist industrialization but potentiated by the stability of nation-state organization that characterize the period of modernity. Amongst the big powers of Europe the process was enhanced by the politically modernizing influences of the seventeenth century English "revolutions" and their transferral of state power to elected assemblies. To this one must add the dual influences of the declaration of independence by European settlers in America in 1776 and the French Revolution against the *ancien regime* after 1789. Each of these asserted modern republicanism and the principle of citizenship. Robertson (1992, p. 56), following Der Derian (1989), has drawn attention to the coincidence in 1789 of the declaration of the "rights of man" with Bentham's advocacy of the need for the word "international" in the context of a law of nations. These are the transformations to which attention is normally directed but there were other important influences too, such as the development of centralized bureaucracy in Prussia (Rosenberg 1958) or the relatively early assertions of power by a free (non-feudal) peasantry in Sweden (Warne, 1929). Political modernization came with the development of the nation-state and the assertion of liberal democracy by its citizens.

The outcome is the Western model of the nation-state with virtually universal application, albeit that the study of its misuse and corruption is as necessary as that of its form. Today people live in a world order made up of nation-states and they exist as the citizens of nation-states. In fact, to lack such citizenship is to be in the extremely problematic position of a stateless person. In the state-socialist societies where for several decades economic institutions were established alternative to those of Western capitalism, the extra function of total economic planning was achieved by state bureaucracy comparable in form to the orthodox Western model. With the establishment of a resurgent Shi'a Islamic Republic in Iran in 1979, Islamic theology and scholarship were foremost yet the state structure assumed the familiar Western pattern of a political forum served by bureaucratic administration with codification in a legal system and enforcement through the principle of a state monopoly of violence.

The development of the Western state was, however, always connected with the development of capitalism and the creation of the global economy. The capitalist economic mechanism was a fundamental principle in the growth of the European economies and the extension of Western influence in global terms was coincidental with maritime expansionism, the control of international commodity markets and the establishment of an international division of labour. Although it has attracted much criticism of late, it was Wallerstein's (1974; 1979) work along these lines that was responsible for bringing sociology — and especially the sociology of development — into contact with the concept of globalization. In Western development capitalism became accepted as the mainspring of economic activity in mercantile city-states and absolutist monarchies alike, but what Wallerstein neglected was the separation of private sector economic institutions from public sector political institutions at a relatively early stage in the process. This began as the means by which the absolutist monarchs could delegate economic activity as monopolies to chartered companies of merchant adventurers, whilst assuring themselves of a share of the proceeds in revenue. However, the institutionalized distinction between polity and economy became, with industrialization and the commodification of labour, a structural principle of modern class societies. Ever since, the distinction between them has formed the point of contradiction and conflict between socialized labour on the one hand and the private appropriation of profits accruing from production on the other. It is an issue that in one form or another has only rarely been absent from the political agenda of Western states. In the process capitalism became not only accepted by the state but also of such pervasiveness in society as to influence the very nature of social interactions and relationships. Virtually no form of social institution has been unaffected by capitalist market transactions and the commodity exchange values that go with them. In fact, society was changed to such an extent that the activities of the state were extended to provide a supportive role for socialized labour, the welfare state structure. During the twentieth century the lead taken by the USA in the institutionalization of mass production, mass communication and mass consumption, although playing down the role of the welfare state, has only served to intensify and broadcast this model of society and life-style. It is this above all that has given rise to the globalization debate. The populations not only of Western societies but also of those influenced by the West are employed primarily in privately owned enterprises producing and consuming the artefacts of modernity. At the same time the supportive infrastructure for this socialized labour is largely provided by the state through basic public sector institutions of mass education, health care and the safety net of social security provisions.

From the mercantile city-states of the Renaissance, through the maritime expansionism and colonialism of the Reformation and Enlightenment, to the creation of a European "workshop for the world" in the Industrial Revolution, first Europeans and then others reproduced the institutions of an international division of labour and a Western-dominated global economy. Since 1980, however, particularly through the work of Fröbel et al. (1980) a "new international division of labour" has been recognized. This follows the transplantation of some of the original Western industries, and some of the more recently developed ones too, away from the West to other parts of the world and most especially to East Asia. This is the result of the reproduction on a global scale of Western economic institutions. Thus, in the economic sphere as in the social and political spheres, people everywhere become increasingly aware of their relationship to these developments and they take this awareness with them in the day-to-day reproduction of social organization in all of its forms. Globalization has become a part of the institutionalization of society and this is reflected in the forms of social organization which are reproduced.

From our present standpoint at the end of the twentieth century we may also perceive another global dimension. This is concerned with the global environment and the amount of damage that has been done to it as a result of the globalization of production. During the twentieth century the principle of mass participation came to be at the centre of Western ideals originally transplanted to the New World during the eighteenth century. These ideals became translated into concrete terms with the institutionalization of mass production and mass consumption enhanced by mass communication. All of this emanated principally from the USA but was developed on a global scale. Around the world consumption takes place in an uneven and unequal way but the consequence of an increasingly globalized mass consumption society is the extensive depletion of natural resources, the pollution of the atmosphere and the creation of waste disposal problems with resulting environmental damage. Furthermore, the detrimental effects of mass production and mass consumption, as in the example of damage to the ozone layer, threaten to affect all the people of the Earth regardless of the unequal way in which the benefits have been distributed. Now it is widely recognized even in intergovernmental circles, as the Earth Summit at Rio de Janeiro in 1992 illustrates, that there have to be some limitations to economic growth and the further expansion of production and consumption patterns. Yet such limitation threatens the material basis upon which the global inter-societal system has been established and this especially is a sensitive problem at this time of economic recessions and doubts about the future viability of the system. There is also the problem of convincing not only the existing heavy consumers, who are predominantly in the West and in East Asia, but also those in other parts of the world who have hitherto been denied high levels of consumption but would dearly like to indulge. Arguably state socialism collapsed principally through its failure to deliver high consumption patterns to the peoples of Russia and Eastern Europe and in the West it remains difficult for governments to curtail consumption substantially. These negative aspects of globalization, along with their attendant problems, are also increasingly carried by people into the routines of social organization and the reproduction of institutions. We go about our daily lives with images of global pollution in our heads and these are set against other global influences.

Transformations in the Global Context

This chapter pursues the notion of translation in the reproduction of social institutions and of transformations in social organization in the context of globalized institutions. It seeks to establish that the reproduction of social institutions is the basis of everyday social life and that in this day-to-day reproduction lies the capacity for change on the part of human agents. But, inasmuch as the experience of human agents in contemporary late modernity incorporates a familiarity with institutions that are reproduced on a global scale – take such disparate examples as the nation-state or McDonald's fast food – then transformations in social organization will clearly take on global dimensions. People's perspectives have become global and this is reflected in their contributions to the reproduction of social institutions.

The outline of global-scale institutions in the previous section provides examples. Perhaps the most obvious in the present context is in terms of patterns of communication in relation to the global communication system. It can be safely assumed that the preparation of academic work such as this is carried out on electronic word-processors by authors most of whom can communicate with each other through electronic mail networks to which their word-processors are permanently connected. Failing this the machines can be linked up to FAX telecommunications. Word-processors are now often portable and can be used anywhere. Yet they are capable of transferring material into the same network. In less than a decade this has become the norm in many spheres of activity and consequently we nowadays approach the organization of work with such forms of communication as the norm. Transformations in organization have therefore taken place with access to global communication techniques virtually taken for granted. Many dimensions of the global communication system embrace satellite transmission stations, television and radio broadcasting, intercontinental telephone systems, optical fibre cabling, etc., and these forms have been extended into several forms of globalized media including music and the cinema. In a world that includes mass produced and mass marketed personal computers, compact disc players and video-TV combinations, the various technologies of communication increasingly overlap. As with other aspects of globalization the distribution of these resources around the world is clearly uneven and yet increasing numbers of people everywhere have access to the global communication system in some form or other. No one can fail to be aware of this if they have visited a Third World village where the inhabitants commonly sit around a communal television. The broadcasts are received from a local station which relies almost totally on programmes purchased from Western networks and satellite broadcasting systems because it cannot afford the high cost of making programmes of its own. India has become one of the largest consumers of satellite television from the Hong Kong based Star system and the owners of receivers rent access to others by cable. It is in the nature of global communications to involve virtually everyone and this is both enabling and constraining. Access to universalized knowledge is emancipating and although the distribution of benefits and disadvantages is determined largely through the nation-state system and the global economy, sometimes these can be bye-passed.

In the system of nation-states, the 1980s saw a process of "rolling back" of state institutions in Western countries. That is to say, many state undertakings were privatized as part of attempts to reduce the burgeoning cost of public sector borrowing requirements and transfer this financial burden on to the private sector. This is an example of a trend in state administration which has become institutionalized in the politically and economically powerful countries and reproduced on a global scale. It has influenced many people's approaches to their day-to-day activities in a world made up of the Western type of political and economic institution. Measures instigated in one country as a political response to economic conditions enter into the global knowledge not only at the level of the financial markets but also at the level of mundane domestic activities and they become institutionalized.

Ironically, far from producing an increase in the power of private sector organizations, the converse has tended to be the case. Since the late 1980s some of the largest trans-national corporations have suffered severe reversals in their economic performance. General Motors and Ford, for instance, have experienced losses that would have destroyed firms without huge reserves and even IBM, which in the early 1980s was held up as *the* prime example of organizational excellence (see Peters and Waterman, 1982), has since been performing badly. The reaction to this is varied. According to some observers (e. g. Hirst, 1993), the number of corporations of truly trans-national proportions has been greatly exaggerated and the notion of globalization is itself a myth. However, this approach does I think suffer from the same kind of economistic shortcomings as Wallerstein's work. Socio-cultural and politico-military institutions are neglected. Above all, globalization should be about the relationship between the human agent and a range of institutions which have become globalized. For instance, it is noticeable that the same period has seen a resurgence in the influence of that long dormant global representation of the nation-state system, the United Nations. During the Gulf War of 1990−91 unanimous resolutions of the Security Council were carried out as never before in the history of the UN and in other points of conflict elsewhere its authority has heightened. The outcome may not always be as desired but the determination to work through the UN is undeniable. The reasons for this resurgence are commonly given as economic recession and the desire of even the powerful nation-states to share the burden of international peacekeeping, especially with the demise of the Soviet Union and the end of the Cold War. These developments should serve as reminders that there is little that is evolutionary in the reproduction of social organization and its institutions. The collective actions of human agents determine the outcomes of history, albeit that to a great extent they are the unintended consequences of such actions and that the aggregate of human actions on a broad scale is difficult to monitor or predict. There is a relationship between the individual and the global even though the individual may feel alienated by the scale of global institutions.

Transformations in the global economy and the nation-state system are not of course detached from each other. There will always be overlaps in social institutions that for purposes of analysis are, in work like this, conceptually separated. For instance, the trans-national corporations have increasingly engaged in global manufacturing networks to supply global markets both of which straddle the borders of nation-states. Basically the *raison d'être* of the trans-national corporation is to range the world in search of raw materials and labour in order to provide voracious global markets with more attractive products at more competitive prices. Advanced communication and transport methods make it possible for new combinations to be exploited and the result is lines of production which do quite literally span the globe. We need resort only to the example, already cited, of the technology utilized in the word-processing of this paper. The electronics industry was established on a global basis with certain production sites having access to research and development and specializing in the development of ever more effective microprocessors; other sites having access to competitively priced labour and specializing in the wiring up of "consumer durable" products to mass-produced microprocessors; and yet more sites conveniently situated for final assembly to the requirements of specific markets; etc. (Henderson, 1989). Electronic communications have made possible a global communication system to transform international financial dealings, investments, commodity prices and their "futures." The main London, New York and Tokyo financial centres operate on the basis of instantaneous communication with each other and with the many other financial markets around the world (King, 1990; Budd and Whimster, 1992). The predominance of Europe, North America and East Asia, connected with these three financial centres, has lead to suggestions of the "triadization" of the world (Ohmae, 1985; Esser, 1992; Robertson, 1992, pp. 184–185). This development has been linked to the exigencies of the political climate during the 1980s and therefore to economic difficulties, widespread privatization, heightened competition for production and investment locations and the failure of GATT negotiations. I have argued elsewhere (Spybey, 1992, pp. 208–209) that Japan might be perceived as setting itself at the head of an Asian bloc, possibly an Asian Free Trade Area or even an Asian Economic Union. The USA is making closer economic ties with Canada and Mexico in a North American Free Trade Area, but with business ties with the rest of Latin America already well developed. The existing European Union, EU could possibly take a greater responsibility for Africa and the Middle East through the legacy of past colonial connections (Ohmae, 1985, p. 143; Esser, 1992, p. 13). On the other hand the existence of outsider cartels can hardly be ignored, especially in the principal and perhaps unique case of OPEC with its influence over energy resources and its Islamic cultural background. An alternative view is that of Dicken (1992) and others who predict a shift towards the Pacific Basin with the twenty-first century as the "Pacific Century," this category to include not only East Asia and Australasia but also the western seaboards of the USA and Canada. In any case the economic monitoring organization of the advanced industrial nation-states, the OECD, has during the past few years given birth to an "elite of the elite" grouping known as G7. This is made up of the seven largest and therefore most powerful economies (the USA, Japan, Germany, France, Italy, Britain and Canada) which meet from time to time to deliberate about the global economic condition. Despite the obvious inequalities anyone involved in economic and financial dealings, at whatever level including that of the individual consumer, approaches day-to-day transactions involving the reproduction of economic or financial institutions with some awareness of the global dimensions. For instance, if coffee prices go up we are aware of the connection with the international market in coffee beans or if faced with adverse exchange rates when travelling we have some idea of the workings of the international money markets. It is part of the emancipatory effects of global communications that this should be the case.

At the same time, during the past two decades people's economic considerations have been increasingly beset with concerns about the environment.

The Green Movement has become institutionalized (Yearley, 1994) and its concerns are predominantly global. The various dangers to the environment that have been identified are inherently global dangers and in aggregate they amount to concern about the very future of the planet and human life upon it. There is little that could be more global than this in its consequences. Furthermore, concern for the environment engages with the extraction of raw materials, their transformation in manufacturing, the consumption of finished products and the ultimate disposal of waste products. These stages of commodity processing of course form the activities of the trans-national corporations in the global economy. In fact, at the heart of the issue is the doubt that has arisen over modernity itself. What once promised through increased technological production to eliminate want altogether now appears to threaten the environment in which we all live. Such concerns become institutionalized and become part of our lives. They enter into the way in which we as human agents reproduce society on a day-to-day basis. The transformations in social organization that this tendency has brought about may not be sufficient to satisfy committed environmentalists but they have become a feature of life in the late twentieth century. Social organization in the global context involves the way that human agents view their interactions against the global environment. As individuals we live our lives against a background that includes globalized institutions. The micro-level forms of organization in which we as individuals live and work operate amongst macro-level networks of globally extended organizational forms. This is characteristic of Western civilization and the culture which it has forced and persuaded upon the whole world. The ways of dealing with this that human beings develop in the routine of their lives constitute processes of translation of social institutions extended through time and space. Society changes but only through the actions of its members as they translate the conditions of yesterday into the terms of today with consequences for tomorrow.

Change in Social Organization

The concept of globalization may be seen in relation to the classical sociological distinction between traditional and modern society and Parsons' presentation of this in a "pattern variable" dichotomy of particularism and universalism. Thus, change in traditional society takes place through the day-to-day reproduction of social institutions that are for the most part locally determined, whilst in modern society the parameters tend to be global in extent. The difference is attributable to a number of things but clearly the development of communication, capitalist industrial production and modern state administration are all crucial. The human agent in modern society has access to multiple channels of communication, to extensive markets in commodities and finance but is subject to much greater levels of state surveillance and intervention. There are a great variety of sanctions facing the human agent in different aspects of social organization. These include the group pressures involved in family, education, work, leisure, etc.; a variety of citizenship responsibilities imposed by the nation-state and its legal system including the consequences of *world order* imposed through the global military balance of power. All of these impinge upon the individual and at the same time elicit responses. It is as much a part of the reproduction of institutions to be oppressed as to be the oppressor. In this way and in other related ways the individual *is* linked to the global and although it may appear that global institutions are not of the human scale it can be demonstrated that the individual *is* involved. For instance, greater concern for the (global) environment in the face of mass production and consumption brings the individual into contact with extra dimensions to existing institutions of communication, economy, polity and law. It is essential to include these linkages as concepts in any social theory of the contemporary world if it is to be meaningful, just as it is essential to maintain links between ourselves as individuals and global forms of organization in order to keep them subject to social monitoring and controls. As Robertson puts it,

> rather than emphasizing the crystallized structure of the world system, a voluntaristic theory remains sensitive to empirical developments, and thus stresses the processes of globalization and the continuing contentiousness of global order. One of my basic points is that varying responses to globalization influence that very process, so that its direction and outcome, and hence the shape of the global field itself are still very much 'up for grabs' (Robertson, 1992, p. 62).

This is very close to Giddens's position in structuration theory when he stresses that processes of globalization although difficult to control are still the result of human actions and must be conceptualized as such. See for instance his analogous reference to "riding the juggernaut" (1990, pp. 151–73) summarized as follows:

> a runaway engine of enormous power which, collectively as human beings, we can drive to some extent but which also threatens to rush out of our control and which could render itself asunder. The juggernaut crushes those who resist it, and while it sometimes seems to have a steady path, there are times when it veers away erratically in directions we cannot foresee. The ride is by no means wholly unpleasant or unrewarding; it can often be exhilarating and charged with hopeful anticipation. But, so long as the institutions of modernity endure, we shall never be able to control completely either the path or the pace of the journey. In turn, we shall never be able to feel entirely secure, because the terrain across which it runs is fraught with risks of high consequence. Feelings of ontological security and existential anxiety will coexist in ambivalence (Giddens, 1990, p. 139).

However, Robertson has criticized Giddens rather heavily, claiming that he exaggerates the processes of globalization as part of modernity and neglects the particularistic tendencies of postmodernity (see Robertson, 1992, pp. 138–145). This criticism refers back to Robertson's argument's for seeing globalization as the interpenetration of universalistic Western global institutions and particularistic local reproductions of them, which was mentioned earlier. In fact the central principle of structuration theory is that the social structure is created precisely through the actions of human beings which reproduce social institutions. Within the act of reproduction there is the scope and capability for human beings to "make a difference." This is the essence of the principle of human agency which structuration theory is intended to address. As the juggernaut analogy is intended to convey, the outcome of social interaction does not always go in the way that the human agent intended, particularly with the scale of social institutions in globalized society. Nevertheless without human agency there could be no reproduction of social institutions at all. The capacity of human agents to make a difference in the reproduction of social institutions, therefore, will always bring about some particularistic tendencies in the face globalistic influences. This is very close to Robertson's requirement for a voluntaristic theory, sensitive to empirical developments.

In the face of the scale and diversity of global structures it is important to retain the view of the individual as a human agent routinely engaged in the reproduction of social institutions, but with the capacity to *translate* them in the course of day-to-day activities. Increasingly, social interactions are connected to structures connected globally but the structure to social life is that which is routinely reproduced in day-to-day activities. In these acts of reproduction there remains the capacity for human agents to translate the structure and it is in this way that change takes place in social organization.

In structuration theory this is seen in terms of the *duality of structure*. The structure to society is *distanciated* in time and space in the form of social institutions but these can have only a virtual existence at any precise moment in the passing of time. At that moment they are subject to routine reproduction by human agents experiencing the progression of historical time as day-to-day life (Giddens, 1984). Therein lies the human capacity to *make a difference* and this aggregates as social change.

Put another way, at any point in historical time there is a conjunction of structure and action as human agents actively reproduce society. Structure has a virtual existence by being carried through time and space in the memory traces of human agents. In "civilized" societies this is aided by literacy and those institutions which literacy makes possible. Latterly, the various electronic media which record culture have added to the store of knowledge at our disposal. Face to face interaction involves *social integ-*

ration in conditions of co-presence but *system integration* exists in social structure extended through time and space (Lockwood, 1964; Giddens, 1984). However social structure is only realizable in the passing moment of time – through social interaction when human agents actively reproduce society – thus exercising their capacity for change through translation.

Any form of social organization is reproduced in this way – by human agents through their *translation* of the institutionalized content of society – as reproduced by other human agents at other points in time and space. We orientate our actions to the actions of others past and present in order to achieve social integration, yet we retain our capacity to make a difference and in so doing we further extend social institutions in time and space. This is achieved not passively but actively. With global communications and global culture, social institutions have become increasingly globalized and the individual increasingly translates the day-to-day in terms of the global. The anthropologist, Jonathan Friedman, refers to this broadly as "transformations of being-in-the-world and global process" (1990, pp. 323–327). Institutionalization becomes globalization, in effect.

I have argued elsewhere that as society has moved from the traditional to the modern the forms of social organization have become increasingly subject to a frame of meaning that has moved from the particularistic to the universalistic (Spybey, 1984). The points of orientation for social organization have changed and this has been reflected in the way in which human agents reproduce the form. Through access to electronic communications of many kinds, the channels of communication have become a global communication system. Through a new international division of labour involving geographically extended production lines, economy has become global economy and the trans-national corporation, the archetypal form of economic organization. However, these are referred to as *trans-national* corporations precisely because they have the facility to transcend geo-political entities which remain organized as nation-states in a global nation-state system. Connected with this are the concepts of world order (involving a global military order and balance of power) and environmentalism (involving concern for the future of the planet and species). This is the contemporary nature of the connection between the individual human agent and social institutions in a rolling process of translation, the reproduction of society.

When Organization Travels: On Intercultural Translation

Richard Rottenburg

Prologue

When I was travelling up the Nile from Kosti to Juba in 1976, a journey which then took fourteen days, for me it was a journey to the heart of Africa. I would never have hit on the idea of becoming in the slightest interested in the organization of the shipping company. What did impress me on the boat was the captain's mysterious ability to travel at night without headlights or radar, guided only by the light of the stars. For the rest, I was concerned with the world views of the people of southern Sudan, and I looked for these in the hinterland, as far away as possible from the transport arteries of a country that was far off the beaten track itself.

If someone were to anounce these days that he or she was travelling to Africa with this kind of motivation, they would lose credibility and I would be sceptical too. Nevertheless, thanks to this attitude, I ended up with the Lemwareng (as the Moro-Nuba of Southern Kordofan call themselves) in 1979, where I lived for three years, learning things that have since become more important to me than any other experience.

In the meantime, civil war is again raging in southern Sudan, so that the almost forty years of the post-colonial epoch have known only twelve years of peace (1971–1983).[1] Whatever individual explanations we may offer, in the end we must conclude that the Sudanese have become fatally entangled in the economic and socio-political order which they have built up since colonial times. At the core of this order stands bureaucracy and the model of formal organization.

My first ethnographic works on the Lemwareng (with a few exceptions that are irrelevant here) were formulated on the basis of a concept of culture that might be summed up as a post-modern celebration of a carnevalesque arena of diversity. I attempted to stylize the Lemwareng as virtuosos of accretion (Rottenburg, 1989; 1991). Now, in view of the present situation

---

[1] See Africa Watch (1991); Amnesty International (1993); Moszynski (1993); Deng (1994); Ryle (1994); Gruiters and Tresoldi (1994).

in the Sudan, no other interpretation could appear more cynical. I therefore cannot stop asking myself what went wrong with the patchwork.

If my understanding of the present debates in and around anthropology is not completely mistaken, an additional remark is required here. Although the worldviews of small, face-to-face societies living at some distance from the "big events" of this world are no more "noble" or "authentic" than those of regions where social exchange is more dramatic, they can at times simply have a more captivating effect on those concerned with cultural critique. And this is unlikely to change in the future either, despite certain demands of political correctness. A person who only questions his or her own world view in places where the relevant processes of globalization and cultural syncretism are taking place, will in the end get just as distorted a picture as a person who seeks his/her inspiration only with the people of the eternal past, out in the remote hinterland. Just as we construct an exotic Arcadia if we overlook the interrelations with global processes, we also make a false assessment of global processes if we do not move to the sidelines occasionally.

Perhaps since Malinowski this move to the remote sidelines and alterity enabled anthropologists to adopt what Lévi-Strauss coined as the *regard éloigné* to practice cultural critique. As far as I can see, this will continue to be the main business of anthropology for some time to come – albeit with some sensitive changes and additions. One of these changes is attempted here. In this essay I want to try out one possible route of recapturing the *regard éloigné* by linking it to the present debate on constructing alterity in post-colonial anthropology: I shall look into processes of cultural translation and accretion, i. e. into processes where otherness is not part of the anthropological discourse but already part of the actors' discourse. Furthermore, I shall concentrate on a field usually ignored by anthropology: the translation of modern organization as the citadel of western cultures.

Mimetic Organizational Isomorphism

It is possible to roughly predict the administrative structures of peripheral nations without any detailed knowledge of the respective society or culture. For example, a certain difference might be noted between two African countries, specifically between their bureaucratic systems and the administrative styles cultivated within them. One would not be going far astray if one initially linked this difference to the former colonial powers – as in the case of the linguae francae.

The import of western artifacts, ideas and models has, of course, not come to an end with the liberation from colonial rule. Even Tanzania's post-colonial Ujamaa system, which has often been called an authentic expression of African tradition, was not only influenced by European socialism, it was actually engineered under the guidance of a western management consultancy (Max, 1991, p. 84). However, the fact that the model of formal organization has spread all over the world also leads us to a second, apparently equally self-evident observation: the structures modelled on those of the western, usually the ex-colonial powers, function totally differently in practice.

Take the example of a middle-class citizen of Dar Es Salaam whose water supply has been cut off by accident — or in an attempt to extort a bribe — and who would like to have it re-connected. Not having received any reply from the responsible authority several weeks after reporting the fault, there will be no doubt in his mind about the difference between the model and practice alluded to here. Another example: the same city's biggest hospital has been in arrears with its water bills for several months. Since it is considered immoral to cut off the water supply, the responsible ministry disconnects the hospital's telephone instead. Whichever way you look at it, it is obvious that there are some unpleasantly practical and tangible issues involved here. This assessment is confirmed by entrepreneurs in most African countries who, for instance, need electricity to operate their expensive machines at an economic level. Yet many African state power-generating companies only supply electricity sporadically and are not even able to say in advance when the next power cut will be (a good ethnographic example is found in Streck, 1995). Not only Coca-Cola and beer breweries have their own water and electricity supply, every large company tries to be as independent as possible from the services provided by the state.

It is a frequently made observation that peripheral nations are far more similar in their administrative and organizational patterns to the industrialized nations of the west than any comparison of the economic, political and the socio-cultural structures would lead one to expect. Peripheric cultures are generally considered more isomorphic than those of the more powerful centres. For the purposes of this essay, "isomorphic" primarily means that the forms of organization resemble each other in a way and to an extent that cannot be deduced from the mechanisms of market competition and related efforts to raise efficiency. The exemplary forms are the types of organization that are presumably used in the "First World" in comparable situations (Hirschman, 1967).

DiMaggio and Powell submitted the first explicit observations on the phenomenon of organizational isomorphism. Concentrating exclusively on the western world — where, as it is usually assumed, the bureaucratic rationalization of society as an aspect of differentiation has been more intensive and extensive then elsewhere — they demonstrate that today models of formal organization are spreading without necessarily raising efficiency.

In their analysis, DiMaggio and Powell (1983) distinguish between three mechanisms by which organizations increasingly grow to resemble each other. If, for example, the state introduces or changes certain regulations (e. g. labour laws, environmental protection stipulations, subsidy policies, etc.), the organizations affected will have to adapt. In this case *coercive isomorphism* is taking place. This category also includes adjustments to expectations from society at large which, at least to begin with, are not always laid down by the law (like for example the notion of what may be decided democratically and what may be ordered by the boss, the admission or exclusion of females from certain jobs, or the admission of homosexuals to the army).

For this reason, the distinction between this mechanism and *normative isomorphism*, which according to DiMaggio and Powell results from the professionalization of the *organization field*, seems rather artificial. The actors are socialized within certain notional worlds in their professions and subsequently spread these ideas in their organizations. Both coercive and normative isomorphism mean that the environment that is relevant for an organization defines certain expectations which the organization cannot disappoint if it is to survive in the long term. Reduced to this common denominator, however, there is nothing paticularly original about the idea of organizational isomorphism.

However, the authors have also observed a so-called *mimetic isomorphism* which is more interesting for my purpose. What is meant here is that organizations operating in a field full of ambiguity and nothing but unreliable, incalculable factors, take their orientation from a model which is successful from their perspective. The two American sociologists also speak of *modelling* to describe this imitation of an apparently successful player.

With this essay I propose analysing the transformation processes in the sphere of the formal organization of African society under the paradigm of mimetic isomorphism. I shall not go into more detail on the aspects of coercive isomorphism in the form of the standards prescribed by global macro-actors like the World Bank and the International Monetary Fund, as well as smaller lenders and other political actors. I only mention them here because they are an important piece of background against which the processes described might appear more plausible. As an explanation, however, they do not suffice. Similarly, and for the same reasons, I do not study normative isomorphism in greater detail either. This type of isomorphism already ensues, for example, from the western training of managers, to mention only the most obvious aspect. What predominantly interests me is mimetic isomorphism, an orientation towards images from the First World, which are presented by all parties as contextually independent, infallible models.

In my argument I expand upon the paradigm as presented by DiMaggio and Powell in two ways: first, I try it out outside of the western world, and second, I relate it to the model of formal organization itself, and not to a selected aspect of organizing. The two authors had touched upon this possibility, but then lost sight of it as a result of their comforting choice of Japan as their non-western example. In their portrayal, the imperial Japan of the late 19th century appears to be a perfect example of their mimetic isomorphism. Japanese experts travelled to the western world to select the best models of social modernization based on formal organization − such as the military, police, courts, banks, schools, etc. − and to combine them in the best possible way for Japan (DiMaggio and Powell, 1983). However, the same process looks quite different from the African point of view.

This difference needs to be considered in any generalizing statement on mimetic isomorphism. Otherwise the impression is gained that the Japanese import of western models, like any other transfer of new and foreign ideas and artefacts, is simply an intentional and rational attempt at picking up a few clever tips from identified models. In this line of reasoning, the main issue remains unresolved: how does an image become a model that others imitate and translate into action in the first place. Unless it falls from the sky, an image becomes a model by being imitated, i. e. it is created by its imitators. An analysis of mimetic isomorphism can therefore hardly start from a given model. It must rather pursue the question of how the model is constructed in the course of its imitation.

When the organizations of a field increasingly resemble a model, in the end resembling each other, this makes them appear more modern and rational. In the course of this process they initially and above all alter their outer appearance, their standing, irrespective of what is otherwise sought or achieved. The main and prior goal here is increasing acceptance and legitimacy. Raising efficiency is something derived, even if it is considered to be the ultimate goal. This way of looking at organizational isomorphism means, however, that the *surface* or the *façade* is being rehabilitated following its modernistic denunciation. *Saving face*, an attitude which modernists like to ascribe to "irrational" individuals and "pre-modern" societies, re-appears as something important and, in a sense, reasonable. Honour and shame are now discovered − of all places − where cool economic rationality was expected.

The issue is more complex, though, since the ideal face of modernity indeed corresponds to function. Imitating *modernistic organizational faces* accordingly means imitating the supremacy of functionalistic organizational forms. The switch from, on the one hand, explaining organizational isomorphism by straightforwardly referring to the economic success of models to, on the other hand, explaining it with reference to a discourse of legitimacy, meaning and aesthetics may thus appear minute, if not insignificant. In the end, one might critically remark, the result is the same anyway. However, the difference, even if minute and only referring to the process and its motives and not to the result, is fundamental, as I shall try to demonstrate. Under the paradigm of mimetic isomorphism, formal organization is presented as a model which, like other models and images, is constructed and spreads through imitation.

Now that this door has been opened, astonishment at what comes to light should not tempt us to close it again. At any rate, it is not enough to carry on regardless, still applying the familiar patterns of sociological explanation. Presumably, purposeful and reflexive imitation is quite a common phenomenon. Actors who do not fully understand their positions will naturally take orientation from someone else who is near at hand and creates a secure and successful impression. But in the end, it is always a matter of a more fundamental form of appropriation of the new and the unknown, a preliminary step, so to speak. For how else is the decision made on which image is to become the model if not by imitation? Or does anybody really believe that the present worldwide craze of "privatization" is based on a verifiable superiority of the model? The choice and designing of a model can only be the consequence and not the precondition of imitations and translations. It is not only because of the circularity of the argument that it is impossible to reduce the isomorphism of organizations to the purposive imitation of ostensively given models. DiMaggio and Powell (1983) themselves hint at this when they speak of a "universality of mimetic processes." However, they break off here by reducing mimesis to a strategy for the avoidance of uncertainty.

By selecting a public sector enterprise from West Africa instead of from Japan, I had a better opportunity to see that mimesis is sometimes fundamentally different from a well-thought-out orientation towards an example or model. The modelling of the Lake Transport Company which I shall use as a case in point does not lead to a reduction of uncertainty, but to an increase, and business success fails to materialize too. The actors continue mimetic isomorphism as though totally unmoved by this.

Czarniawska and Joerges speak in a comparable context of a "magic attraction" and agree with Sahlin-Andersson when she describes Sweden's large-scale projects as the "totem" of a certain fashionable wave of organizational design. In other words, they assume that the actors experience the images as being equipped with power, and that this is why they exert such an attraction on them. In this essay, however, I cannot make this peculiar attraction the direct subject of my study. Rather, I have to start with a preceding question: how is mimetic isomorphism related to the politico-cultural translation of globally circulating ideas and artifacts into local political arenas?

In the next section (The Story of the Lake Transport Company) I present a preliminary version of my case. In doing so I shall follow the state of the art in organizational studies relating to what used to be called the "Third World." Following a discussion of an exemplary text by Larissa Lomnitz in the third section (Established Explanations), I advocate making formal organization structures an object of anthropological observation, thus removing them from the sphere of an ostensibly unquestioned rationality. In the fourth section (A Fresh Vocabulary) I then critically extend the crucial point made by John Meyer (that organizational survival is the result of skilful institutionalization in the sense of embeddedness) and the point made by DiMaggio and Powell (that mimetic isomorphism is the clever imitation of a given model). I justify these extensions above all with the assistance of Callon and Latour's *translation model* (who borrowed it from Michel Serres), their concept of *obligatory passage point* and with the reference to the heterogeneity of culture. From the viewpoint thus established, organizational mimetic isomorphism proves to be a process of politico-cultural construction of an obligatory passage point and a macro-actor. In section five I use this interpretative pattern to retell the story of the Lake Transport Company. In the final section (Façades/Practices) I attempt an outlook on how to conceive organizational change by drawing a sharper distinction between legitimacy discourses and practice.

The Story of the Lake Transport Company

When I came to the West African Lake Transport Company in the summer of 1992, there was one dominant subject of conversation within the company.[2] Everyone was saying that not enough freight business was being attracted to cover costs. Of course, the attributions of blame heard in the course of these discussions varied greatly according to the speaker's perspective and context. I shall only mention the most important ones here. Some people said the marketing department was responsible, because they were not aggressive enough in their dealings with customers. Others maintained it was the transport department, who were unreliable and thus drove customers away. Then the management was to blame for everything, because they cared more about lining their own pockets than for working for the company. Another complaint was that the lower income members of staff stole so much that the company was bleeding to death. The easiest

---

[2]   I spent six weeks within the company, where I collected the material presented here by way of participating observation, interviews and the study of files. I spent two further weeks in the country in order to get a better idea of the relevant economic sector and the company's political and economic environment.

way to achieve a consensus was of course to blame the decline in business on the government, who supposedly gave preferential treatment to road transport through their tax and infrastructure policy, so that inland waterway transport was bound to fail. Another popular theme was that the Levantine businessmen who dominated road transport gave bribes to the mainly public-sector customers.

A second *leitmotiv* came up again and again in many conversations on these issues. A few years ago, there was apparently a bitter conflict between the workforce and the management. I heard reports from all sides about an ominous *nucleus* of staff, who were supposedly still active. Some mentioned a death in this context, which they described as a mysterious result of the conflicts at the company. The general tenor was that I could not understand the present debates and conflicts because I was not familiar with this story. So I attempted to find out about it as best I could.

In 1966, the biggest river in the West African country was dammed close to its sea estuary, forming a lake four hundred kilometres long. While the main purpose of this gigantic project was to generate hydroelectric power, it became necessary to provide ferry links between the east-west roads that had been cut by the new lake. This also created an opportunity to transport bulk goods (such as fertilizers, cement, fuel, cotton seeds, etc.) between the north and south of the country by ship, especially since neither stable roads nor railway lines were available.

In 1970, the River Authority responsible for the hydroelectric power station and the development of the lake area formed the Lake Transport Company in collaboration with a private European firm. The European partner withdrew by 1976, because various state regulations apparently made profitable business operations impossible. Three years after the European managers had left, the ships were out of service and the firm's survival was hanging by a thread. In 1979, the parent company felt obliged to initiate the dissolution of the company and the dismissal of all the staff.

The government sought foreign assistance, and at the last moment found a source of credit, a western bank that was not involved in the dam project, so that it saw this as an opportunity to demonstrate its presence in the organization field of development agencies. A so-called rehabilitation programme was launched in 1980 to repair the old ships, buy new pusher tugs and lighters, and completely reorganize the company with the help of European experts. The plan also involved a merger with the previously independent lake ferry service and the parent company's department of navigational safety.

The combination of the business crisis, the merger and the externally directed restructuring led to a series of events at Lake Transport that further deepened the mutual distrust of the people concerned.

A particularly precarious aspect was the fact that a new formal hierarchy was set up with the help of the foreign advisers. This meant that the established informal coalitions lost their importance, at least for a while. For example, career prospects cultivated over years became obsolete overnight. The most delicate situations cropped up wherever someone new was brought in from outside and put in charge of a long-serving employee. The new managing director came from the parent company, which also had the last word on the Board of Directors. At that time there were four managerial positions on the second level of management, and none of them were filled with long-serving employees. The only old candidate ended up one level lower, because the new applicant had political connections, as the story goes.

As a result of these interferences in the social framework of the company, competition between staff belonging to the three original firms soon lost its significance. It was eclipsed by antagonism between old and new. In order to discredit the new people, who bore the most responsibility together with their "collaborationists," who were also soon on the scene, the old staff even went so far as to sabotage equipment. Rags were stuffed into motors and electric cables severed in inaccessible places; major jobs remained undone for weeks and months until the new man was on holiday — then the job was done in record time.

In addition, a grievance that had been irritating everyone since the company was formed in 1970 but which most people had almost grown accustomed to, resurfaced as a result of the hiring of outsiders to top management positions. The management of Lake Transport resided in the parent company's ostentatious building in the distant capital. Even the part of the administration that was located at the southern end of the lake had its offices not at the harbour, but in the nearest town about ten kilometres away. Hence, the management and higher employees were even geographically separated from the commercial and shipping staff. In the harbour and on the river, this topography was a source of additional ill-humour in addition to the merger and reorganization.

The staff accused management of indifference, blamed them for the continuing crisis and seemed to be increasingly determined to take things into their own hands. The solidarity that grew in this context transformed the polarization between old and new into a confrontation between "us" and "them." To use the dominant legitimacy idiom of the complex society, the *patron-client relations* had come apart at the seams and needed to be renegotiated.

In late 1984 and early 1985, the mood seems to have hit rock bottom. There had been a long-standing agreement between Lake Transport and the hospital in the town at the southern end of the lake, according to which the hospital gave free out-patient and in-patient treatment to all Lake

Transport staff and their family members and subsequently sent the bills to the firm. Because Lake Transport stopped paying these bills sometime in 1984, the hospital no longer felt bound by the arrangement and started demanding cash in advance from employees. Then the firm stopped paying its employer's share of a pension fund for the employees. The result in early 1985 was that Lake Transport had to pay a heavy fine, which was an additional burden on the still ailing balance sheet.

The next scandal involved the embezzlement of company resources by higher employees – at least this was the version told by a a few people who felt cheated. The company treasurer, to whom the ships' captains handed over the cash receipts from tickets and cargo, is supposed to have disappeared with a large sum of money. Yet for practical reasons alone, the story cannot have been that simple, because cash is regularly deposited at the bank precisely to avoid large sums accumulating. For this reason, a different version is considered more plausible by the Board of Directors: a coalition between the people who handle the cash receipts – in particular ticket sellers, inspectors, captains and finance department staff – must have been conspiring to embezzle company revenue over a long period. Because the new structures being set up in the finance department would sooner or later have led to the discovery of the fraud, the only option left in early 1985 was to have one member of the coalition run off as a front man and take the blame for the total loss. According to this version, the people who in retrospect were interpreting the case as further proof of management corruption, were not loyal, simple members of staff, but themselves members of the suspected coalition acting out their plan.

Against the background of the financial and technical difficulties at Lake Transport, the complications caused by the merger and the interpretation of the above-mentioned crises and scandals as a consequence of management corruption and incompetence, the workforce staged an occupation of the company and locked out the management. This took place in May 1985 under the leadership of the company revolutionary committee. The government feared that the rehabilitation and expansion project that had already been launched might be interrupted if the western lenders were to learn too much about the revolt. So they did their best to ensure that "orderly conditions" returned as soon as possible.

The occupation of the company was ended by the government. They took the workforce's complaints about management corruption literally and promised a new and competent management. The political actors pretended on the surface to know nothing about the existence of clientele coalitions or how they worked; they also denied knowledge of their indisputable legitimacy. Subsequently one manager returned to the parent company, another one handed in his notice, and a third, a former military man from the navy, was transferred to a special post.

However, before the committee of inquiry was able to announce its solution, the tragedy took place about which I had been informed so cryptically. The fourth manager, the General Service Manager, died in a car crash on his way from the southern harbour to the capital; one of his children also died, and the rest of his family were taken to hospital with serious injuries. Today, there are many versions circulating in the company to explain this sad occurrence; all of them assume that it cannot have been a coincidence. Among managers, one frequently hears that the workers had driven the colleague to his death by magic or psychological terror. Those who sympathize with the occupiers point to God, who had dispensed retributive justice.

Of the four managers of the company, the man who died had been at Lake Transport the longest, and he knew conditions at the company better than anyone. The claim made by the former occupiers that he had been responsible for some shady dealings himself is not seriously doubted by anyone. In addition to the above-mentioned disappearance of a large sum of money, there was apparently a story about the misuse of some trucks for which he was responsible. The man's clientele within the company must have felt betrayed when the rumour went about that he had exposed irregularities at the committee of inquiry, in order to divert attention from his own role. Some of the former occupiers today admit that they threatened the General Service Manager in the ensuing weeks. Their wives reviled and jostled his wife, who like the others worked as a trader at the market, and his children were victimized at school.

However, what appears as treachery in the legitimacy idiom of clientelism, appears as the proper statement of a witness in the idiom of formal organization. The report of the manager who later had the fatal accident apparently revealed the "true" purpose of the attempted revolutionary renewal of the company structure: it was to save established coalitions from being destroyed by the restructuring of the company and to put the blame for any cases of corruption that were revealed during this operation on a few old patrons.

According to the logic of the formal structure, a "new beginning" was possible at the end of 1985, and evidently everyone acted as though it had always been their aim to create "clean conditions." As a first step, a new Managing Director arrived in January 1986, and one of the most important criteria for his selection by the parent company and the country's political leadership was evidently that he should have the diplomatic skills required to win back the workforce and encourage them to identify with the company. Under his direction, the four vacant posts, as well as two newly created posts on the second level of management, were filled during 1986 — again with managers from outside the company.

Under the new management, and with the help of the expatriate experts — who were still there to rehabilitate the fleet, build up workshop facilities, train technicians and restructure the company — Lake Transport was able to survive up to the days of my visit in 1992. However, as I have already mentioned, the company was performing poorly and the permanent problem was the small amount of cargo it could attract. The new and expensive facilities were continuously underused and could therefore not be run profitably. The whole investment by the foreign development bank thus became questionable and the entire organizational set-up doubtful.

To sum up: the informal arrangements of everyday practice that had evolved since the formation of the company in 1970 aimed above all at coming to terms with the model of formal organization. Asymmetrical relations created by the formal hierachy were defined according to the valid ethos as *patron-client relations*. The reverse side of this appropriation consisted in using tactical positions of the formal hierarchy as the hardest currency in patron-client exchange. The company crises, the first in 1979 and the second in 1985, but also the notoriously poor performance of the company were at least partially consequences of this form of appropriation.

Told in this manner, the story of the Lake Transport seems to confirm the established explanations of the malfunctioning of formal organizations in the former Third World.

Established Explanations

Formal Systems and Informal Networks

The contradiction between the broad distribution and popularity of a particular organization model on the one hand, and its manifest ineffectiveness in many parts of the world on the other, is the point of departure for Larissa Lomnitz's article "Informal Exchange Networks in Formal Systems" (1988). In this chapter I shall use her excellent text to briefly summarize what can be considered the state of the art.

Lomnitz, a Mexican anthropologist, sketches a sequence of events that is set in motion in many non-western societies by the fact that (firstly) the objectives and structures of formal organization run counter to historical and socio-cultural realities in these societies. This (secondly) makes the organizations themselves ineffective, which induces people (thirdly) to satisfy their needs by helping themselves in ways that are illegal according to the rules of the system. This, of course, makes the formal organization even more inefficient and further boosts the importance of informal exchange. She concludes: "The degree of formality and the inability of the formal system to satisfy societal needs give rise to informal solutions" (1988, p. 54).

This line of reasoning is open to question. What "societal needs" are cannot be stated in advance of the analysis as an Archimedean point and cannot therefore be used to explain actions either. It also seems unfounded to equate the distinction between formal and informal ways of doing something with the difference between "rational" and "socio-culturally embedded."

Lomnitz is endeavouring to move the debate on informal networks out of the periphery of complex societies (Eisenstadt, 1961) into their centre. She would like to prove that it is not a matter of separate spheres, but different dimensions which are not only to be found in the countryside or the urban slums, but also within the administrative machinery of the modern sector in complex societies. Her examples come from Chile, Mexico and Georgia.

However, while the Mexican anthropologist is concerned with informal networks in formal systems, I suggest turning the question around and asking: what are the conditions governing the emergence of formal organization systems in the context of informal networks? And then more particularly: what role do new ideas and artefacts play in this process? Ideas and artefacts floating around in a global discourse that are picked up by certain actors to be translated into their local context. Is formal organization one of these ideas and artefacts? But first I shall look into the established pattern of explaining informal relations.

Bureaucracy and Gift Exchange

Following the framework of institutional analysis (in the tradition of Marcel Mauss and Karl Polanyi), Lomnitz looks mainly at exchange relations. Her paradigmatic transactions take place between partners who consider their dealings to be based on mutuality, i. e. to be legitimated by the norm of generalized reciprocity or by an "ideology of kinship and friendship," as she puts it. On this basis people engage in what in anthropological parlance is called gift exchange. In accordance with the classical tripartite model she moves on to redistributive exchange and market exchange.

Like most of her predecessors she overlooks one crucial aspect of reciprocity. When people believe their dealings to be based on generalized reciprocity and relate this to an ideology of kinship, it does not mean that the partners of these dealings actually are equals exchanging equal values. It is rather the other way round: in societies that praise generalized reciprocity, people have an indisputable right to be different and to be treated differently. This basic right is established mainly outside and prior to the exchange and relates to aspects like gender, seniority, descent, and social status. Bureaucracy and market society are challenging this right to be different.

For Lomnitz the point of departure is the exchange of *favores* between members of the middle classes in Chile and Mexico. These favours always consist in the donor bringing his or her influence with the formal system into play to illegally set aside a scarce resource. The recipient may not respond immediately with a quid pro quo, and certainly not with money. Such behaviour would destroy the symbolic content of gift exchange. This content consists in the mutual trust in the reliability of the respective partner to bindingly profess his or her allegiance to the system of mutual assistance, not for the sake of a short-term advantage, the assessment of which might change radically from one moment to the next, but on the basis of an ethic of reciprocity in the sense of a holy duty. In essence, it is a matter of the *confianza* (trust) one is most likely to expect from close family relatives.

If a person does not have the right connections to get hold of a desired object that is inaccessible by legal means, he or she can use a friend as an intermediary who enjoys a relationship of trust with the distributor of the resource. The entire society is crisscrossed in this way with networks established through relations between individuals which are made to resemble kinship relations. Gift exchange thus fills in the gaps of modern society, like grass that spreads between flagstones.

The donor of a gift, however, is involved in a conflict of loyalties, since the setting aside of resources for a friend means breaking the rules of the formal system, as in the case of the director of a telephone company who has a phone installed for a friend who would otherwise have been on the waiting list for two years. The practice of allocating telephone lines, like any other practice, requires a *representational mode*, a theoretical construct defining how things should be in a specific field.[3] This model has two different tasks in the present case.

On the one hand, it is supposed to make the practice of allocating telephones look like the implementation of a plan that is rationally oriented towards the principle of efficiency. On the other hand, it is supposed to make practice look fair and legitimate in the eyes of as many people as possible. From the point of view of the telephone company, which has been commissioned by the society to supply people with telecommunications, the representational model consists, among other things, of the waiting list with its fixed set of special regulations (e. g. priority for fire-fighters, policemen, doctors, etc.). But many people consider another representational model of practice to be equally important. It points to family and group solidarity, *noblesse oblige* and chivalry. These are justification patterns for practice which are quite differently, but for this reason no less closely geared to the public interest and therefore appear legitimate and meaningful precisely for this reason.

---

[3]   Holy and Stuchlik (1983) distinguish between action (the real activity), action model (which states how something can be achieved in a specific situation in everyday routine) and representational model (as the most abstract notional level).

Hence, the problem lies in how the actors handle the tension between bureaucratic allocation and their obligations towards friends and relations, how − to use Weberian terminology − they mediate between *formal and material rationality* (Weber, 1973, p. 437). We learn that in South America it is usually a skilful balancing act between what I should like to call two *legitimacy discourses*.

On the one hand, a legitimacy discourse is built up that makes practice appear reasonable and moral, as long as the ethos of *confianza* is confirmed in countless exchange events. However, people will, if need be, act contrary to this ethos if it appears opportune to do so in a certain situation. Yet the actors will continue to profess allegiance to the ideal despite this − or precisely for this reason. They will often justify their deviating behaviour by saying that they had no choice under the circumstances and will endeavour to put things right later. In other words, this representational model does not begin to crumble or become obsolete as a result of being repeatedly exposed as unrealistic by the *action model* (the recipe for situation-related routine action) and concrete practice.

On the other hand, a legitimacy discourse is built up according to the same pattern which makes practice appear reasonable and ethically correct if the principles of efficiency and the bureaucratic demand for symmetry (treating all cases equally) are respected. Virtually any particular action that appears rational and legitimate in the light of one discourse can be de-legitimated by relating it to the other one, and vice versa. Consequently, successful situational manoeuvring means alternating from one discourse to the other at the right moment. For the purpose of analysis, therefore, it is important to have detailed knowledge of the relationship between practice and the two diverging legitimacy discourses, as well as the switching by actors between discourses. The above-mentioned and several other examples are interpreted by Lomnitz as though ethos and rationality were diametrical opposites. I argue, by contrast, that both discourses contain ethical and rational dimensions and both can equally be used tactically by the actors.

Nonetheless, societies, social contexts and development phases evidently differ in the way the individual discourses are expressed, in the possible transitions between and accretions of the discourses, and in the links with practice. Some of Lomnitz's examples show that growing social distance between actors has an effect in this sense. Many exchanges of assistance that were previously explained using the rules of reciprocity, mutate in this way to become exchanges that are justified by the market rules according to which a service is available for money. At the same time, an increase in social distance can also lead to the emergence of patron-client relations containing a special kind of reciprocity that Lomnitz calls "asymmetric" (in Polanyi's well-known terminology: redistributive exchange).

Bureaucracy and Patronage

Whenever a member of an informal network is promoted within the formal system, it becomes difficult for the exchange partners to reciprocate the contributions of this member in the same currency and with the same amounts. Furthermore, the promoted person is more likely to be interested in loyalty, which he or she can best build up by leaving his/her exchange partners in the "shadow of indebtedness" (Gouldner). A patron-client relationship starts to develop in this way. One side, the patron, offers access to sought-after positions or contracts, political protection or help in times of need. The other, the clientele, reciprocates with personal loyalty, especially in political and ideological matters, with small services and information from areas that are no longer accessible to the patron because of his/her elevated position, but on which he/she is particularly dependent.

An apt example is the university graduates of a certain year who graduated from the same department or studied together a long way from home, say in Leipzig or Manchester. In the "developing countries," where this kind of elite is still small, the members of such an "old boys' club" (it really is nearly always boys, after all) are more likely to pervade a considerable part of the civil service and the big state enterprises than elsewhere and can normally use their network to assert themselves successfully. The awareness of being dependent on such connections alone is enough to make a person stick to the rules. As soon as a member of the group succeeds in attaining a higher position, for example that of a director at the tax office, he, or more rarely she becomes the patron of a network of former fellow students, which in turn increases the power of the network.

The Mexican anthropologist emphasizes the subversive character of such arrangements. It can be argued, however, that such arrangements do not necessarily undermine or change formal organizations and their hierarchies into something else but rather tame and reduced them to a humane measure. Networks make it impossible for individuals or alliances to exploit the hierarchy at will for their own advantage. The effect of this kind of appropriation can be seen as a special form of "democratic" control of the bureaucratic machinery. Seen from the opposite point of view, it is the bureaucratic machinery that creates the conditions in which patronage can flourish. Patronage and networks would otherwise be redundant or at least would be something else.

With a reference to Ronald Dore (1984), who writes about informal relations in the Japanese economy, Lomnitz expands her argument in a direction which the reader had probably already been expecting. Everywhere, not only in the so-called Third World, formal relations between certain role-bearers are only one dimension of an extensive bundle of human relations between people. In every society, behind the decisions of administrations, organizations and enterprises, there often lie reasons that are hardly ever mentioned officially, even though everybody knows about them (Lomnitz, 1988, p. 49). These reasons are connected with cultural issues such as loyalty, keeping face, conscience, ambition, jealousy, envy, machismo and, not least, fashion, and seem foreign to the legitimacy discourse of formal organizations.

The road on which the two discourses can meet and also be officially linked is very narrow, however, at least in the western market economy. Essentially, it is a matter of the passion for the cool selection of the best means to pursue certain interests which are considered to be in accordance with the common good.[4] There is no other representational justification for organizational decisions available but this form of "passionate" objectivity (*Sachlichkeit*). Whatever the reasons for making a decision may have been, what will subsequently be announced will always be something like: "... because it has been proved that the means chosen are demonstrably the best for the given purpose." Any other outward representation would reveal the coincidences and uncertainties of decision-making. This would in turn undermine the legitimacy of the procedure and allow the players to see how thin the ice is on which they are walking.[5]

The question is, therefore, why, in the case of Japan, do we hear so much about the supposedly outstanding effectiveness of informal relations compared to the bureaucratic model? And why, on the other hand, are informal relations predominantly seen as strategies of subversion when they occur in South America, Asia and Africa?

Theoretically, both tendencies must exist everywhere, since each society contains the two corresponding legitimacy discourses. However, this does not clear the problem out of the way, as a simple observation by Victor Ayeni (1987) shows. Like other countries, Nigeria has a government agency for the control of the state bureaucracy, to which citizens can turn if they feel their rights have been infringed by the state. However, the Nigerian Public Complaints Commission has developed into a monolithic bureaucracy itself and systematically undermines the official reason for its own existence. In the corresponding agency in Canada, a handful of employees process several thousand cases a year, whereas in Nigeria 1,800 employees are needed to deal with a third to a quarter of this number. Ayeni concludes with the laconic remark: "This is certainly ridiculous" (Ayeni, 1987, pp. 314−317).[6]

---

4   On the question of passion for the cool rationality of formal organizations, cf. Hischmann (1977) and Albrow (1992).

5   The fact that in post-modern conditions it can perhaps be decisive to communicate precisely the uncertainties of decision-making is an issue I can ignore here without loss for my argument.

6   In 1988 the *International Political Science Review* had a special issue on bureaucracy where further instructive examples can be found, see especially Olowu (1988) and Rohr (1988).

Within the paradigm offered by Lomnitz, one cannot go further than the cultural-relativistic and cultural-deterministic statement that some cultures spawn informal relations that support the rational, formal system, and others, by contrast, bring forth informal relations that work in the opposite direction. While the issue at the beginning of her text was that "culturally determined loyalties to kin and local groups" (Lomnitz, 1988, p. 42) run counter to bureaucratic rationality and cause inefficiency, at the end we find ourselves confronted with the opposite conclusion where Japan is concerned. There, it seems, primary relations strengthen organizations built on formal rationality.

Lomnitz understands the formal system of society as something rational in itself and legitimate simply for this reason, without reference to political and cultural processes. By assuming that when the formal system fails, the actors tactically resort to informal relation patterns from the sphere of the reciprocity ethic she creates the impression that only this frame of reference is politically and culturally constructed. As a result, she logically only endeavours to explain this part of the story, while omitting the rest from analysis, along with natural and technological aspects. She takes it for granted that the flagstones do not need to be explained, only the grass in-between. Although probably contrary to her good intentions, the end result is that the western world emerges as the normal case, while all other civilizations are apparently just trundling along in a deficient mode.[7]

Coming back to my case, we cannot understand it by relying on the state of the art. The story of Lake Transport, but also the material supplied by Lomnitz, suggest a different interpretation. Hierarchies are padded out with patron-client relations not because something or other is not working properly, but because asymmetries in the social exchange only appear to be acceptable under the guise of protection and loyalty between people. And if the reciprocity ethos among people who perceive themselves as belonging to the same "community of brothers" still holds sway in situations where, from a western perspective, transactions ought to be carried out according to quite different rules, then this primarily points to certain social obligations being regarded as *holy* − as Lomnitz herself says. They cannot be neglected without considerable negative consequences.

The reciprocity ethos is only a representational model, though. There is always enough scope in practice for people to see to their own advantage. Perhaps the most important way to seek gain is by disputing the definition of a given situation: is it a case for reciprocal, redistributive or market exchange? Cases where all parties to an exchange agree on the same defini-

---

[7]   Dalton (1959) presented a different analysis of the various combinations between formal and informal systems in western society.

tion of their transactions are rather exceptional. The important thing here is the politics of interpretation.

Above all, however, Lomnitz leaves out one aspect that is continuously present in her material, as it is in my case study. She ignores the fact that the formal structures are built up intentionally by people. And certainly, the actors involved do not only intend to open a *discourse of equal rights and opportunities*, and to establish an effective service to the public interest. They are probably just as interested in improving their own individual lives via the positions and action opportunities of the formal system. In concrete terms, this often means strengthening their role in the informal network via a role in the formal system. For this they need and want the formal system. It is not so much a matter of two separate worlds as of two types of discourse which are continually intersecting and traversing each other: one cannot exist without the other and vice versa.

In an outstandingly well-researched analysis on the appropriation of rural development projects in the Sudan, Kurt Beck (1990) goes beyond the usual dichotomy of formal and informal relations. He emphasizes how during the process which he calls "tribal appropriation" not only the appropriated object, but also the actors are re-constructed. From this perspective, the tribe does not appear as a stable context into which something new is brought, but as a flexible construct. This construct only takes shape during the appropriation process, and this shape can easily be changed under different circumstances. Equally, the rural development project does not appear as a rational organizational instrument to achieve certain goals. It only takes shape and becomes real during and by the process of appropriation which unavoidably means transformation.

In the remaining part of this text, I should like to attempt a more detailed narrative of the relationship between the discourse of equal rights and opportunities and the discourse of the right to be different, of their various intersections and their relevance for practice. For this purpose, in the next chapter I shall first introduce a different vocabulary.

A Fresh Vocabulary

Formal Organization and Modernity

Within the overall theme of this book, the topic of this essay is the intercultural journey of the notion and practice which, despite some difficulties of definition, can be called "formal organization." In other words, I am not investigating the spread of special ways of organizing, nor the spread of ideas that can be important for organizational actions; rather, I am investigating the spread of the idea of formal organization itself.

Formal organizations are deliberately not conceived as autonomous, monolithic corporate groups or systems that are self-explanatory or can be understood through their objectives. Without wishing to dispute any value of such a viewpoint − especially since it is unavoidable within the limits of judicial discourse − I follow those who prefer to speak of *fragile, complex constructs* which are loosely composed of more or less institutionalized action and interpretation patterns, some of which contradict each other (Czarniawska-Joerges, 1992).

Considering the purpose of this essay, it seems useful to add the liberal ideology as an additional aspect to the definition of formal organization. This ideology is related to the emergence of the bourgeois society at the end of the 18th century and as such is expressed in three characteristics of formal organization: (1) unrestricted freedom of the members to enter and leave, (2) unrestricted freedom to shape structures and processes depending on the respective situational opportunity, and (3) unrestricted, free choice of purpose. Seen in this light, the topos of *formal rationalization* constitutes the core of formal organization.

Ernest Gellner (1983), in his study on nationalism and modernity, drew attention to the fact that social rationalization is based on a linking of two principles: the principle of efficiency (cool selection of the best available means for given, isolated purposes) and the principle of symmetry (treat identical cases in an identical way, maintain regularity and coherence, create and set down in writing a well-determined set of rules for action, create optimum transparency and predictability). To this I would like to add in Weberian manner that the essence of this order is a special definition of reality made possible by the principle of keeping files. Accordingly, only phenomena that correspond to filed rules and regulations are valid, real and can be used in court. In turn, each change of relevance can only be implemented in the form of files and of new, written and codified rules. Such an order is above all designed to eliminate uncertainties and specific criticism.

To a certain extent, the emphasis on formal rationalization and freedom of decision stands in contrast to the above-mentioned emphasis on the societal embeddedness of formal organization. In the one case, the aspect of institutionalization is emphasized, in the other, through freedom of decision, deinstitutionalization. It proves useful, however, to incorporate this ambiguity into the definition. On the one hand, formal organizations must be made up of institutional building blocks if people are to be expected to hold them together in the long term. On the other hand, they are designed by the actors for manipulating these building blocks and inventing new ones − otherwise they would probably not come into being in the first place. From this viewpoint, formal organizations are equally characterized by the need for institutionalization and the possibility and intention of dein-stitutionalization. They thus belong to the core repertoire of modernity.

In the next step, I shall heuristically contrast cultures in order to make visible a second important socio-structural and cultural precondition of modern formal organization.

In anthropology, *social organization* refers to the complex interconnec-tions between *institutions* which provide social practice with a certain amount of orientation. Institutions are conceived as a kind of sediment of previous transactions and as materializations of ideas which have become indisputable and "natural"; they are taken for granted and sometimes be-come unnoticed. Institutions in anthropology are primarily production and ownership structures, rules of descent, succession and inheritance, family and marriage patterns, systems of age classes and neighbourhood patterns. Social organization, which has perhaps preoccupied social anthropology the most intensively and the longest, has no formally organized central agency and no formally organized enforcement staff (Fortes and Evans-Pritchard, 1940; Middleton and Tait, 1958; Sigrist, 1967).

The institutions of so-called segmentary (or "acephalous" or "stateless") societies always simultaneously incorporate economic, legal, political, socio-structural, moral, aesthetic, religious and mythical aspects and are therefore "embedded," to take up Karl Polanyi's central metaphor (1944, p. 75). While a simple dichotomy of embedded/disembedded economic forms is certainly misleading, a dissimilarity does, after all, exist here. But what exactly is this difference which reveals the fundamental precondition of formal organization in modern society?

We can continue to credit Weberian modernization theory with drawing attention to this point. We can do so even if we distance ourselves from the notion of a historical one-way street to modernity because we prefer not to have historical inevitabilities. Max Weber's central argument itself is de-signed around the differentiation mentioned here. According to his ideal-type construction, the pursuit of profit in the so-called tribal society is lim-ited to trade with strangers. The basic economic principle of utility maximi-zation appears here in its purest, most differentiated form. External moral-ity (Weber: *Außenmoral*) applies, and the end justifies the means.[8] The out-side world thus defined is confronted by the clear-cut inner world where economic action is subordinated to the regulations of the ethic of brotherli-ness. Precisely this division of the social world into two is abolished in principle in the market society.

Here, in the market society, disembedding and the thematic purging of one logic from the logics of the other societal spheres respectively, relates

---

[8] Elwert (1987) discusses this phenomenon from a different perspective and explains the increase in venality as a consequence of the spread of market economy.

to a universal, and thus also *internal* differentiation.[9] We are thus talking about the *universalization* of differentiated logics that have in principle been disentangled. However, this leads in turn to their mutual *permeation* – and this is the important thing here. The fact that a rational capitalist also charges his brother interest is offset by the fact that he charges a stranger the same rate of interest as his brother. After Benjamin Nelson (1949) captured this pattern in the slogan "from tribal brotherhood to universal otherhood," Richard Münchünch – (1984) succeeded particularly well in highlighting the difference between embedding and "permeation" (he follows Parsons in speaking of interpenetration; Rottenburg, 1994).

Accordingly, the embeddedness of economic action amounts to the ideological subordination of its aims and interests to the premises of community action. By contrast, the permeation of economic action with the logics of the other spheres should be understood as a forever temporary compromise between contrary logics involved in an insoluble conflict. Seen from this standpoint, the special social and ideological space in which modern formal organization can emerge is the zone of permeation, i. e. the ever-provisional, controversial and loose coupling of divergent types of discourse. This is the second precondition of formal organization and the cardinal difference mentioned above. Seen against the now given background, formal organization becomes visible as a characteristic project of modernity relating to the meta-narratives of progress and emancipation.

The feudal societies and other non-modern, comparably undifferentiated societies, where some rights and opportunities differ according to birth and social position, have primarily generated legitimacy discourses emphasizing above all *the ascribed right to be different* (*Sonderrechte*). Status differences and asymmetric relations are predominantly attributed to principles that lie *outside* of transactions and are looked upon by the people concerned as part of a sacred, never-changing order (gender, age and descent are the most important categories here). The legitimacy discourse of the market society, which primarily promulgates *equal rights* (*Rechtsgleichheit*), represents precisely the opposite (Ignatieff, 1984). This society attaches importance to offering all citizens the same opportunities, and the only status differences it recognizes as legitimate are those that prove to be good for business. Hence, performance becomes the status criterion par excellence; as a result, everyone *de jure* has an equal chance of attaining status.

However, this contrast must not be understood in the sense of Sir Henry Maine's famous dictum "from status to contract," i. e. as a law of evolution. Since Meyer Fortes we can assume that both legitimacy discourses play a part in every society. The decisive factor is therefore: "What is (...) their

---

[9]   Luhmann (1970) speaks of a system with its own decision logic with reference to the capitalist economy, being a differentiated societal sphere.

relative elaboration and differentiation, their relative weight and scope in different sectors of social life" (Fortes, 1969, p. 220). And most importantly, it must be noted that the contrast refers to legitimacy discourses and not to social practice, as I have now repeated several times.

In this section I have specified the cardinal difference between the modern, formal organization and other forms of organizing. To make this point I have recalled the difference between *embeddedness* and *permeation.* To consider organizations legitimate and rational as long as they appear institutionally embedded is something fundamentally different from regarding organizations sound and morally acceptable if they seem to accommodate conflicting logics from the various societal spheres by permeation. This difference mainly becomes manifest in the way in which modern, formal organizations legitimately pursue change up to the point of disembedding certain practices by referring to the ideas of progress and/or emancipation. The simultaneous existance of conflicting legitimacy discourses between which actors can switch strategically makes it necessary to add an excursus on the question of social and cultural heterogeneity.

Translation and Accretion

The illusion of being able to distinguish between "pure" and "compound" cultures, or at least find the "original" of an intellectual or material work, was dropped long ago in anthropology. Although even today some ethnographies still create the impression that they are describing local, self-contained worlds, even the authors of these works do not dispute that every culture comes about through diverse *syncretisms* and *syntheses.* It is generally accepted that we are dealing exclusively with imitations and literally *hybrid* social structures and world views, and that these hybridizations are continually developing further (Barnett, 1940; Kroeber, 1940). Kroeber's statement that "every culture is an accretion" has become part of common knowledge to the extent that it is quoted in Webster's Dictionary (1986) as an illustration of the term *accretion.* During the long dominance of functionalistic, structure-functionalistic and structuralistic models, with their penchant for societal integration and static orders, the question of how this process of accretion or hybridization actually works was not considered to be particularly interesting in anthropology.

It was not until the end of colonialism and the post-structuralistic turning point (perhaps marked by Lyotard, 1987), that discussion began on the post-modern, multicultural society, and the ethnographic lens was able to focus on what became known as patchwork or collages (Clifford, 1988). Not much later, however, the politically explosive nature of the relationship between cultural syncretism and societal synthesis has also come into the limelight − not least as a result of the violent conflict in the former Yugoslavia, the disintegrating Soviet Union, and the seemingly endless crisis in Africa which has entered a new period of incredible aggravation in the last ten years.

Allow me continue with cultural heterogeneity and the spread of ideas and artefacts in general. When new and foreign ideas and artefacts join together to form collages, the individual parts inevitably change the meaning they had in the previous context. The metaphor *translation* characterizes the process: in order to bring an idea into a local cosmos from any part of the outside world, one has to use a cultural code. This presumes the existence of a deep structure which seems to be concealed within the motley and inconsistent patchwork of culture, like grammar in language. Probably both statements are true: both the observation that cultures are patchworks of only loosely fitting and partly contradictory parts, and the assumption that there is something that has an ordering function, comparable to grammar in language.

However, and this is the decisive point here, it is not necessary to imagine this cultural grammar as a uniform and genotypical code that determines the phenotypical surface. There is much to support the assumption that each culture has several mutually contradicting codes which are made available to individual people like alternative repertoires for thought. Each code has a different explanation of how the world is ordered, how you can recognize it, what you can do in it and what meaning results from it all, if any. Because of the contradictory nature of the various codes, it is not possible to completely deduce the patchwork of the cultural phenomena from them. The codes themselves are not unalterable either. Because they are continuously incorporating new elements, they change in a way that is analogous to the translated elements, which are no longer what they used to be after they have been translated. As a result of these observations, we can only speak of a code – or rather the metacode – of a culture at all because the available choice of repertoires and their tangle of relations somehow differ from one culture to another.

Translation aims at the *appropriation* of an external thing, which is then given another function, an altered meaning and often a new shape in the new context. The constructivistic "sociology of translation" as advocated by Michel Callon and Bruno Latour (1981; Latour, 1986) offers an image which can help us to understand appropriation and contextualization processes. While the classical anthropological diffusion model (Ratzel, 1896) assumes that ideas and artefacts move through social space and across borders under their own steam, it is more accurate to imagine this process as a kind of ball game. Only if the actors catch the ball and pass it on, i. e. if they collaborate, can the game continue. In the case of the movement of ideas and artefacts through time and space, each actor therefore takes the "thing" into his or her own hands and gives it the shape and direction that best corresponds to his/her context and intentions. In this way, we move from the *trans-mission* of a thing that remains the same to the *trans-formation* of the thing.

Transformation also means that people turn a thing that they initially experience as non-authentic into an authentic component of their local life. In this way, a *rational choice*, or *mimicry*, *imitation* or *simulation* can lead to the emergence of a *fashion* and this in turn to a *social institution*.[10] People can then no longer imagine the world without what used to be a new thing; it has become a natural part of their repertoire. In the course of the process from initial appropriation to institutionalization, an "authentic way of handling the non-authentic" (Bausinger, 1990) may occur.

The Lemwareng (as the people with whom I lived in the early nineteen-eighties in the Sudan call themselves) hang the New Testament wrapped in a plastic bag under the apex of the straw roof of their houses to fend off unexpected visitors and evil forces. In the way in which they authentically handle the Holy Scripture and naturally integrate it into their cosmos, they attribute to it a different meaning from the one that the missionaries had in mind when they distributed the printed paper (Rottenburg, 1989; 1991). The point of this observation is vital to my thoughts on the transformation of the model of formal organization: like the New Testament, it too finds itself transported from one cultural context to another.

In the same way that the appropriated elements are transformed, the *context* also changes. It is permanently taking in new elements, so that conditions slowly alter. Under favourable conditions, which from a historical viewpoint is perhaps the "norm" − at least it is the most pleasant case for the people concerned − this process passes off virtually unnoticed. Under different conditions, there can be violent modernization or retraditionalization processes; and in some cases the latter can be a cover for the former.

In the sense of the accretion processes sketched here, every culture is a composite picture made up of disparate parts. The important point here is that these parts never perfectly grow together, but for ever remain somewhat contingent and inconsistent. Particularly since accretion is a process of morphogenesis that is never completed, a culture can be more accurately characterized by its inconsistencies and specific forms of transformation than by the relatively homogeneous and stable components of its structures. All this, however, does not mean that accretion is a completely haphazard

---

[10] See Czarniawska and Joerges (in this volume) on the transition from fashion to institution. Using the example of clothing among the Lemwareng, I (Rottenburg, 1989) showed how the process runs from mimicry (dressing in order to not be conspicious) via status symbol (hoarding clothing to gain prestige) to institution (being ashamed of going about without clothing).

process where anything goes. Without returning to structural-functionalism one can well distinguish between more or less successful translations as I shall try to show later on.

Politico-Cultural Translation

Some processes of cultural translation are driven by curiosity and by the desire to try out, simulate and imitate things. Others are propelled by efforts by individual actors to increase their resources or numbers of supporters through new ideas. In many cases these two types of motivation cannot really be distinguished; it does not really matter here whether the passion for novelty, the hunger for truth or the greed for power came first. The point is that cultural translation is usually linked to political translation and power. The above-mentioned translation model introduced by Michel Callon and Bruno Latour aimed at conceptualizing this phenomenon with the emphasis on power.

They recommend the heuristic reversal of the line of argument that has been popular ever since Durkheim. According to their reversal, it is not like in Durkheim where society holds the people together; rather, it is people who hold the society together. As Hobbes originally proposed, all actors are thus declared *isomorphic*. The only way for anyone to become greater or more powerful is by transaction with other people. Greatness and power are thus initially always passed on upwards from below and are, as a consequence, not a fixed component of certain social positions. The main aim here is to avoid further obscuring and fortifying via sociological analysis the advantage and position of the so-called *macro-actors*, who largely determine the lives of the so-called *micro-actors*.

Unlike in Hobbes, in Callon and Latour's view, the transactions that lead to the emergence of a macro-actor do not consist primarily of contracts, but above all of *translations*. In this way, they are continuing Durkheim's argument that societization is impossible without a minimum of classificatory solidarity; at the same time they give it a radically performative touch. The latter, in turn, is reminiscent of Max Weber's charismatic power and very close to Bourdieu's (1984) proposal to link power and culture through the process of reality definitions and interpretations.

The suggestion here is to apply heuristically the type of argument as presented by Callon and Latour in the context of bureaucratic rule. In this way, we are able to show that macro-actors − including bureaucratically legitimated macro-actors − cease to exist when they lose their following. And they lose their following as soon as they are no longer able to translate and package the ideas and interests of those who make up their following. In short, macro-actors basically only exist − as long as they exist − in the minds of the micro-actors. Attention is thus steered away from the power mechanisms of bureaucratic machineries to the invisible, but much more effective power of definitions of reality. This is not playing down the importance of the "iron cage." On the contrary, it makes it seem even more threatening, with everyone contributing to building their own cage.

Conversely, only in this way can the weak spots be found where the tools of deconstruction can be applied, making it possible to escape apparent inevitability after all. To find the weak spots means to offer different definitions of reality which provide different passage points for micro-actors to achieve their goals by avoiding the old passage points. Borrowing from military parlance, Callon (1986) speaks of an *obligatory passage point* if someone has convinced others that they cannot get what they want unless they pass through a narrow passage that can easily be controlled and utilized to generate power. The social sciences are just one of several voices that contribute to an ongoing competition about reality definitions and ensuing passage points.

The main assumption in this translation model is that the actors are isomorphic. To claim the true *isomorphism* of all actors in the capitalist-bourgeois society would be absurd. It should be understood as a heuristic device, because of course Callon and Latour are also aware that the world is pre-structured by macro-actors, or more precisely: always appears to the individual in this form. On the other hand, the assumption that all actors are principally isomorphic does come quite close to one aspect of segmentary societies in Africa.

In these, as in any other societies, there are de facto differences as regards wealth, prestige and influence. The right to be different is in fact unchallenged here. But at the same time some of the attributes of difference are extremely ephemeral. The instruments with which the actors try to build on asymmetries that seem advantageous to them are awfully weak and transient. No one succeedes in developing a durable power machinery to perpetuate existing dependencies.

Callon and Latour's "blackbox" metaphor can be aptly applied in segmentary societies: macro-actors immediately depend on opportunities and means of translating the viewpoints and interests of potential followers into something that is to their own advantage. They then try to bundle these ideas and lock them away in black boxes, so that at least for a while, everyone regards reality thus defined as perfectly natural. At best no one hits on the idea of questioning the state of affairs and opening these boxes to re-sort the contents in a way that might be more advantageous for them. The maximum advantage for these new actors who challenge the established reality definitions would be to open new passage points obligatory for everyone else.

In other words, the point here is that in segmentary societies, every group of followers has to constantly reconstitute itself politically without the support of any device which would give this process a notion of objectivity. Among the Lemwareng during the rainy season, when everyone goes to the fields every day, this state of affairs is directly visible: all the men and women stand in front of their houses practically every morning and consider which invitation to collective work they should follow. Besides the reciprocity norm, factors influencing their decision include debts, calculated advantages, feelings of liking or dislike, but never inescapable dependencies laid down in contracts. As in other spheres of their society, there is no perpetual macro-actor involved here. It is hardly possible for anyone who has reached above-average wealth to multiply it through others, since there is no social machinery or technology available for this purpose.

On a different level, the spirit mediums of the Lemwareng also illustrate this distinction between differentiated societies − which have substantial durable devices to black-box reality definitions and petrify social relations − and other, less differentiated societies − which have fewer such devices. The always female mediums re-sort old, conventional and taken-for-granted notions; they bring in new, unfamiliar ideas from the outside world with the help of foreign spirits that possess them. However, they are only able to tie these up in the above-mentioned black boxes as long as they have the consent and help of their clientele. They have no additional devices at hand to seal the boxes and assemble them in such a way as to forge more durable obligatory passage points. If their new solutions and reality definitions are no longer convincing, the people can stay away and choose other passage points without coming to any harm. In the same way that the political leaders of the Lemwareng have no enforcement staff, the mediums too have no machinery − like a church, for instance − to perpetuate their spiritual leadership. On the Lebu mountain where the Lemwareng live, people lose allies and followers as quickly as wealth; everything is as transient as the mud houses. Obligatory passage points change more easily and frequently than in other societies.

The most refined black boxes ever invented to build obligatory passage points are perhaps bureaucracy and technology, which often go together and distinguish modern society. Bureaucracy with its system of keeping files excludes any idea or occurence that cannot enter a file and thus become a true "case." It works like this: to be successful, any attempt at re-defining reality has first to become a case. However, in most instances the translation into a case is unavoidably equivalent to the loss of the re-definition of reality. Hence bureaucratic black-boxing is virtually immune. Similarly technological systems encapsulate social relations which thus become opaque and appear unalterable, since their *raison d'être* looks as natural and objective as the machines themselves. At the same time, though, modern society encourages change and progress more than any other society.

Market culture does not accept any final truth, but only best-selling ideas and artefacts.

Anthropologically speaking, Callon and Latour are suggesting approaching bureaucratic power machineries as though they were acephalous, segmentary societies that only allow charismatic positions of power, if any.[11] Otherwise, according to their assumption, there is an acute danger of equating power with rationality, instead of analysing its social construction and thus revealing possibilities for its deconstruction and thereby opening up alternatives.

Summing up: in the above section, I elaborated on the specific ambiguity of the modern organization which pursues deinstitutionalization while it remains − or more poignantly: in order to remain − legitimate and institutionalized. The distinction between two types of legitimating discourses was the cardinal point here: a rhetoric of representing organizing activity as something truely embedded was contrasted with a rhetoric of representing organization as a permeation of conflicting logics.

Next, I said that any kind of organization is always also an attempt at bundling up a larger number of small activities into a collective, coordinated action. This process is evidently a mechanism of political translation. However, political translation presupposes cultural translation as an attempt to find definitions and interpretations of reality which make joint decision-making possible in the first place. My proposal therefore is to speak of *politico-cultural translation* at the end of which someone has established him- or herself as an obligatory passage point for others for a while, and at least in certain contexts is allowed to speak with one voice for everybody concerned.

Seen against this background, the eminent specificity of the modern, formal organization is the durability of its black boxes. As a result of this effectiveness, the few who manage to define, occupy and control the obligatory passage points that others have to use to achieve their own goals are remarkably powerful. Micro-actors have comparatively great difficulties in challenging the dominant reality definitions. At the same time, however, the preeminent modernist discourse on equal rights encourages all attempts to challange the status quo, to bring about change and progress. Coming to terms with this new and paradox situation is perhaps the main issue in the story on Lake Transport.

Having recourse to the translation model, this section has above all made it clear that organizational change is not invariably and necessarily the result of prior changes in the institutional surroundings − these being considered to be the macro-level − to which the organization then adjusts on the

---

[11] Callon and Latour themselves do not seem to see the analogy with the segmentary society.

micro-level. Rather, the process of change that is more interesting for my argument here — and for modern society in general which is, after all, composed largely of formal organizations — works the other way round. Everything revolves around the fact that new forms of organization are created (by politico-cultural translations) which can, and indeed are meant to, change social institutions, or at least alter their relevance and meaning. A distinction between the macro- and micro-level is not possible here since the emphasis is on processes that fuse both levels.

Looking at Lake Transport from the common and popular perspective sketched in the third section, one perceives on the one hand a formal system based on instrumental rationality which is beyond anthropological analysis. On the other hand, one discerns informal networks that develop within the formal system and cause considerable damage to this system. The informal networks are thus conceived to be socio-culturally moulded and can therefore be subjected to anthropological analysis. The almost inevitable question at the end of such observations is "how can one make the two systems fit together?." In Third World studies the tacit implication is often, "how can one eradicate the informal networks."

By contrast, I believe that we must change the perspective. The decisive point is to look at how formal organization is built up from within the horizon of informal networks. We have to replace the metaphor of the yoke by the metaphor of self-entanglement. Using the vocabulary established in this section, I should now like to retell the story of Lake Transport as a story about the intercultural travel of the formal organization model.

The Story of the Lake Transport Company Retold

In a sense, the story of Lake Transport is a story of *failure*, since the re-embedding of the formal organization model does not really succeed, or at least results in something quite different from what anybody had desired. Failure is certainly not intended to mean that the model receives another meaning in the course of its transfer. That is inevitable, as the extreme example of the New Testament as a magic instrument of protection beneath the straw roofs of the Lemwareng was intended to show. Transmission always means trans-lation and trans-formation.

On the level I want to argue, success or failure can only relate to the course of the politico-cultural translation itself. If previously existing ways of smoothly switching between and productively combining divergent legitimating discourses of collective action are broken off as a result of the translation of a new model, then the translation is a failure. A failure is given when previous ways of negotiating solutions and collective actions, established institutions, and checks and balances are disturbed, while no new forms are put in their place. In this negative case, political translation (as the construction of macro-actors who can make things happen) is at odds with cultural translation (as the construction of shared ideas and the specific ability to agree on common decisions and obligatory passage points).

An Outside Political Influence

We remember the simplified version of the plot: a company is about to pass away, an externally financed rehabilitation programme is started, the company is merged with two other companies and restructured; the crisis continues, the new management is locked out, government exchanges the management; seven years later the company is still unprofitable, and the foreign experts are still there doing their rehabilitation programme. I now start the new interpretation of the story by adding one aspect that comes in at the beginning.

The economic crisis in the West African country in the late seventies and early eighties led to a change of government.[12] In 1981, a National Defence Council came to power by a *coup d'état* and began restructuring the country along socialist lines. Militant workers' councils were formed in the factories and organizations, and the executive boards of strategic enterprises were temporarily replaced by bodies in which the lower-income groups had a guaranteed majority. There were sporadic, violent riots against representatives of the old elite; in the military these culminated in the spontaneous execution of some officers by the lower ranks.

The revolutionary, socialist zeal did not last long, however. In 1983, the new rulers acceded to the demands of the World Bank and the International Monetary Fund in order to gain their support. The socialist managing boards of the state-owned companies were dissolved again in 1983/84. Their "workers' councils" were renamed "revolutionary committees" and integrated into the machinery of the state. Each department of a company elected four shop stewards from among its staff; in turn, these departmental representatives directly appointed four representatives for the entire company, and one of these became the chairman of the company revolutionary committee. At Lake Transport this practice actually continued, at least in theory, until 1992. Unlike trade unions, this revolutionary committee was supposed to represent the public interest, or to put it in the words of one of the people involved, they "helped the government."

Seen in retrospect and from a bird's-eye view, one can say that the elite that ruled before 1981 had sawn off the branch they had been sitting on. They had failed in their task of steering the country's industrialization pro-

---

[12]   Carola Lentz kindly helped me to avoid factual mistakes in this section.

cess. Above all, however, they had failed to establish the envisaged trans-formation of social relations as a legitimate and desirable objective in the semantic fields (Berger and Luckmann, 1966) of the people affected. To use the terminology of Callon and Latour, the elite no longer translated the will of their followers, and thus lost their legitimacy. This is why the fighters of 1981, who were recruited from the lower classes, especially from urban society and from youth, found it relatively easy to oust the old elite from their role of macro-actor and controller of the obligatory passage points.

Under the influence of both their origins and the expectations of their followers, the new rulers were sensitive to the sorry state of the public administration and the economy, as regards both efficiency and the degree to which it was embedded in political-social and cultural life. They felt it necessary, at least in the early stages, to stabilize their role by trying to link up the society's formal organization with the established institutions. A major issue in this context was the shaping and legitimation of asymmetri-cal relations, i. e. how to link earnings and status with performance. The central political symbol was, of course, an anti-corruption campaign.

On the company level as analysed here, this strategy resulted in two new levels of authority being imported: the revolutionary committees and the socialist managing boards (although the latter did not last long). Yet these were hardly any closer to the legitimacy discourse of the complex society (which favours the *principle of ascribed difference*) than other forms of for-mal organization (which favour the *principle of equal rights*). Patron-client relations and forms of solidarity justified by primary relations look just as counterproductive to a socialist formal organization of society as they do to the capitalist model. The socialist boards were therefore the first attempt at rooting out existing patronage relations − prior to the 1984 reconstruc-tion of the Lake Transport Company under the supervision of an expatriate consulting firm.

We can conclude: between 1979 and 1986, the parent company and the state machinery undertook two attempts at giving direction to the process of translating the model of formal organization. Although these attempts were ideologically opposite, they were nonetheless very similar in their dis-tance from the dominant legitimacy discourse. The introduction of socialist managing boards and revolutionary committees pursued mainly one objec-tive: to allow the formal rationality of organization to unfold without hin-drance. Similarly, the primary aim of the plan to restructure Lake Transport under the supervision of foreign experts was to prevent the spontaneous, uncontrolled appropriation of the model. The intention was that in the future, the practice should be determined by the formal structure, in order to secure the success of the company in this way. Trans-mission and not trans-formation was the target. As one might have expected, new conflicts arose and old ones escalated whenever these attempts at planned control, which were one-sidedly oriented towards the efficiency principle, contradicted the notions and interests of the people concerned.

At the same time we have to understand that the model of formal organization was not and is not simply forced on the actors. Rather, the actors − all of them − actively take part in building up formal structures. The individuals and coalitions compete with each other for influence and resources. And they take up the discourse of equal rights and formal structure as an argument in this struggle.

The Inevitable Recovery of Patronage

With the backing of the parent company, the responsible Transport Ministry and the national revolutionary committee, in the years after 1986 the managing director persevered in pursuing a policy aimed at integrating all forces into the decision-making machinery of the company according to the rules of the formal structure. He also consciously tried to achieve a positive link between the formal structure on the one hand, and the semantic fields and in particular the legitimacy notions of the people concerned on the other. He was thus acting as a professional agent of modernity pursuing a rationalization programme in the (Foucauldian) sense of linking power and reason. Perhaps it was on this grounds that he liked to be referred to as "MD" for short, showing his affinity for the anglophone world of management.

As far as concrete action was concerned, he initiated round-table discussions between the revolutionary committee, the works council and the management. The aim was that elements tending to detract from the purpose of the company should be not excluded, but transformed into constructive commitment by encouraging participation. There were regular meetings between 1986 and 1991, at which important decisions were discussed. The 1990 revolutionary committee election was won for the first time by staff who considered the socialist orientation of the body to be a mistake left over from the past and who kept their distance from the former "nucleus" mentioned in the first version of the story.

Nevertheless, the managing director's efforts met with little success. While the rhetoric of commitment to the company was being cultivated at the round-table discussions, and the idea that performance should be the sole criterion of earnings was being praised as the only legitimate solution, day-to-day work had to continue. There the actors went on transforming hierarchy into patron-client relations − partly unintentionally and in some cases actually contrary to their intentions, as we shall see later − while doing their best to conceal this fact.

The example of a concrete management initiative can show where one of the initial difficulties lies when an attempt is made to divert an established type of translation. The most obvious flouting of company rules of behaviour is when members divert resources. And the crudest variant of this is when money and other valuables like fuel and spare parts are actually stolen. The euphemistic term used for this in the company jargon of Lake Transport is "leakage." A monitoring team was founded in 1986 to reduce the number and scale of such losses, which had by no means declined after the 1985 revolt. The MD introduced a rotating chairmanship in an attempt to prevent this instrument of control from also becoming a tool of coalitions. The revolutionary committee and works council were involved in the monitoring team. The hope here was that this would prevent company members who felt unfairly treated from taking their complaints to political bodies outside the company. At the same time, this measure also formed part of the rationalization programme, i. e. the reason why the professionally trained MD had been hired at Lake Transport in the first place.

The monitoring team concentrated its spot checks on the Traffic Department, since this was where the most leakages took place. One day, however, the responsible manager felt affronted because the interventions in his field of responsibility were so frequent. Furthermore, the then chairman of the team was unable to fully hide his real intentions. He is said to have been less interested in company resources than in settling an old score with the manager concerned. Some of the team's powers were thus misused and subsequently withdrawn by the MD. However, the manager of the Traffic Department still failed to get the situation under control, and the fact that he soon handed in his notice gave rise to speculation about his true role. This in turn gave his old opponent some satisfaction.

In the following years, the problem smouldered on, escalating periodically. In 1992, during my stay at Lake Transport, the losses had become so great that even the well-meaning members of the Board of Directors could no longer remain silent. New negotiations were started to revive the meanwhile defunct "monitoring team." In the meantime, however, there were conflicting ideas on the make-up of the team, who should have the authority to activate it, and who should become its chairman. The end result was a clumsy gesture of punitive power: precisely what the MD with his modern ideas had sought to avoid.

From the viewpoint of a simple employee, it seemed in the end that anyone who was high enough in the hierarchy could carry out any controls he or she wanted. It was insinuated that a self-styled controller will always ensure that he finds the rule-breakers anywhere but in his own sphere of responsibility. Some maintained that the whole idea was to divert attention away from the leakages in certain people's own territory and to direct suspicion towards other coalitions. This meant that the attempt at rationalization by identifying all forces with the object of the company had not only simply failed; it had also provided further proof that completely different principles persisted and were still effective.

The failure initially has to do with the following translation: while the discourse of formal organization is based on the assumption that performance is monitored by the hierarchy and, conversely, hierarchy is legitimated by performance, these two dimensions fall apart in practice at Lake Transport. Whenever there is talk of control or monitoring, the managers automatically think of surveilling the use of resources by the lower ranks. Their conception of monitoring is that of a manager casually walking through the firm and catching perhaps a ticket-seller cheating, some fork-lift drivers playing cards in the shade of a tree, or a mechanic asleep under a truck.

Within the top levels of management, on the other hand, it would seem extremely out of place if anyone should try to systematically instruct colleagues on the same level or directly below him and then monitor their performance. Politeness and respect for the honour of a person on the same or a similar level make it impossible to treat him or her like an immature or suspicious person. Similarly, the alternative of using monitoring instruments in such a way that the person applying the instrument is monitored at the same time while he tries to control others, is not taken up for the same reason.

It is the function of hierarchy to separate different levels in the division of labour and to only link them at precisely defined points, in order to make it possible to work undisturbed on tasks. At Lake Transport, this function is exploited as far as possible, so that in the end, the points linking the levels become invisible or appear arbitrary, thus increasing uncertainty instead of reducing it.

What this practice boils down to is that no member of staff can be monitored in the sense of the official goal by his or her immediate superior, even though the latter might be directly responsible for that employee's actions. This also means that the superior is unable to prove his (it is always men) own performance either, especially if his main job is to supervise precisely this member of staff. In such a situation, the best way to win colleagues for a task is to engage in either symmetrical reciprocity relations or patron-client relations, depending on social distance. By acting in this manner, the managers of Lake Transport are suspected of undermining, whether they intend to or not, the claim to legitimacy of their own high position, as well as that of the formal structure as such, based as they are on the principle of equal rights and opportunities. And it makes it all the more difficult to convince anyone in the company that earnings and status improvements should really be a reward for excellent performance. This is the first cause of the peculiar combination of hierarchy and patronage at Lake Transport.

A second cause of this process is perhaps more intentional – or at least shows a different direction of intention. When the new heads of department started work, the hopes that had been expressed by all sides in the rhetoric that had accompanied the new beginning were not fulfilled. Rather, like their predecessors after the merger of the three companies in 1984, they were greeted with massive distrust. All kinds of obstacles were placed in the path of the "intruders," and attempts were made to discredit them by way of skilfully launched rumours. This animosity forced the new players to look for allies wherever they could find them, and especially lower down in the hierarchy. For it must have seemed to them that there was no other way of making a success of their work at Lake Transport. Conversely, the potential clients had achieved precisely what they wanted: they had evaded the hierarchy and instead opened a discourse in which they held the better cards.

In such circumstances, however, the same vicious circle inevitably develops as before: by having to fall back on informal collaborators, a manager is himself contributing to the development of further clientele relations. Their biggest effect then consists not in the eradication of clientelism – which in some cases perhaps really was the true intention – but rather in distrust being further nurtured and becoming habitualized. In the final analysis, the motives for the establishment of patron-client relations are of little importance for practice. After a certain period of time, it is impossible anyway to tell whether the motive was "good intentions" to strengthen the hierarchy, or perhaps to undermine it, which is, after all, a good intention from a different perspective. All that remains is that the people involved can interpret virtually any event as evidence of the effect of coalitions undermining the interests of the company. There seems to be no easy way out of this self-perpetuating interpretation pattern.

Up to now, we have concerned ourselves with the observation that all attempts at establishing a formal hierarchy and thus legitimating asymmetrical relations with the criteria of the discourse of equal rights and opportunities, usually led to a strengthening of elements of the discourse of ascribed difference – i. e. patron-client relations – although this remained hidden. In the above examples, the initiative for the establishment of formal structures came from the top. In some cases the recourse to patron-client relations also came from the top. In all cases the intentions pursued by the actors did not make any difference. Whatever one does, it can and will be interpreted as proof of dubious machinations intended to undermine the formal structure.

The initiative for the establishment of formal structures, in fact, comes just as much from simple employees. And this aspect is even more important for the argument on self-entanglement in formal structures. Within the interpretation attempted here I now come to the third cause of the transformation of formal organizations.

Political Translations

People who felt disadvantaged reacted to the prevailing distrust at Lake Transport in two ways. These presumably exist in various forms in every company in the world, but seem to develop particularly well in this West African state enterprise. The first technique is having all aspects of personnel policy laid down in a catalogue of regulations, so that all the responsible manager needs to do in a specific situation is to look it up. In this context, making exceptional payments for outstanding performance is a particularly sensitive issue.

In early 1988, the story got around that the company had bought new furniture for one of its employees. Some of his colleagues found this piece of news scandalous and forced the management to call a special meeting. Many months of toing and froing followed, all of which — in scrupulous application of the bureaucratic rules — was documented in files (which I was able to study). Finally it was declared that this had been a rumour started by people who had felt disadvantaged since the events of 1985.

Precisely because the story is most probably based on fabrication, it demonstrates particularly clearly the mechanism of self-fulfilling prophecy that is effective here. The criticism levelled is that if anyone deserves to receive furniture, then it should be the person with the longest service. Otherwise a company agreement must be concluded first, in which the works council, the revolutionary committee and management agree on the criteria by which furniture may be handed out. Since none of the regulations defined according to this logic were followed in the present case, it could safely be concluded that this was yet another case of a swindle.

This line of argument on the part of the critics represents a remarkable renunciation of patron-client etiquette otherwise held in such high esteem and often practiced by them. The customary privilege of the patron to bind a client even more closely to his or her favour by higher *remuneration* is categorized here as favouritism. Since this category does not make much sense in the vocabulary of patronage, we must conclude that a change of discourse has taken place.[13] On the other hand, according to the rules of the discourse of formal organization, it is legitimate and desirable to honour a player for exceptional performance. Company management does not require symmetry as an end in itself, but only to the extent that it raises or

---

[13] An additional explanation might be necessary at this point. In every society and in particular in every formal organization, people frequently pursue other aims than the ones to which they will openly admit. I am not describing this as a peculiarity of Lake Transport or calling it reprehensible. Rather, it seems to be a fundamental prerequisite of freedom and autonomy. In symbolic interactionism, the possibility of acting a part has been seen to depend on role distancing, without which an individual cannot develop his or her unique identity.

at least stabilizes efficiency. Yet it is precisely this context that the staff want to ignore when they demand not fair managers but, strictly speaking, bureaucrats who do nothing but passionately follow the symmetry demands of rational bureaucracy.

In other words, neither of the representational models justifies the exclusion of performance bonuses. Only the particular link between the two models, the type of syncretism selected, leads to a situation in which nothing more can function in this direction. If excellent performance is to be rewarded, this has to be done secretly within the discourse of ascribed difference, where its effect will again be a source of distrust. Which brings us back to the beginning of the furniture story, where a deviation from the rule – if necessary an invented one – serves as proof of the machinations of coalitions that are ruining the company.

It cannot be excluded that the employees who protested against the alleged furniture purchase in the first place simply wanted to embarrass another coalition which, from their viewpoint, was more successful. Nor can we know the true background to the gifts of furniture, which did indeed take place, at least in other cases. However, none of these speculations are really relevant to my argument. The point I am trying to make is that such intentions are not necessary to lead to the present result. Irrespective of the intentions of the actors concerned, the suspicion arises, according to the principle of self-fulling prophecy, that the arguments of formal rationality are being used to play false.

The second above-mentioned technique used by simple employees to cope with the prevailing atmosphere of distrust consists in roping in official bodies from outside the company. The usually written complaints to the local revolutionary committees, or sometimes straight to the Secretary of State for Revolutionary Committees at the "Castle" (as the seat of the Party headquarters and government are called even in the party-line press), always follow the same pattern. It is claimed that the action of a certain manager was self-privileging and arbitrary, not legitimated by any fair criterion such as performance, loyalty or length of service. The outside revolutionary committees seldom reject complaints with the advice that an attempt first be made to settle the matter internally using the available arbitration mechanisms. Rather, the management is usually called upon to make a written statement or to come for a meeting at the Castle.

Here is an example. In June 1989, the director of a north-eastern harbour reported to the local police the theft of certain articles from the spare parts store. He accused a technician who had just returned to the firm's main workshop at the southern harbour. The man was questioned by the police, who then handed the case over to the courts. A few weeks later, the Castle, evidently at the request of the person who had been accused, suggested to the MD that the charges be dropped and the case settled internally in an amicable fashion. The Castle perhaps alleged that it was probably a case of internal intrigue that was unworthy of the courts. This time, however, the company withstood the pressure. It made a tactical statement to the effect that it did not wish to interrupt the proceedings at this late stage; otherwise the impression might be created that Lake Transport did not trust the legal institutions. More than six months later, the court found the accused not guilty.

As might be expected, this was not the end of the case. The formerly accused man felt that the wind had turned in his favour and now claimed in another letter to the Castle that he had been the victim of intrigue from the outset and that a certain colleague had even tried to bribe the court to get him out of the way. He also claimed a certain sum of money on the grounds that he had had additional expenses as a result of having to travel to and from the court. The company in turn tried to prove that some of the alleged expenses were fictitious. For example, the dates on the submitted hotel bills did not fit the dates of the court hearings. As a result, the man was again accused of acting with fraudulent intent. And so the story goes on and on until a new one is found. The fact that the courts were brought in shows how intractable the situation is. The actors do not expect reliable support from any side. They feel hopelessly entangled in a jungle of shady dealings.

Contrary to the declared intention of wanting to create conditions based on equal rights, the simple employees' appeals to political institutions reduce the efficiency and legitimacy of formal structures. As in the previous example, where the actors were ostensibly fighting for bureaucratic principles, here too, the intention does not seem important; i. e. whether a cunningly disguised appeal is made to the discourse of equal rights, while the true, covert aims being pursued are firmly within the realm of the discourse of ascribed difference. This kind of politics can never be completely excluded. Even if someone acts with serious intent within the official discourse, no one will believe him and he will bring nothing but suspicion on himself.

Patron Managers and Client Employees

In this case study, translation consists mainly in incorporating the formal structure related to the principle of equal rights into negotiation processes related to the principle of ascribed difference, processes that did not declare themselves as such. The selected examples involve tactical shifts between hierarchy and patronage.

One reason for the inevitability with which patron-client relations develop at Lake Transport is that the formal structure lacks legitimacy in the eyes of the actors. One of the main causes of this legitimacy deficit is the justification of status and earnings primarily by performance, as derived from the logic of the formal structure.

For them, a person's status is for the most part an ascribed dimension belonging to the discourse of community, and may not be directly subordinated to the cool deliberations of economic efficiency. Although it also seems to be possible and desirable to improve status by performance in the local legitimacy discourse, higher status is mostly achieved by redistributive generosity. For this reason, the actors translate the company hierarchy into personal reciprocity obligations and appropriate it in this way.

On the other hand, this transformation process also has an instrumental dimension which is perhaps more important. In public, all actors endorse only the representational model of the formal structure because they would suffer disadvantages if they did not. Conversely, they also expect advantages from this behaviour. Above all, however, falling back on the arguments of the formal structure is often the only way they can respond to the ploys of the other players. This practice develops a special dynamism of its own which generates distrust as a self-fulfilling prophecy.

If the new figure of the patron-manager created by politico-cultural translation adhered mainly to personal loyalties, and allowed himself to be publicly controlled by the clientele according to this yardstick, we would be dealing with a slightly altered patron. His action would be primarily sanctioned by the legitimacy discourse of the complex society centered around the principle of ascribed difference, which would continuously be slightly altered in the course of public negotiation processes − probably in the direction of the legitimacy discourse centered around the principle of equality.

However, the patron-manager whom we have got to know here hides his role as a patron. He officially relates his action to the rules of formal organization. In this way, he can improve his position by pursuing the aims of a patron with the means of a manager and vice versa. For example, he can sporadically apply the performance principle to the clientele as a criterion of earnings. In this way, the patron can violate his obligation to protect and care for his clientele with impunity, and successfully transform generalized reciprocity into negative reciprocity − at least this will be the effective insinuation.

A literally hybrid asymmetry of this kind can only be successfully asserted if the people affected by such tactics themselves actively participate in the game. In public, clients act only as employees and do not throw any arguments from the representational model of patronage into the debate. Having chosen such a position, it seems ill-advised to publicly demand that the patron fulfils his obligation to care for his clientele, or to praise one's own loyalty as a client. Anyone doing so would only discredit himself.

Instead, clients − like patron-managers − can use arguments from the context of formal structure to defend and improve their chances. Whenever the patron-manager stresses the performance principle in the sense of the formal organization, the client-employee can counter by referring to the principle of symmetry and coherence. According to this principle, all cases must be treated equally. For this reason there can theoretically be no performance sanctions without a set of bureaucratic regulations. As the examples have shown, this set of bureaucratic regulations is interpreted above all as a weapon in the struggle of the individual actors and coalitions for interests rooted in the principle of ascribed difference.

Up to this point, the analysis presented here corresponds to Callon and Latour's bilateral translation model. On the one hand, the actors translate the foreign, "uncivilized" idea − according to which earnings must be exclusively related to performance, and status is detached from redistributive generosity − into their institutional context. On the other hand, through this translation they transform − altogether intentionally − the existing allocation rules of earnings and status, which they derive from the historically more strongly established system of patronage. The emergence of a form of patronage that can sporadically and highly effectively fall back on a formal structure is something fundamentally different from a form of patronage that cannot.

Behind the backs of the actors, these translation processes lead to an undermining of communication in the company, which in turn leads to an erosion of trust. In the end, even serious attempts to keep to the rules of the formal structure are not recognized, but even appear suspicious. Conversely, attempts to secretly continue to orientate actions towards the system of patronage and clientelism also repeatedly fail. In short, the conditions for translating the will and ideas of individual, small actors and bundling them together to form a common project prove to be problematic at Lake Transport.

I have proposed seeking the reason for this in the following: the intercultural translation of some new and foreign elements into a well established, taken-for-granted, and hence familiar context can impede the local, political translation and bundling of micro-actors to form a macro-actor. This in turn seems to be connected to the fact that formal organization itself is a model of translation of many small, particular ideas into a common, larger idea and action. If this model is transferred into a different institutional context, then we are dealing with a special case of institutional translation, *the translation of a political translation model*. Under the historical and socio-structural circumstances given in the case of the West African organization, this initially leads to an obstruction of all forms of political translation.

The socio-structural principle at work in the background here is embeddedness. The only transactions that appear legitimate and desirable are those that forge a link with comprehensive sociality, thereby confirming a kind of invisible bond that holds the actors together.[14] Such a dominance of communitarianism makes companies that base their legitimacy on the rationalistic model of formal organization appear in an unfavourable light — the model is, after all, specifically designed to de-institutionalize. On the other hand, communitarianism favours coalitions that are legitimated by an ethos of reciprocity and face-to-face obligations.

Not until the economic, communal and political logics have become mutually permeated is formal organization legitimated as a model of political translation. Yet it would seem that it is difficult to initiate this permeation via the introduction of formal organization if the latter in turn can only emerge as a consequence of this permeation. Nevertheless, everyone is busily working on precisely this, because "we have to do business as business is done." It seems that no-one can fully evade this trend and find a better way out.

Interjection

The story of Lake Transport indicated that not every accretion of new and old ideas and artefacts must necessarily be a success or at least not an immediate success. A different issue arose as a result. Could it be that occasionally the power generated by the formal organization model blocks the local politico-cultural translation processes and thus prevents the emergence of legitimate macro-actors? Is this the area where we have to look for answers to the question raised in the prologue: i. e. what went wrong with the patchwork? This question does not fit smoothly into the present debate on creating otherness through anthropological writing. But then, having no answer, what is so attractive about the assumption that translations are always successful, that the local and the translocal naturally enrich each other by hybridization and that therefore alienation is no longer an issue? I believe, we are dealing here with a "control point" (Mary Douglas) that directs attention and supresses questions which would disturb absolute presuppositions and cherished master ideas.

Façades/Practices

However, the topic of this essay is more modest. I have discussed the translation of the modern notion of formal organization into an African context in order to learn something about this notion in general: by looking at it

---

[14] Dettmar (1995) shows how in Nigeria the rhetoric of communitarianism is the only legitimate medium to present private entrepreneurship to the public.

from afar. This anthropological technique helps us to grasp nuances which are otherwise easily overlooked. It is now time to turn the view back to the citadels of western cultures as they are at home.

Formal Structure as Ceremonial Façade

My whole argument was based on the assumption that all social practice is traced back by the actors to patterns which give it meaning and legitimacy. However, because the available orientation patterns of a culture represent opposing semantic fields and institutional orders, and therefore contradict each other, each actor is given various opportunities — there is always a considerable amount of scope. This scope is substantially increased by a second, perhaps even more consequential phenomenon: the possibility to pick up and translate into the local discourse new ideas and artifacts not existent in local time/space but circulating in a global discourse. In turn, it follows that the significance of the orientation patterns lies not only in restricting action opportunities, but also in being used by the actors post hoc to attribute new ways of doing things with legitimacy and meaning.

To use the language of neo-institutionalism common in organizational studies, it is said after Karl E. Weick (1969) that the two levels are "loosely coupled." On the first level there are the concrete actions, on the second the recipes for action, ideologies, symbols and myths which give people's actions transrational meaning and the necessary recognition. In the case of formal organization, however, several selected orientation patterns are laid down in a condensed, intentional way in the *formal structures*: the hierarchy and the overall system of rules which are supposed to steer the work routine, i. e. the action level or practice.

John Meyer and Brian Rowan (1977) attempt a more precise definition of the state of "loose coupling." To emphasize that practice is not determined — in the narrow sense of the word — by formal structures, although these structures are more than an empty sham or a swindle, the two authors introduce the metaphor "ceremonial façade". Although Meyer and Rowan only intended this term to cover the formal structures of so-called "institutionalized organizations" (meaning, for example, hospitals and schools as opposed to companies), it is widely agreed today that a more general phenomenon has been identified here. Although companies serving the maximization of capital are different in significant respects, even in their case it would seem helpful not to lose sight of the loose coupling of the two levels.

The use of the word *façade* to describe the outer appearance of a collective actor takes up a metaphor from architecture. The face of a building directed towards the street as a public space is meant for the eye of the observer, it is said that the façade is "a gift for the street." It reveals little about how the building looks like inside. A building's façade can be changed several times, and, vice versa, the same type of façade can be used for many different buildings in different periods. The façade is just as important as the building itself, albeit with reference to a different purpose, namely the design of public spaces and the images of actors. The façade achieves its effect by the ceremonial expression of ingeniously selected cosmological ideas and values. Both, the façade and the building, must also be securely fixed together, technically speaking; they will collapse if they separate. The one cannot exist without the other.

If the type of façade is not entirely derived from the technical makeup of the building but rather ceremonially displays the aesthetic expectations of (at least some) observers, then even in architecture one can borrow Meyer and Rowan's terminology and aptly speak of "ceremonial façades." They stand in the middle, between functional and aesthetic requirements, and are not fully integrated into either. The point of calling a façade "ceremonial" is to emphasize that in contrast to the everyday language of modernity one does not want to talk about shrewd camouflage, nor about the mask as the opposite to the inner self, nor about the scenes that supposedly conceal "real" life which only takes place behind the scenes. Analyzing ceremonial façades is to look at appearances, surfaces and scenes in their own right, as phenomena loosely coupled to social processes and the identity of the actors. Like post-modernist architecture, which tries to overcome the modernist denunciation of the façade, post-modernist social science sees itself above all as post-structuralist, i. e. more concerned with appearances, surfaces and images in their own right, not just as depictions of something else.

In other words, according to Meyer and Rowan − at least implicitly, since they do not elaborate this point − the analogy between building and organization is the following: concerning the outside appearance, the aesthetic requirements from the field of architecture correspond to the shared ideas about how a sound organization should look like, how it should formally be structured. Here the cosmology and the institutions of the society come into play as a frame of reference. Although one cannot fully deduce the formal structure from the institutions, it must correspond sufficiently with them in order, in this way, to receive its vital legitimacy. Formal organizational structure is thus classified as a legitimating façade.

Concerning the inside, the technical makeup of the building corresponds to the practice of an organization. Practice means functional requirements, efficiency, survival and simply keeping things going. In the same way that a façade does not reveal much about the inside of a house, we cannot read everything about practice from the formal structure of an organization − i. e. from the abstract regulations on action routines and the command hierarchy that is supposed to be functionally related to these regulations and to practice. However, like any other metaphor the façade metaphor contains a distortion: while organizational practice is a rather messy process, the technical makeup of a building is usually uncompromisingly structured.

After one has accepted this way of distinguishing between façade and building and the analogy to organization façade and practice, the interesting question is how these two aspects or levels relate to each other. I can start again with architecture.

Some modernist buildings consciously and radically do without all forms of ornament. The "FFF ideology" ("form follows function") emphasizes sober functionality and claims to have overcome the façade as a supposedly pre-modern and superfluous phenomenon. Yet the distinction between function and symbolic meaning cannot be overcome arbitrarily. The outer appearance of a modernistic building ends up as a façade anyway, despite all its self-claims to pure functionalism. It is simply a rationalistic façade which, like any other façade, relates to the ideology of the observer and the intended reputation. It does not result directly from the functions of the building. Like any façade it is there primarily to furnish legitimacy and identity and not functional efficiency. Functional efficiency can be achieved with many different appearances. This quintessence of the façade is clearly expressed by the mirror façade. The observer's look is returned, so that his or her assumptions about the world are hardly called into question by the experience. A fascinating development of the mirror façade is to be found in Japanese projects of "interactive architecture," where house façades are huge video screens showing what is going on in the flow of urban life. But how can we use this image for organizations? How to envisage the relation between practice and organizational façade?

Ceremonial Façades and Practice

Through the metaphor of the ceremonial façade, neo-institutionalism has succeeded in bringing back into the analysis of formal organizations Max Weber's second major topic after the rationalization of the world: the legitimacy of social forms. Modern organizations − like the modernistic façades of the architects − do not exist and survive simply and exclusively because they are functional and effective. They must also be anchored in the institutions; they must be legitimate. By definition this involves being embedded into a semantic field which only indirectly has anything to do with purposive rationality and efficiency. However, these two dimensions of organization are evidently not mutually independent. It is helpful to separate them analytically, since they point to different discourses. But in the final analysis, the interesting questions refer to the various crossings and combinations between these discourses. This is the point I am trying to make here.

John Meyer and Brian Rowan (1977) concentrate on western society. They neither explain nor question the fact that this society is thoroughly rationalized and differentiated; they take it for granted. In their pioneering essay they speak of the institutions of this type of society as "rationalized institutional structures" which are considered to be "myths," myths in the sense of narratives of certain events and of certain aspects of the world which are of crucial importance for a culture. If we disregard the slight terminological mess of this argument, the authors say that institutions are linked to myths. Myths are narratives which make institutions appear proper, adequate, rational, necessary, and, I would add, natural. To be legitimate, organizations must incorporate institutions as their "building blocks." In fact, these blocks can be assembled with little entrepreneurial energy into formally structured organizations.

On the one hand, this position has helped to lead the analysis of organizational change out of the blind alley of trying to explain organization solely as a set of purpose-related and rational instruments for achieving an objective. Along this route one inevitably ends up with a discussion of unintended consequences, "underlife," and the cultural patterns of those who seem to deviate from the official goal.

On the other hand, however, any one-sided emphasis on the discourse of institutionalization and legitimacy might induce organization studies to remove organizational change from the organizations themselves, so that in fact other disciplines become responsible for it (DiMaggio and Powell 1991, p. 27 and passim; Friedland and Alford, 1991, p. 243). There is also a temptation in this paradigm to underestimate how formal rationality comes into being as a source of legitimacy in the first place, how it works, how it manages to last and how it is part of a global discourse that can be tapped by any actor around the world. This temptation probably has to do with the enthusiasm about the (re)discovery that rationality functions above all as a legitimating *myth* and consequently is disseminated mainly via irrationality.

Max Weber already made a clear reference to this, and his entire theory lives precisely on this paradoxical relationship between rationality and irrationality. In a footnote to the *Protestant Ethic*, he writes: "If this essay contributes to anything, then hopefully towards revealing all the diversity of the only ostensibly unequivocal concept of the 'rational'" (1976; author's translation from the German original, 1972, p. 35). Or later on (German original, p. 62): "At this point we are particularly interested in the origin of that irrational element that lies in this and every concept of 'vocation'" (*Berufung*). Weber is writing here about the Protestant concept of vocation, according to which a person exists for his business and not vice versa, so that the rational capitalist spirit is based on irrational "vocation fulfilment" (*Berufserfüllung*).

The most condensed expression of the paradoxical relationship between rationality and irrationality can be found in Calvinist teaching, as presented by Weber. Anyone who wishes to influence his fate, in particular his fate after death, by his own deeds, is discredited by Calvinism as a magician. The only person who is rational is the person who draws the ultimate conclusions from his eternally unchangeable inability to recognize God's will. This means that his deeds cannot be a *means* of influencing his state of grace, but only *signs* of the same – which can of course also be deceptive. If, however, these signs spread among the people, under the premises of Calvinism they can only do this via imitation, since otherwise it would again be magic.

Meyer and Rowan's (Calvinist) definition of intentional organization structures as ceremonial façades – i. e. ritual reproductions of institutionalized orientation patterns that are generally regarded as rational and legitimate in the surrounding society – can now be critically extended. I have applied the concept of ceremonial façade outside the western world, where dramatic transformation processes are taking place, in order to bring it back to western society.

For it makes a considerable difference whether the myth of rationalization – declaring that it is possible to formally rationalize the world – is at the centre of the actors' world view or somewhere out on the fringe. An observation made earlier on can be reinforced by this distinction: the difference between non-modern and modern societies does not lie in the fact that the organizations of one society (e. g. clans) are embedded and therefore irrational, while the organizations of the other (e. g. companies) are disembedded and therefore rational. It is ultimately impossible to entirely deinstitutionalize a practice, i. e. to restrict it to its inherent rules, because every form of purposive rationality always assumes a given, transrational meaning. Rather, the difference is that most forms of social organization in modern society are legitimated in the main by the myth of formal rationalization.

The crucial point here has to do with the special type of institutional anchorage that is involved. Institutionalization based on the rationality myth results in ongoing purposive-rational processes of change, which, paradoxicaly, are considered legitimate precisely because they deinstitutionalize established ways of doing things. In this way, the myth of formal rationalization gives the modern world a fundamental ambiguity which distinguishes it from other societies and constitutes its historical "improbability" (Mühlmann [in his essay on Max Weber], 1966, p. 13): deinstitutionalization has become institutionalized. This dialectic of rationalization, mentioned above as the intended but never completed confluence of façade and function, is one of the central themes of Michel Foucault, whom I shall briefly bring in here for clarification and support of my argument.

In *Discipline and Punish* (Foucault, 1977), he describes, for example, how in modern prisons disciplining as a repressive measure has become invisible and simultaneously much more effective. The authorities began to subject the measure to a logic that was taken from its intended effect, instead of being antagonistically contrary to it, as in the times of absolutism. If prison inmates regularly engage in productive work, their own action seems to them to be only determined by the inner logic of the work, and the true effect − i. e. that they are being disciplined − no longer strikes them as an act of repression. They are more likely to experience this activity as a relief from the monotonous isolation of the cell and hence participate actively in their own disciplining. In the same way, a "true politician's" power is based on his committing his followers to himself with the chains of their own ideas. By linking the end of this chain with the "order of reason," he makes the chain invisible and all the more durable (Foucault 1977, pp. 242 ff). If rationalization is the central characteristic of modernity, Foucault deciphered the meaning of this ambiguous process for us.

The particular manner of creating legitimacy via reason, can easily slip through the net of organization studies, as long as we concentrate our attention on embeddedness. This has been recognized within neo-institutionalism. In their introduction to the 1991 reader, DiMaggio and Powell, for example, underline the important challenge represented by Friedland and Alford's contribution. These two authors show that as far as the characteristic feature of the modern society is concerned, the issue is not a choice between institutionaliztion or deinstitutionalization, but rather "the appropriate relationship between institutions," and the question of "by which institutional logic different activities should be regulated and to which categories of persons they should apply" (DiMaggio and Powell 1991, p. 30; Friedland and Alford 1991, pp. 256 and elsewhere).

If this is true, however, then in addition to the loose coupling between practice and formal structure, conceived as a ceremonial façade, to which Meyer and Rowan have referred so insistently, there is a second loose coupling: between the formal structure of an organization − still conceived as a ceremonial façade − and its institutional surroundings. And indeed, in the line of argument of the previous section I constantly had to imply this second loose coupling to present the story of Lake Transport. It can now be outlined more precisely, and the harvest of our excursion to the West African lake can be brought home.

In every organization's environment there are several institutionalized orders, meaning above all the societal spheres of politics, the economy, community and the family, as well as culture, religion and science. Each of these institutional orders has its own, corresponding definitions of reality − meaning systems of classifications and symbols, as well as action models that give practice its meaning. They also involve more fundamental institutions such as the concept of the self or of formal rationalization itself, which is a prerequisite for legitimating the differentiation between various logics of action. But since there are insoluble conflicts between the various semantic fields of a society, and every action can be related to various orientation patterns, this gives the actors a certain amount of scope − albeit full of ambiguities − for micropolitical processes in which to settle conflicts, modify their power positions, and change their world.

Within the process of these negotiations, heterogeneous social institutions are brought in to justify practice − albeit to a varying extent, in different ways, and with varying interests. In any social context, creative and entrepreneurial as well as all political action consists primarily in attempting to untie traditional conventions and alliances, and subsequently to re-tie them differently, while of course paying attention to personal advantage. The most important source of change is provided by globally floating ideas and artefacts that are selected and translated into local political arenas by potential macro-actors. The formal organizations of the market society are the ideal place for such politico-cultural translations. The world of formal organization is the home of the idea of rationalization, which can annul old privileges and break up well-practised solution methods.

The bare existence of a formal organization is evidence that some actors have been able in this way to launch legitimating discourses which then developed into intentional formal structures. In the image of politico-cultural translation, these actors have succeeded in tying up several definitions of reality in black boxes, in order to keep them out of reach of the others. They have succeeded in establishing an obligatory passage point for many others who now have to pass through this point to achieve their goals: to find employment, to improve their reputation, to obtain a research grant, to have a text published, to cross a bridge or a national border or to be admitted to heaven.

The way formal organizations are constructed also means that as a rule they are composed of several black boxes, certain of which are considered illegitimate by some of the people concerned. The latter may at times not be able to do much about this, because they either do not have any adequate alternative passage points or do not recognize them, or else regard them as unrealistic. At some time or other an organization dies or at least radically changes if the lack of legitimacy and the resulting amount of dissent increase above a certain point, or simply because someone has opend a new passage point which appears more suitable.

However, there is more to this observation than the possible distinction between legitimate and surviving organizations on the one hand and illegitimate and perishing ones on the other. The fact that all organizations contain some elements which are considered illegitimate by some actors − illegitimate because these elements work against their interests and/or violate some of their ethical principles – means that a constant debate and a permanent struggle takes place to change or reinterpret these organizational elements. This state of affairs, about which we learned by following the journey of the idea of modern organization to Africa, has an important impact on what I have called after Meyer and Rowan the ceremonial façade.

If the formal organizational structure inevitably contains contested aspects, the organizational façade cannot be ceremonial in an absolute sense. Some actors, at some occasions, at some time will in fact oppose a number of aspects and implications of the façade, while at the same time they will publicly pretend to respect these aspects. In these cases the façade becomes at least for some actors a shrewd camouflage to achieve certain goals in practice which would otherwise be out of reach. At this point I am back to where the everyday language of modernity situates the word façade.

An early contribution to this topic came from Prince Potemkin. He knew how to exploit the fact that the meaning of the façade is in the eye of the beholder. In 1787 he invited Czarina Katharina II, who was well-disposed towards him, to visit the Crimea, which he had conquered only a few years previously. To conceal the rather meagre achievements of his colonization and development projects, he had the now (at least in German language) proverbial Potemkin villages built along the road: neat façades with no houses behind them. The journey of inspection was a success, the Czarina was impressed and did not ask to be shown the "real life" which went on somewhere else.

Since any organizational façade is only loosely linked to both sides – institutions and practice – it is nearly always impossible to clearly distinguish between a ceremonial and a Potemkin façade. There are very few cases that one can undoubtedly classify as belonging either to the Potemkin or to the ceremonial tradition.[15] Normally any façade contains elements of "authenticity" and of "charlatanry," no matter to which society and culture the organization belongs. Therefore, the more interesting question is about the various combinations of the two dimensions and about how, if at all, they can be distinguished. In the meantime, the only safe conclusion would appear to be the following: a certain degree of charlatanry is the prerequisite for envisioning new possibilities and making changes.

---

[15] An exceptional and remarkable example is given by Groffebert (1995) who presents the ingenious tricks used by so-called *ONG-Bidon* (literally: "fake NGOs") in West Africa to increase their resources that mainly come from the rich countries.

Otherhood:
The Promulgation and Transmission of Ideas in the Modern Organizational Environment

John W. Meyer

The studies above present a rich set of arguments and observations on how ideas and models about organizing evolve and travel in modern environments, and how, when, and why they enter into the life of specific organizations. These studies work from a number of sources in contemporary thinking in the social sciences and to some extent the humanities. A principal starting point is contemporary sociological institutional (or neo-institutional) thinking (e. g. Meyer and Rowan, 1977; DiMaggio and Powell, 1983; Meyer and Scott, 1992; Powell and DiMaggio, 1991; Scott and Meyer, 1994).

In this line of thought, modern social, scientific, legal, and cultural environments contain expanding sets of rationalized models, scripts, or ideologies: e. g. accounting standards, professionalized personnel rules, japanified styles of work organization, or computerized technologies. As this occurs, new rationalized formal organizations can spring up in the relevant domains, and extant organizations are driven to incorporate the new models: new or expanded accounting or personnel departments, and so on. The environmentally-developed model of rationalized organizational actor is created and expanded, and specific organizations incorporate the expanded rules of this expanded and collectively-defined actor. The incorporation can be ritualistic, with little practical implementation or consequence (one sort of decoupling), but may often penetrate rather deeply into organizational life. The incorporation may also occur in practice without much structural or policy adaptation (another sort of decoupling), as when fashionable new accounting practices routinely promulgated by accounting firms or consultants and built into software packages flow into firms without much by way of decision or policy.

The typical American version of this line of theorizing starts with a typically-American conception of organizations and the people in them as sharply-defined and often fairly rational actors. These actors have prior purposes, clear boundaries, definite technologies, unified sovereignty, clear internal control systems, and definite and discrete resources to employ. This starting point makes it difficult to think about institutional processes as involving the travel of ideas (see e. g. the concerns expressed in Chapter 1 of Powell and DiMaggio, 1991). In each step of such travel, one must give a proper account of why these hard-wired and sharply defined entities chose to (or were constrained to) adopt or pass along the new ideas. Prior strong motives are assumed to exist, and must be used to explain any deployment of or modification in ideas. Thus, American research on institutional ideas has been strong in demonstrating that collective rules and ideas of various sorts do in fact travel down into particular organizational structures and sometimes their practices. It has been weaker on showing the processes involved in the rise of the ideas in question, the transformations these ideas go through over time at the collective level, the further transformations they go through as they travel down into particular organizations, and the nature of the social processes involved in adoption or incorporation. The positivist research designs favored by the American researchers amplify these problems: but these designs really parallel and reflect underlying cultural and social scientific models stressing the reality of bounded purposive actors. The culture involved sets more limits than does the research design it prefers.

In the American tradition, it is understood that people and organizations are not always, or often, like this. Boundaries are unclear, sovereignty weak, and purposes opaque. The hard wires that connect the sovereign, through the control system, down to each activity are broken, missing, or overloaded. Similarly, the hard wires that run from resources through means-ends technologies to purposes are often shadow production functions rather than real ones.

Thus, dialectically, the same American tradition that takes very seriously the reality of sharply-defined actors in individual and organizational life, must spend much time and effort dealing with the problem of what is called "uncertainty." A favorite idea is that ideas and their variations − and thus the whole panoply of institutional effects − become especially consequential under conditions of "uncertainty." An assumption of this kind is routine in organization theory, and also in the sociology of culture (Swidler, 1986).

Pronounced limitations arise with this approach: ideas get separated from (indeed occur in a kind of opposition against) a putatively real social world. They matter episodically, or interstitially: they matter in the least important and most epiphenomenal situations. And the ideas considered tend to be in the expressive periphery of a society that is in reality instrumental: they are attitudes, beliefs, sentiments, values, and so on. In a more perfectly rational and controlled world, there would be no free-floating ideas or ideologies, and no need for them.

In fact, in this tradition, external ideas and rational action tend to be alternatives to each other. The truly hard-wired actor would be almost immune to external ideas. Thus, if the institutionalists show empirically the impact of external ideas on organizational structure and practice, one must find very special conditions ("uncertainty" is the favorite) or motives (external requirements, normative rules, or special considerations of prestige) for them. Without an analysis in terms of true actorhood or agency (the underlying principles of American culture), the story is thought to be incomplete (Powell and DiMaggio, 1991, Chapter 1).

The Soft Actor

The chapters in this book, in contrast, have a European flavor. The term actor is less often used to describe people and organizational entities. And when it is used, fewer assumptions about the hard-wired and bounded character of the actor are employed. People (and organizations) are understood to be constructed and to act in light of socially-constructed and defined identities, which are understood to be made up of cultural ideas. Their purposes, technologies, and resources are social constructions, and change with changing ideologies and models. Their sovereignty, boundaries, and control systems are similarly embedded in cultural material. The fundamental materials of actorhood, in short, are culturally dependent in the first place.

This permits the enriched discussion of the travel of ideas found in the chapters above. Organized social life itself is conceived to be made up of ideas that may flow and change: it is translation, editing, and dramatic enaction more than action (Czarniawska; Joerges; Sevón; Rottenburg). Even fundamental identities, naturally cultural, vary with cultural flows (Sahlin-Andersson; Forssell and Jansson). The adoption of ideas follows the patterns of fashion (Abrahamson; Røvik). And since rationalized ideas are now strongly patterned (e. g. in the sciences and professions) at the world level, they follow general worldwide trends (Spybey).

Incorporating the assumption that both identity and activity are intrinsically cultural relaxes the American requirement that one must find a motive behind every adoption or change in ideas, and the further requirement that one can only anticipate the creation or penetration of ideas at the margins or interstices of an incomplete ("uncertain") action situation. Actors are embedded in culture, and change with variations in the flows and fashions of this culture.

Also relaxed is the American requirement that social activity, by definition, be seen as (usually fairly rational) purposive "social action" – tied down to the calculated purposes of tightly-defined actors. In this tradition, there is either active purposive social action or there is passivity, as when people and organizations under uncertainty are driven into passive conformity with institutional norms and definitions (through coercion, norms, or passive mimesis, in the terms of DiMaggio and Powell, 1983). The chapters above deploy a much looser conception of social activity, since identities and behaviors are seen as embedded in the first place. So the travel of exogenous ideas into organizational life can be quite an active process: behaving people are translating and interpreting exogenous ideas (Czarniawska and Joerges; Sevón; Abrahamson; Røvik); they edit these for their situations (Sevón; Sahlin-Andersson; Rottenburg); they negotiate and change identities (Sahlin-Andersson; Forssell and Jansson). This is not a special search process under uncertainty, but intrinsic to the nature of people embedded in sociolinguistic identities and models: strong principles of motive and choice do not need to be invoked, and the analysis is enriched. The core principle is that identity and activity always involve ideas, which always have exogenous aspects, and that organizational behavior involves the routine use and modification of them.

Actors and Others

In one respect, however, the papers in this book remain fairly traditional. The focus of the analysis is on the now-softened "actors" — the people who behave in organizations, who carry out the specific behaviors involved, and who edit and translate and use ideas in the process.

A natural extension of the perspective here, in future research, would be to contemplate more completely the other participants in the process of the flow and deployment of organizing ideas. There are behaving organizational participants, to be sure. But there are also the people who form and change and carry the ideas involved in the wider environments surrounding organizational life. We understand from the chapters in this book why organizational participants routinely translate, edit, and employ exogenous ideas, and respond to shifts in their availability and fashionability. But why are there so many ideas out there to be so used in the modern organizational environment?

The perspective developed in this book is useful, not only for analyzing the use of ideas in activity, but also for analyzing the modern tendency to reify activity in ideas. It is, in other words, useful for discussing both those who act and those who talk (Brunsson, 1989): Actors, and what may be called Others. Others, in this scheme loosely derived from George Herbert Mead, do not take action responsibility for organizational behavior and outcomes. They discuss, interpret, advise, suggest, codify, and sometimes pronounce and legislate. They develop, promulgate, and certify some ideas as proper reforms, and ignore or stigmatize other ideas. Who are these Others, and why are so many of them, out there in the modern organizational environment?

In pushing forward the arguments in this book, I consider simultaneously two issues: a) the forms taken by modern organizational Others, and b) the factors that expand their numbers and range.

The Organizational Stratification System

Clearly, the chapters in this book see organizations as providing models for each other. Arguments about why and how people in organizations employ these models are well developed. I consider here, not the demand for models, but the supply. Why do modern organizations put themselves forward as general models, and promote the copying process? I treat it as obvious that they do this, frequently encouraging internal and external professionals to communicate their practices as general models for others. It seems, in fact, a general characteristic of modern rationalized Actorhood that Actors easily parade as Others, giving friendly advice to the world around them.

The question, seen in historical and comparative context, is more puzzling than it may seem. In most societies at most times, competing organizations keep their successes to themselves: they see few advantages in helping aliens and competitors. Secrecy seems more rational than publicity. Why does this change in the modern organizational world, so that organizations glory in depicting themselves as successful instances of organization in general, or in being so depicted by the relevant professionals (e. g. consultants and business school professors)?

A general answer, here, runs through the chapters of this book. Because modern organizations legitimate themselves as specific instances of models (i. e. sets of ideas) that are universally true, progressive, and rational, they not only use exogenous ideas, but turn their own structures and practices into such ideas. They live by the standard of universalistic rationality, and gain strength and stability by promoting themselves as instances of this standard. Further, they spread their models widely − the more consensus they can build around their universalizable validity, the stronger and more legitimate they are. The advantages accrue to their internal legitimacy (convincing their members that the organizational model is really true) and their external legitimacy (convincing the environment of the same thing).

Both the opportunity to market one's Actorhood as an Other to the entire neighborhood, and the advantages of doing so, are greatest under some obvious conditions. (Røvik and Abrahamson discuss parallel points from the point of view of consumers: here we look at the producers of ideas and models.) First, high status and successful organizations can in this manner store up and stabilize their prestige and success − this is the obvious dimension of organizational stratification at issue. But second, organizations at the "innovative" margins of standard organizational populations have special needs and opportunities to so legitimate themselves. Various types of radical nation-states do this in world society; other organizations similarly compete to be properly-recognized "innovators."

These two factors together help produce the fashion cycles that Røvik and Abrahamson discuss above. Fashion is structured by status and prestige, but also by a continuing pressure for innovation and change: the result is cyclic change within some general parameters.

Associational Structures

Modern organizations routinely enter into associations with other organizations conceived to be similar. Some of this, of course, reflects common material interests in shared goods (e. g. access to the state). But much of it reflects the dependence of modern organizational Actors on the legitimation provided by exogenous ideas: an organization's existence and stability are enhanced by the ideas and models provided externally. Immersion in common association helps dramatize the similarity of the organizations with the general models, and thus with each other. Sahlin-Anderson stresses the importance of such similarity in promoting the diffusion of ideas from the consuming Actor's point of view: here, we stress the producer side. Associations provide loci for models and ideas: they and their members gain stability and legitimacy from this role.

Social Movements

Organizations create associations that act as Others promoting rationalistic ideas for organizational improvement: so, in the modern system, do their internal and external critics. In another world, organizations were, with a few exceptions in centralized religious and state institutions, seen as illicit conspiracies – something to be eliminated, not expansively reformed. In the modern world, anti-organizational social movements take the role of rationalized Others proposing ideas for elaboration, reform, and improvement, rather than elimination. If organizations are thought to oppress their labor forces, we create movements with ideas – not to eliminate organizations but to elaborate their personnel structures (grievance procedures, union rights, internal labor markets). If organizations are thought to suppress innovation, we create movements with ideas for institutionalizing research and development. If organizations are thought to be inefficient mechanisms, we create movements with ideas for improved accounting and control. If organization destroys community, we create rationalized ideas for improving community in organization. All these processes expand the stock of ideas for organizing and organizational improvement, expansion, and change.

Sciences and Professions

The chapters above frequently discuss ideas for organizing as carried by these most perfect Others of the rationalized society. The contemporary world is filled with organizational consultants, business schools, and scientific and professional fields, all carrying ideas for organizational expansion and change. The focus of the chapters above is mainly in their impact on the demand side – on the consumers of organizational ideas. What accounts for the extraordinarily expanded supply of these professional Others?

Obviously, consumer demand is one answer: modern organizations, legitimated by the standard of universalistic rationality, search externally for consensual and scientifically "valid" standards. But a more complex answer lies in the wider cultural and political system, which itself validates universalistic rationality as a collective good – not simply a good for each particular organization. The consultants and scientists and professionals involved are not simply servicing a market of particular consumers. They serve what is seen as a higher set of truths: scientific, universal, and inherent in the laws of nature (and sometimes the moral order): and they thus serve the whole societal collectivity that is seen as a rational project under such laws. Just as modern organizations themselves are legitimated (e. g. in the law) as instruments of general principles of the collective good, so are the rationalistic bodies of ideas on which they depend.

The Joys of Rationalized Otherhood

All of the answers suggested above to the questions of the forms and expansiveness of rationalized Otherhood – the many sources, and extraordinary amounts, of cultural materials providing ideas for organizing and reorganizing – return ultimately to the argument that the modern system gives great cultural credence to abstract and universalistic ideas of a rationalistic sort. The point needs little defense, and is often treated as a truism. I comment here, first on some implications of the credence involved, and then on the fact that it is cultural (rather than organizational or material).

The Modern Credence

Students of social stratification, by and large a very serious lot, argue about whether the modern inequalities rest principally on organized power (ultimately, the state) or exchange (ultimately organized class relationships). In fact, their empirical studies cast much doubt on either idea: in practically every modern stratification system that has been studied, the most prestigious and rewarded and apparently influential occupations are the professional carriers of what we have called Otherhood. In the modern system, the carriers of ideas have more standing than the carriers of action. This means that in the organizational transactions between responsible actors and professionalized Others the latter have interactional advantages. It also means that people who have both roles are likely to take more seriously, ceteris paribus, their membership in the world of ideas than their experience as actors.

The same effect arises from the fact that modern stratification systems, rather uniformly, select people for advancement and organizational leadership heavily on the basis of abstract education rather than concrete experience and competence. As is well-known, success in the educational system depends heavily on, and produces skill in, the manipulation of abstract rationalistic ideas rather than effective actions (in fact, it is unclear empirically that action capability, in most roles, is much affected by education − though credentialing rules make job selection dependent on education in any case). We select and promote people in organizational life, in other words, on their inclination to think in terms of rationalistic ideas: this naturally makes organizations depend heavily on such ideas, and increases the inclination that practices will be stabilized and legitimated inasmuch as they can be constructed into generalized ideas.

The universalistic character of modern assumptions underlying rationalistic ideas about organizing creates large-scale arenas for the development and communication of such ideas. An organization can legitimately adopt ideas that come from places (organizations and countries and professional bodies) that no member has ever been in direct contact with. The authority of scientific ideas, for instance, rather clearly transcends local circumstances and experience: the ideas discussed in the chapters above routinely come from very distant places. The idea market is much larger, and contains much more usable material, than the market of actions and transactions.

The Cultural Character of Organizing Ideas

In one primitive sense, of course, ideas are inherently cultural, in that as symbols they ordinarily occur at a more macroscopic level than their local material referents. This is not very useful: it implies, for instance, that the general specifications for a particular bolt are more cultural than are the measurements of that bolt. In a more useful sense, ideas may be cultural in that they are rooted in models of meaning rather than in particular social structures (at whatever level of analysis and social structure).

Organizational ideas, in the chapters above, are cultural in this latter sense. They are rooted in models of scientific and moral meaning − often quite complex ones − rather than in particular technical or control systems.

To carry the point further, the types of organizational ideas under discussion here − and generally in theorizing on the subject − are rooted in and legitimated by truth value, generalized moral laws, and the like. They are not principally rules put forward by dominating states, powerful economic forces, or overriding organizations: modern social science sees little to explain in the travels of such rules. The problem of the book is to explain the travels of ideas of a cultural kind, located in meaning rather than concrete power. And as we have noted above, ideas of this cultural sort, along with their standard promulgating and transmitting Others, are of great importance in modern organizations.

One reason for this lies in a peculiar property of modern rationalistic and universalistic culture. It carries, depicts, and assumes principles that the true ideas and knowledge about organizational life are universal − located in natural and moral law. But there is no corresponding universal organization to carry, control, and enforce this culture. (If there were, there would be little problem, and probably no book, here.)

This property of modern rational ideas about organizing − that they are highly valued and little controlled by any superordinate organizational structure − helps account for the profusion of organizational ideas, models, innovations, and reforms in the modern system, and for the profusion of people and groups behaving as Others in transmitting them to actors. It is all highly valued, and nobody is in a structural position to stop it.

Imagine, counterfactually, that there were a closed and controlled imperium, in the modern world, policing which ideas are acceptable and which are not. And policing which Others − self-advertising actors, associations, social movements, and scientific and professional consultants − could properly advocate and disseminate organizing ideas. It should be entirely clear that the number and travels of organizing ideas would decline very sharply, and that the processes discussed in this book would weaken dramatically.

Two implications follow: One is that the proliferation of organizing ideas and their Other advocates is enhanced by the fact that the wider legitimating culture is not under close organizational control. A more interesting point, discussed by Spybey, is that the rise of the modern worldwide or global system of communication about organizations dramatically increases the number and travel of rationalistic organizational ideas (Meyer, 1994). Because world society is under peculiarly little unified organizational control (it has, the convention has it, no state), globalization amplifies the modern explosion of organizing ideas. If ideas could be put forward, and travel, only within the context of a given nation-state, the state could and would be likely to greatly constrain them. (To some modest extent, this situation probably described organizational life in the Communist bloc and Soviet Union: a context known to have limited the development and travel of organizational ideas.)

A related way to put the same point may be useful. Great incentives exist for cultural elites, in the modern system, to create and disseminate new organizing ideas. The rationalities involved are highly valued, and this value is built into great incentive systems. Scientists and professionals (e. g. in business schools) gain status and preferment by doing this. Consulting organizations and business associations similarly benefit. There are few costs for success in this enterprise for such people, and great benefits.

But many of the new ideas involved do involve costs: creating brave new departments in firms (personnel, research and development, safety, and so on) and assuming new responsibilities (the environment) is likely to be very expensive. But who bears these costs? The actors bear all the costs of the new ideas, not the Others who only gain by producing them and distributing them. In the modern world, a few long-haired scientific Others can journey to Antarctica, discover that the earth's life force is leaking out through a hole in the ozone layer, and gain enormous status and publicity by defining this problem: the actors of the world then must bear all the costs of remodeling the production and use of refrigerators. One can easily imagine the reluctance with which an organized world imperium would honor such troublemakers: they would more likely be buried alive than granted the dignities of academic tenure and status.

The expanded flow of organizing ideas, and expanded numbers of Others producing and transmitting them, is thus greatly enhanced by the combination of world-wide rationalistic culture and the absence of overall collective organizational control. There is no agent in a position to stop progress.

Types of Ideas

The studies above focus on the people dealing with ideas − using, editing, translating, adopting, changing, and rejecting them − and not much with the content of organizing ideas. But a natural extension of this work, in future research, would be to develop arguments, not only about the people and organizations involved, but about the contents of the ideas that travel and don't travel. Obviously, some types of ideas travel better than others. We can develop, here, a few of the implications of the studies in this book for this general question.

It seems obvious that organizing ideas linked to central rationalistic values travel better than ideas less linked to these highly legitimated goals. Organizations are to produce outcomes rationally, efficiently, and effectively: this is centrally legitimated in terms of the Western, and now world, project of progress. Thus ideas justified in terms of enhanced organizational outcomes travel better than ideas justified in other terms (e. g. in terms of human comfort, lowered conflict, or other possible goals). And the tighter the theorized linkage between a given idea and progressive outcome, the stronger the likely flows of the idea: a clear and effective new technology might travel quickly, and a more distant one (e. g. improved personnel practice) might travel faster if justified in terms of established economic theory (e. g. human capital theory). Thus the more elaborate and rationalized the theorized identity of a given organizational model, the more new ideas can spread, and spread rapidly.

A second core value, along with collective Progress, in the modern system is justice (often some form of equality) for individuals. Much modern rationalization is around worker, citizen, and human rights — considerations that directly derive from the ancestral Western celebration of the individual soul. Ideas legitimated in terms of such rights — to equal treatment, to the celebration of individual merit, and so on — probably travel fairly rapidly too (an example would be the rather rapid worldwide spread of ideas about the rights of women in organizations).

A third core value in the modern rationalistic system is rational organization itself: the doctrine the properly socialized humans (and their collectivities) can and should construct perfected purposive structures to accomplish highly legitimated ends. Thus ideas proposing more organization — more complex roles and relationships — have advantages over those proposing less organization. This produces the well-known phenomenon that any collective social activity is increasingly likely to be organized in more complex and differentiated forms as time goes on.

Which kinds of organizing ideas are less likely to be developed, and if developed, to travel? Clearly, those rooted in cultural materials outside the rationalistic system: ideas grounding organization in collective principles are given little standing. Thus ideas about organizing activity around families and familial relationships, distinct ethnic or national cultures, gender, communal relationships, or distinctive religious understandings, are not likely to be successful. Such entities and forces seem irrational in modern culture. Few business consultants would put together organizational packages proposing to take advantages of socially "natural" role differences between men and women in restructuring a firm (even in a traditional cultural context): many would supply packages for the selection and assignment of personnel on more rationalistic bases. Even the modern ideas about organizational culture, on inspection, involve quite rationalized conceptions of persons and their proper relationships: the technologies may celebrate very broad aspects of the humans involved, but these are likely to turn out to be analytic properties that can be assessed by personality tests.

An Implication

Our discussion here of the properties of ideas likely to be produced and to travel produces an implication that runs against many other lines of causation (and argument). In most lines of thought, ideas that really work are likely to be produced and to travel. But in a system that differentiates Actorhood and Otherhood, and organizes the latter around highly general and abstract purposes, this may less be the case. If ideas are produced and transmitted in terms of criteria of abstraction, generality, and universality, it is not at all obvious that "working" in local situations distinguished by their particularity is likely to be a consequence. The things that make an idea a good idea may often, in fact, run against making the idea good practice. To properly develop and travel, an idea must be organized in terms of great abstract truths, not mundane realities.

This line of thought can help explain a subsidiary theme that runs through the studies of this book: the travels of ideas in and around organizations is often highly decoupled from actual organizational practice. And the decoupling involved is not necessarily highly problematic: the hypocrisies involved may make up a kind of rough organizational equilibrium (Brunsson, 1989). In any society, Durkheimian reasoning would have it, there are inevitably great and stable differences (hypocrisies) between collective social rules and individual life and behavior: in the modern rationalistic cultural system, these would naturally focus around the culture and models of rationality.

Conclusion

The studies here focus on the ways culturally embedded people and organizations (social actors in a very soft sense) employ, change, and depend on ideas in maintaining and changing organizational life. They can easily be extended to consider two closely related questions: the factors involved in the development of the idea-creation and idea-transmission system in the environment (what is called here, Otherhood); and the properties of ideas that enhance their potential to travel.

References

Abrahamson, Eric (1989), Fads and fashions in administrative technologies. Unpublished doctoral dissertation. Stern School of Business, New York University, New York.

Abrahamson, Eric (1991), Managerial fads and fashion: The diffusion and rejection of innovations. *Academy of Management Review,* 16: 586−612.

Abrahamson, Eric (in print), The emergence and prevalence of employee-management rhetorics: The effect of long waves, labor unions and turnover, 1870 to 1992. *Academy of Management Journal.*

Abrahamson, Eric, and Fombrun, Charles (1994), Macroculture: Determinants and consequences. *Academy of Management Review,* 19: 728−755.

Africa Watch (1991), Sudan destroying ethnic identity. The secret war against the Nuba. *Africa Watch News Bulletin,* December 10.

Agger, Ben (1991), *The decline of discourse.* New York: The Falmer Press.

Ahrne, Göran (1994), *Social organizations. Interactions inside, outside and between organizations.* London: Sage.

Albert, Stuart, and Whetten, David A. (1985), Organizational identity. *Research in Organizational Behavior,* 7: 263−295.

Albrow, Martin (1992), Sine ira et studio or do organizations have feelings? *Organization Studies,* 13(3): 313−329.

Amnesty International (1993), Sudan: The ravages of war: Political killings and humanitarian disaster. Ai-Index AFR 54/29/93.

Andersen, Benedicte, Gjerde, Ragnhild, Magnussen, Anne Mette, and Olsen, Johan P. (1990), Domstolene som institusjoner: Reformforslag, verdier og situasjonsforslag. Bergen: Norwegian Research Centre in Organization and Management. Research Paper 21/90.

Argyris, Chris, and Schön, Donald (1978), *Organizational learning: A theory of action perspective.* Menlo Park, CA: Addison-Wesley.

Ayeni, Victor (1987), Nigeria's bureaucratized ombudsman system: An insight into the problem of bureaucratization in a developing country. *Public Administration and Development,* 7(3): 309−324.

Bacharach, Samuel, Gagliardi, Pasquale, Pasquale, and Mundell, Brian (1995), Research in sociology of organizations, vol. 13. Greenwich, CT: JAI Press.

Bachrach, Peter, and Baratz, Morton S. (1963), Decisions and non-decisions: An analytical framework. *American Political Science Review,* 57: 632−642.

Baier, Vicky E., March, James G., and Sætren, Harald (1986), Implementation and ambiguity. *Scandinavian Journal of Management,* 2(3/4): 197−212.

Baldwin, John D. (1986), *George Herbert Mead. A unifying theory for sociology.* Beverly Hills, CA: Sage.

Barber, Bernard, and Lobel, Lyle S. (1952), Fashion in women's clothes and the American social system. *Social Forces,* 13 (2): 124−131.

Barley, Stephen R., and Kunda, Gideon (1992), Design and devotion: Surges of rational and normative ideologies of control in managerial discourse. *Administrative Science Quarterly,* 37: 363–399.

Barley, Stephen R., Meyer, Gordon W., and Gash, Debra C. (1988), Culture of cultures: Academics, practitioners and the pragmatics of normative control. *Administrative Science Quarterly,* 33: 24–60.

Barnett, H. G. (1940), Culture processes. *American Anthropologist,* 42(1): 21–48.

Barthes, Roland (1960/1973), Le bleu est à la mode. *Revue Française de Sociologie,* 1 (2). Reprinted in: Wills, Gordon, and Midgley, David (eds.) (1973), *Fashion Marketing.* London: Allen and Unwin, 313–356.

Barthes, Roland (1983), *Fashion system.* London: Cape.

Bateson, Gregory (1979), *Mind and nature.* Toronto: Bantam Books.

Bausinger, Hermann (1961/1990), *Folk culture in a world of technology.* Bloomington: Indiana University Press.

Beck, Kurt (1990), Entwicklungshilfe als Beute. Über die lokale Aneignungsweise von Entwicklungshilfemaßnahmen im Sudan. *Orient,* 31 (4): 583–601.

Beckman, Björn (1987), *Att bilda EOU-organ.* Stockholm: ERU report 51.

Bell, Daniel (1973), *The coming of post-industrial society: A venture in social forecasting.* London: Heinemann.

Bell, Quentin (1976), *On human finery.* New York: Schocken.

Berger, Peter L. (1966), Identity as a problem in the sociology of knowledge. *European Journal of Sociology,* 7: 105–115.

Berger, Peter L., and Luckmann, Thomas (1966), *The social construction of reality. A treatise in the sociology of knowledge.* Harmondsworth, Middlesex: Penguin.

Berger, Peter L., Berger, Birgitte, and Kellner, Hansfried (1973), *The homeless mind. An approach to modern consciousness.* New York: Random House.

Bergler, Edmond (1953), *Fashion and the unconscious.* New York: Robert Bruner.

Bernas, Mary Bellarmine, Sister (1981), The innovation process of individualized instruction in some elementary schools in the Philippines. Doctoral dissertation. School of Education, Stanford University, Stanford, CA.

Bie, Frode (1992), Sykehuset: Fra institusjon til bedrift. Tromsø: Department of Political Science,The University of Tromsø, Norway.

Blakely, Edward J., Roberts, Brian H., and Manidis, Philip (1987), Inducing high tech. *International Journal of Technology Management,* 2(3/4): 337–356.

Blau, Peter M. (1971), *The structure of organizations.* New York: Basic Books.

Blumer, Herbert G. (1968), Fashion. In: Sills, David L. (ed.), *Encyclopedia of the social sciences,* vol. 1. New York: MacMillan, 341–345.

Blumer, Herbert G. (1969), Fashion: From class differentiation to collective selection. *Sociological Quarterly* 10: 275–291.

Boland, Richard J. Jr. (1982), Myth and technology in the American accounting profession. *Journal of Management Studies,* 19: 109–127.

Bourdieu, Pierre (1977/1980), The production of belief. Contribution to an economy of symbolic goods. *Media, Culture and Society,* 2: 261–293.

Bourdieu, Pierre (1979/1984), *Distinction. A social critique of the judgement of taste.* Cambridge, Mass.: University of Harvard Press.

Brenninkmeyer, Ingrid (1963), The sociology of fashion. Doctoral dissertation. Lausanne: University of Lausanne.

Brint, Steven, and Karabel, Jerome (1991), Institutional origins and transformations: The case of American community colleges. In: Powell, Walter W., and DiMaggio, Paul J. (eds.), *The new institutionalism in organizational analysis.* Chicago: Chicago University Press, 337−360.

Brown, Roger (1973), *A first language: The early stages.* Cambridge, MA: Harvard University Press.

Bruner, Jerome S. (1957), On perceptual readiness. *Psychological Review*, 64(2): 123-145.

Bruner, Jerome S. (1961), The act of discovery. *Harvard Educational Review*, 31: 21−32.

Bruner, Jerome S. (1986), *Actual minds, possible worlds*, Cambridge, MA: Harvard University Press.

Bruner, Jerome S. (1990), A*cts of meaning.* Cambridge, MA: Harvard University Press.

Brunsson, Nils (1985), *The irrational organization.* Chichester: Wiley.

Brunsson, Nils (1989), *The organization of hypocrisy:Talk, decisions and actions in organizations.* Chichester: Wiley.

Brunsson, Nils (1993), Reforms as routine. In: Brunsson, Nils, and Olsen, Johan P. (eds.), *The reforming organization.* London: Routledge, 33−47.

Brunsson, Nils (1994), Politicization and 'company-ization' on institutional affiliation and confusion in the organizational world. *Management Accounting Research*, 5: 323−335.

Brunsson, Nils, and Hägg, Ingemund (eds.) (1992), *Marknadens makt.* Stockholm: SNS.

Brunsson, Nils, and Olsen, Johan P. (1993), Organizational forms: Can we choose them? In: Brunsson, Nils, and Olsen, Johan P. (eds.), *The reforming organization.* London: Routledge, 1−14.

Brunsson, Nils, and Winberg, Hans (1993), Implementing reforms. In: Brunsson, Nils, and Olsen, Johan P. (eds.), *The reforming organization.* London: Routledge, 109−126.

Brunsson, Nils, Forssell, Anders, and Winberg, Hans (1989), *Reform som tradition.* Stockholm: EFI.

Budd, Leslie, and Whimster, Sam (eds.) (1992), *Global finance and urban living: A study of metropolitan change.* London: Routledge.

Burns, Lawthon, and Wholey, Douglas (1990), The diffusion of matrix management: Effects of task diversity and interorganizational networks. Manuscript, University of Arizona.

Business Week, (1986), Business Fads: What's in and out. July 12.

Callon, Michel (1986), Some elements of a sociology of translation: Domestication of the scallops and the fishermen of St Brieuc Bay. In: Law, John (ed.), *Power, action and belief.* London: Routledge and Kegan Paul, 196−233.

Callon, Michel, and Latour, Bruno (1981), Unscrewing the big Leviathan: How actors macro-structure reality and how sociologists help them to do so. In: Knorr-Cetina, Karin, and Cicourel, Aaron V. (eds.), *Advances in social theory and methodology.* London: Routledge and Kegan Paul, 277−303.

Carman, James M. (1973), The fate of fashion cycles in our modern society. In: Wills, Gordon, and Midgley, David (eds.), *Fashion marketing*. London: Allen and Unwin, 125–136.

Carroll, Glenn R. (1988), Organizational ecology in theoretical perspective. In: Carroll, Glenn R. (ed.), *Ecological models of organizations*. Cambridge, MA: Ballinger, 1–6.

Castorina, Paul, and Wood, Brian, (1988), Circles in the Fortune 500: Why circles fail. *Journal for Quality and Participation*, 11: 40–41.

Child, John (1968), *The business enterprise in modern industrial society*. London: Collier Macmillan.

Christensen, Tom (1991), *Virksomhetsplanlegging: Myteskaping eller instrumentell problemløsning?* Oslo: Tano.

Clifford, James (1988), *The predicament of culture. Twentieth-century ethnography, literature, and art*. Cambridge, MA: Harvard University Press.

Clifford, James, and Marcus, George (eds.) (1986), *Writing culture. The poetics and politics of ethnography*. Berkeley, CA: University of California Press.

Cohen, Michael D., and March, James G. (1974), *Leadership and ambiguity*. New York: McGraw-Hill.

Cohen, Michael D., March, James G., and Olsen, Johan P. (1972), A garbage can model of organizational choice. *Administrative Science Quarterly*, 17: 1–25.

Cole, Robert (1985), The macropolitics of organizational change: A comparative analysis of the spread of small-group activities. *Administrative Science Quarterly*, 30: 560–585.

Collins, Allan, and Gentner, Dedre (1989), How people construct mental models. In: Holland, Dorothy, and Quinn, Naomi (eds.), *Cultural models in language and thought*. Cambridge, UK: Cambridge University Press, 243–265.

Covaleski, Mark, and Dirsmith, Mark (1988), An institutional perspective on the rise, social transformation and fall of a university budget category. *Administrative Science Quarterly*, 33: 562–587.

Crozier, Michel (1964), *The bureaucratic phenomenon*. Chicago: The University of Chicago Press.

Czarniawska, Barbara (1985), The ugly sister: On relationships between the private and the public sectors in Sweden. *Scandinavian Journal of Management Studies*, 2(2): 83–103.

Czarniawska-Joerges, Barbara (1988), *Ideological control in nonideological organizations*. New York: Praeger.

Czarniawska-Joerges, Barbara (1990), Merchants of meaning. In: Turner, Barry A. (ed.), *Organizational symbolism*. Berlin: de Gruyter, 139–150.

Czarniawska-Joerges, Barbara (1991), Culture is the medium of life. In: Frost, Peter J., Moore, Larry F., Louis, Meryl Reis, Lundberg, Craig C., and Martin, Joanne (eds.), *Reframing organizational culture*. Newbury Park, CA: Sage, 285–297.

Czarniawska-Joerges, Barbara (1992), *Exploring complex organizations. A cultural perspective*. Newbury Park, CA: Sage.

Czarniawska-Joerges, Barbara (1994), Narratives of individual and organizational identities. In: Deetz, Stanley A. (ed.), *Communication Yearbook,* vol. 17. Newbury Park, CA: Sage, 193–221.

Czarniawska, Barbara (1996), *Narrating the organization. Dramas of institutional identity.* Chicago: University of Chicago Press.

Czarniawska-Joerges, Barbara, and Joerges, Bernward (1990), Linguistic artifacts at service of organizational control. In: Gagliardi, Pasquale (ed.), *The symbolics of corporate artifacts.* Berlin: de Gruyter, 509–548.

Daft, Richard L., and Weick, Karl E. (1984), Towards a model of organizations as interpretative systems. *Academy of Management Review,* 9: 284–295.

Dahrendorf, Ralf (1959), *Class and class conflict in industrial society.* London: Routledge and Kegan Paul.

Dalton, Melville (1959), *Men who manage. Fusions of feeling and theory in administration.* New York: Wiley.

Dasgupta, Partha (1988), Patents, priority and imitation or, the economics races and waiting games. *The Economic Journal,* 98 (March): 66–80.

Deng, Francis Mading (1994), The Sudan. Stop the carnage. *The Brookings Review,* 12(1): 6–11.

Der Derian, James (1989), The boundaries of knowledge and power in international relations. In: Der Derian, James & Shapiro, Michael J. (eds.), *International/intertextual relations: Postmodern readings of world politics,* Lexington MA: Lexington Books, 3–10.

DesForges, Charles D. (1986), US and UK experience in technology transfer – a comparative analysis. *International Journal of Technology Management,* 1(3/4): 457–475.

Dettmar, Erika (1995), Segregation und soziokulturelle Integration in Joint Ventures. Das Beispiel Nigeria. In: Oppen, Achim von, and Rottenburg, Richard (eds.), *Organisationswandel in Afrika.* Studien 2, FSP Moderner Orient, Berlin: Das Arabische Buch, 79–105.

Dicken, Peter (1992), *Global shift: The internationalization of economic activity* (2nd edition). London: Paul Chapman.

Dill, William (1958), Environment as an influence on managerial autonomy. *Administrative Science Quarterly,* 2: 409–443.

DiMaggio, Paul J. (1983), State expansion and organizational fields. In: Hall, Richard H., and Quinn, Robert E. (eds.), *Organizational theory and public policy.* Beverly Hills, CA: Sage, 147–172.

DiMaggio, Paul J., and Powell, Walter W. (1983), The iron cage revisited: Institutional isomorphism and collective rationality in organizational fields. *American Sociological Review,* 48: 147–160.

DiMaggio, Paul J., and Powell, Walter W. (1991), Introduction. In: Powell, Walter W., and DiMaggio, Paul J. (eds.), *The new institutionalism in organizational analysis.* Chicago: The University of Chicago Press, 1–38.

Dore, Ronald (1984), Good will and the spirit of market. *The British Journal of Sociology,* 36(4): 459–482.

Douglas, Mary (1986), *How institutions think.* Syracuse, NY: Syracuse University Press.

Downs, Anthony (1972), Up and down with ecology: The issue-attention cycle. *The Public Interest,* 28: 38–50.

Dunnette, Marvin, and Bass, Bernard M. (1963), Behavioral Scientist and Personnel Management. *Industrial Relations,* 2: 115–130.

Durkheim, Emile (1915), *Elementary forms of the religious life.* London: Allan and Unwin.

Durkheim, Emile, and Mauss, Marcel (1903/1963), *Primitive classification.* Chicago: University of Chicago Press.

Eccles, Robert G., and Nohria, Nitin (1992), *Beyond the hype.* Cambridge, MA: Harvard Business School.

Eco, Umberto (1990), Fakes and forgeries. In: *The limits of interpretation.* Bloomington, IN: Indiana University Press, 174−292.

Edelman, Murray (1988), *Constructing the political spectacle.* Chicago: The University of Chicago Press.

Edwards, Richard (1979), *Contested terrain.* New York: Basic Books.

Eisenstadt, Shmul N. (1961), Anthropological studies of complex societies. *Current Anthropology,* 2(3): 201−222.

Elster, Jon (1985), Introduction. In: Elster, Jon (ed.), *The multiple self. Studies in rationality and social change.* Cambridge, UK: Cambridge University Press, 1−31.

Elwert, Georg (1987), Ausdehnung der Käuflichkeit und Einbettung der Wirtschaft Markt und Moralökonomie. In: Heinemann, Klaus (ed.), Soziologie wirtschaftlichen Handelns, *Kölner Zeitschrift für Soziologie und Sozialpsychologie,* 28: 300−321.

Esser, Josef (1992), Transnational corporations in a trilateral world. Paper presented to a symposium of the Andrew Schonfield Association in Florence, March 1992 (revised version July 1992).

Fallers, Lloyd A. (1954/1973), A note on the trickle effect. In: Wills, Gordon, and Midgley, David (eds.), *Fashion marketing.* London: Allen and Unwin, 207−214.

Finkelstein, Joanne (1989), *Dining out. A sociology of modern manners.* Cambridge, UK: Polity Press.

Fiol, Marlene, and Lyles, Marjorie (1985), Organizational learning. *Academy of Management Review,* 10(4): 803−813.

Fleck, Ludwik (1935/1979), *Genesis and development of a scientific fact.* Chicago: University of Chicago Press.

Fligstein, Neil (1985), The spread of the multidivisional form among large firms, 1919−1979. *American Sociological Review,* 50 (June): 377−391.

Fligstein, Neil (1990), *The transformation of corporate control.* Cambridge, MA: Harvard University Press.

Fligstein, Neil (1991), The structural transformation of American industry: An institutional account of the causes of diversification in the largest firms, 1919−1979. In: Powell, Walter W., and DiMaggio, Paul D. (Eds.), *The new institutionalism in organizational analysis.* Chicago: Chicago University Press, 311−336.

Flugel, John C. (1930), *The psychology of clothes.* London: Hogarth Press.

Flugel, John C. (1930/1973), Fashion. In: Wills, Gordon, and Midgley, David (eds.), *Fashion marketing.* London: Allen and Unwin, 229−240.

Forssell, Anders (1989), How to become modern and businesslike: An attempt to understand the modernization of Swedish Savings Banks. *International Studies of Management & Organization,* 19(3): 32−46.

Forssell, Anders (1992), *Moderna tider i sparbanken*. Stockholm: Nerenius & Santér-us.

Fortes, Meyer (1969), *Kinship and the social order. The legacy of Lewis Henry Morgan*. London: Routledge.

Fortes, Meyer, and Evans-Pritchard, Edward E. (1940), *African political systems*. London: Oxford University Press.

Forty, Adrian (1986), *Objects of desire. Design and society 1750−1980*. London: Cameron.

Foucault, Michel (1975/1977), *Discipline and punish*. New York: Pantheon.

Foucault, Michel (1980), *Power/knowledge: Selected interviews and other writings 1972−1977*. New York: Pantheon.

Friedland, Roger, and Alford, Robert R. (1991), Bringing society back in. Symbols, practices, and institutional contradictions. In Powell, Walter W., and DiMaggio, Paul J. (eds.), *The new institutionalism in organizational analysis*. Chicago: University of Chicago Press, 232−263.

Friedman, Jonathan (1990), Being in the world: globalization and localization. In: Featherstone, Mike (ed.), *Global culture: Nationalism, globalization and modernity*. London: Sage, 311−328.

Fröbel, Folker, Heinrichs, Jürgen, and Kreye, Otto (1980), *The new international division of labour. Structural unemployment in industrialized countries and industrialization in developing countries*. Cambridge, UK: Cambridge University Press.

Galaskiewicz, Joseph (1991), Making corporate actors accountable: Institution-building in Minneapolis, St. Paul. In: Powell, Walter W., and DiMaggio, Paul J. (eds.), *The new institutionalism in organizational analysis*. Chicago: University of Chicago Press, 293−310.

Garfinkel, Harold (1967), *Studies in ethnomethodology*. Englewood Cliffs, NJ: Prentice Hall.

Geertz, Clifford (1980), Blurred genres: The refiguration of social thought. *American Scholar*, 29(2): 165−179.

Geertz, Clifford (1983), *Local knowledge*. New York: Basic Books.

Gellner, Ernest (1983), *Nations and nationalism*. Ithaca: Cornell University Press.

Gergen, Kenneth J. (1991), *The saturated self. Dilemmas of identity in contemporary life*. New York: Basic Books.

Gherardi, Silvia, and Strati, Antonio (1988), The temporal dimension in organizational studies. *Organization Studies*, 9(2): 149−164.

Giddens, Anthony (1979), *Central problems in social theory: Action, structure and contradiction in social analysis*. Berkeley, CA: University of California Press.

Giddens, Anthony (1984), *The constitution of society. Outline of the theory of structuration*. Cambridge, UK: Polity Press.

Giddens, Anthony (1990), *The consequences of modernity*. Cambridge, UK: Polity Press.

Giddens, Anthony (1991), *Modernity and self-identity: Self and society in the late modern age*. Cambridge, UK: Polity Press.

Giddens, Anthony (1992), *The transformation of intimacy: Sexuality, love and eroticism in modern societies*. Cambridge, UK: Polity Press.

Ginsberg, Ari, and Abrahamson, Eric (1992), Champions of change and shifts in strategy-making: Managerial perspectives on the role of change advocates. *Journal of Management Studies*, 28: 173—190.

Girard, René (1977), *Violence and the sacred.* Baltimore: The John Hopkins University Press.

Gjerde, Ragnhild (1991), *Reformforsøk i domstolesektoren: En studie av moderniseringsforslag for by og herredsrettene.* Bergen: Institute for Administration and Organization Science, University of Bergen.

Gong, Gerrit W. (1984), *The standard of 'civilization" in international society.* Oxford: Clarendon Press.

Gouldner, Alvin (1960), The norm of reciprocity: A preliminary statement. *American Sociological Review* 25(2): 161—178.

Groffebert, Hans (1995), Potemkin in Afrika. Die 'ONGs-bidon": Materialien zum Thema Bluff-Organisationen im West-Sahel. In: Oppen, Achim von, and Rottenburg, Richard (eds.), *Organisationswandel in Afrika.* Studien 2, FSP Moderner Orient, Berlin: Das Arabische Buch, 131—143.

Gruiters, Jan, and Tresoldi, Efrem (1994), *Sudan, a cry for peace.* Brussels: Pax Christi International.

Hall, Peter, and Marcusen, Ann (1985), *Silicon landscapes.* Boston: Allen &Unwin.

Hall, Richard (1982), *Organizations: Structure and process.* Englewood Cliffs, NJ: Prentice-Hall.

Hammer, Michael (1990), Reengineering work: Don't automate, obliterate. *Harvard Business Review*, 68(4): 104—112.

Hannan, Michael T., and Freeman, John (1977), The population ecology of organizations. *American Journal of Sociology*, 82: 929—64.

Hannan, Michael T., and Freeman, John (1984), Structural inertia and organizational change. *American Sociological Review*, 49: 149—164.

Hannan, Michael T., and Freeman, John (1989), *Organizational ecology.* Cambridge, Mass.: Harvard University Press.

Hansson, Lennart, and Knutsson, Bo (1991), Organisation av kommunalteknisk verksamhet. En enkätstudie i början av 90-talet. Lund: Department of Business Administration. Research Report no. 2.

Hawley, Amos (1968), Human ecology. In: Sills, David (ed.), *International encyclopedia of the social sciences*, 4. New York: Free Press, 328—337.

Heckscher, Eli F. (1921), *Gammal och ny ekonomisk liberalism.* Stockholm: P.A. Norstedts & Söner.

Hedberg, Bo (1981), How organizations learn and unlearn. In: Nystrom, Paul C., and Starbuck, William (eds.), *Handbook of organizational design,* Vol. 1. Oxford: Oxford University Press, 3—27.

Henderson, Jeffrey (1989), *The globalization of high technology production: Society, space and semi-conductors in the restructuring of the modern world.* London: Routledge.

Hendriks, Jan, and Kalishoek, A. (1987), Decision-making on cutting back of staff at Dutch universities. Paper presented to the EGPA-conference, May 6—9, Valencia (Spain).

Hilgartner, Stephen, and Bosk, Charles L. (1988), The rise and fall of social problems. *American Journal of Sociology*, 94: 53—78.

Hinings, Bob, and Greenwood, Royston (1988), The normative prescription of organizations. In: Zucker, Lynne G. (ed.), *Institutional patterns and organizations: Culture and environment*. Cambridge, MA: Ballinger, 53–70.

Hirsch, Paul M. (1972), Processing fads and fashions: An organization set analysis of cultural industry systems. *American Journal of Sociology*, 77: 639–659.

Hirsch, Paul M. (1986), From ambushes to golden parachutes: Corporate takeovers as an instance of cultural framing and institutional integration. *American Journal of Sociology*, 91: 800–837.

Hirschman, Albert O. (1967), *Development projects observed*. Washington: The Brookings Institution.

Hirschman, Albert O. (1977), *The passions and the interests*. Princeton: Princeton University Press.

Hirst, Paul (1993), Globalization is fashionable but is it a myth? *The Guardian*, London, March 22.

Hollinger, David (1980), The problem of pragmatism in American history. *The Journal of American History*, 67(1): 88–107.

Holy, Ladislav, and Stuchlik, Milan (1983), *Actions, norms and representations. Foundations of anthropological inquiry*. Cambridge: CUP.

Hood, Christopher, and Jackson, Michael (1991), *Administrative argument*. Aldershot: Dartmouth.

Hoplin, Nancy K., and Schiffer, Betty (1948), The limits of fashion control. *American Sociological Review*, 13: 730–738.

Horn, Marilyn (1968), *The second skin: An interdisciplinary study of clothing*. Boston, MA: Houghton Mifflin.

Howe, R.B.K. (1994), A social-cognitive theory of desire. *Journal for the Theory of Social Behaviour*, 24(1): 1–23.

Huff, Anne S. (1982), Industry influences on strategy reformulation. *Strategic Management Journal*, 3: 119–131.

Huff, Anne S. (1990), *Mapping strategic thought*. Chichester: Wiley.

Hughes, Everett C. (1939), Institutions. In: Park, Robert E. (ed.), *An outline of the principles of sociology*. New York: Barnes and Noble, 283–347.

Hurlock, E.B. (1929), *The psychology of dress*. New York: Ronald Press.

Iacocca, Ian, and Novac, W. (1984), *Iacocca, an autobiography*. New York: Bantam Books.

Ignatieff, Michael (1984), *The needs of strangers*. London: Chatto & Windus.

International Business Week (1985), The counterfeit trade. December 16: 48–53.

Isacsson, Ulf, and Knutsson, Bo (1992), Styrsystem i förändring. En studie av målstyrning. Lund: Department of Business Adminstration Research Report no. 12.

Jacobsson, Bengt (1989), *Konsten att reagera: Intressen, institutioner och näringspolitik*. Stockholm: Carlssons.

Jansson, David (1989), The pragmatic uses of what is taken for granted: Project leaders' applications of investment calculations. *International Studies of Management & Organization*, 19(3): 47–62.

Joerges, Bernward (1976), *Beratung und Technologietransfer: Untersuchungen zur Professionalisierbarkeit gesellschaftsüberschreitender Beratung.* Baden-Baden: Nomos.

Joerges, Bernward (1994), Expertise lost: An early case of technology assessment. *Social Studies of Science,* 24: 96–104.

Johannessen, Truls (1993), Kommunal fornying eller språklig fornying. En studie av en kommunal omstillingsproces. Master thesis. Tromsø: University of Tromsø, Department of Public Policy and Administration.

Johansen, Steinar (1994), *Ikke bare fanges,men også selges: En organisasjonsteoretisk studie av markedsorientering i fire fiskeindustribedrifter.* Tromsø: Institute of Political Science, University of Tromsø.

Johansson, Johan (1988), *Kommundelsnämndsreformen i Sverige.* Paper presented at Statsvetenskapliga Förbundets Årsmöte, Förvaltningskonferens, Mariehamn, Åland, October 3–5.

Kahn, Herman (1979), *World economic development: 1979 and beyond.* London: Croom Helm.

Kamens, David H. (1977), Legitimating myths and educational organizations: The relationship between organizational ideology and formal structure. *American Sociological Review,* 42: 208–221.

Kanter, Rosabeth M. (1983), *The change masters.* New York: Simon and Schuster.

Kerr, Clark, Dunlop, John T., Harbison, Frederick, and Myers, Charles A. (1960), *Industrialism and industrial man. The problems of labor and management in economic growth.* Cambridge, Mass.: Harvard University Press.

Kervasdoue de, Jean, and Kimberly, John R. (1978), *Hospital innovation explanation in France and the United States: Organizational versus institutional analysis.* New Haven, Connecticut: Yale School of Organization and Management.

Kimberly, John (1981), Managerial innovation. In: Nystrom, Paul, and Starbuck, William (eds.), *Handbook of organizational design,* vol. 1. New York: Oxford University Press, 84–104.

King, Anthony D. (1990), *Global cities: Post-imperialism and the internationalization of London.* London: Routledge.

King, Charles (1963/1973), A rebuttal to the trickle-down theory. In: Wills, Gordon, and Midgley, David (eds.), *Fashion marketing.* London: Allen and Unwin, 215–228.

Kingdon, John W. (1984), *Agendas, alternatives and public policies.* Boston: Little, Brown and Company.

Klapp, Orrin (1969), *Collective search for identity.* New York: Holt, Rinehart and Winston.

Knorr-Cetina, Karin (1981), *The manufacture of knowledge.* Oxford: Pergamon.

Knorr-Cetina, Karin (1994), Primitive classification and postmodernity: Towards a sociological notion of fiction. *Theory, Culture and Society,* 11: 1–22.

Kogut, Bruce (1988), Joint ventures: Theoretical and empirical perspectives. *Strategic Management Journal,* 1: 84–104.

Kommunenes Sentralforbund (1977), *En revurdering av nemdstrukturen i norsk kommuner.* Oslo: Kt-report no. 2.

Kondratieff, Nikolai D. (1916/1935), The longwaves in economic life. *Review of Economic Statistics,* 17: 105–115.

Koplin, John, and Schiffer, Barbara (1948), The limits of fashion control. *American Sociological Review* 13: 263−289.

Kramer, Fritz (1991), Patchwork. Zwischen Struktur und Anomie. In: Kramer, Fritz W., and Streck, Bernhard (eds.), *Sudanesische Marginalien. Ein ethnographisches Programm*. München: Trickster, 7−16.

Kroeber, Alfred L. (1940), Stimulus diffusion. *American Anthropologist*, 42(1): 1−20.

Kroeber, Alfred L. (1923/1948), *Anthropology*. New York: Harcourt, Brace and Co.

Kønig, Rene (1974), *The restless image: A sociology of fashion*. London: Allen and Unwin.

Lash, Scott, and Urry, John (1987), *The end of organized capitalism*. Cambridge, UK: Polity Press.

Latour, Bruno (1986), The powers of association. In Law, John (ed.), *Power, action and belief*. London: Routledge and Kegan Paul, 264−280.

Latour, Bruno (1988), The politics of explanation: An alternative. In: Woolgar, Steve (ed.), *Knowledge and reflexivity: New frontiers in the sociology of knowledge*. London: Sage, 155−176.

Latour, Bruno (1992a), The next turn after the social turn... In: McMullin, Ernan (ed.), *The social dimensions of science*. Notre Dame, IN: University of Notre Dame Press, 272−292.

Latour, Bruno (1992b), Technology is society made durable. In: Law, John (ed.), *A sociology of monsters: Essays on power, technology and domination*. London: Routledge, 103−131.

Latour, Bruno (1993), *Messenger talks*. Lund: The Institute of Economic Research Working Paper, No.9.

Latour, Bruno, and Woolgar, Steve (1979/1986), *Laboratory life*. Princeton: Princeton University Press.

Lauer, Jane C., and Lauer, Richard H. (1981), *Fashion power: The meaning of fashion in American society*. Englewood Cliffs, NJ: Prentice Hall

Lawler, Edward E. III (1971), *Pay and organizational effectiveness: A psychological view*. New York: McGraw-Hill.

Lawler, Edward E. III, and Mohrman, Susan (1985), Quality circles after the fad. *Harvard Business Review*, 63(1): 65−71.

Lawrence, Paul R., and Lorsch, Jay W. (1967), *Organization and environment: Managing differentiation and integration*. Boston: Harvard Business School.

Leiser, David, Sevón, Guje, and Lévy, Daphna (1990), Children's economic socialization: Summarizing the cross-cultural comparison of ten countries. *Journal of Economic Psychology*, 11: 591−614.

Levitt, Barbara, and March, James G. (1988), Organizational learning. *Annual Review of Sociology*, 14: 319−340.

Linton, Ralph (1936), *The study of man*. New York: Appleton-Century-Crofts.

Lockwood, David (1964), Social integration and system integration. In: Zollschan, George Z., and Hirsch, Walter (eds.), *Exploration in social change*. London: Routledge & Kegan Paul, 244−257.

Lomnitz, Larissa A. (1988), Informal exchange networks in formal systems: A theoretical model. *American Anthropologist*, 90(1): 42−55.

Luhmann, Niklas (1982a), The world society as a social system. *International Journal of General Systems*, 8 (July): 131−8.

264   References

Luhmann, Niklas (1970/1982b), *The differentiation of society.* New York: Columbia University Press.
Luhmann, Niklas (1991), Sthenographie und Euryalistik. In: Gumbrecht, Hans-Ulrich, and Pfeiffer, Karl-Ludwig (eds.), *Paradoxien, Dissonanzen, Zusammenbrüche. Situationen offener Epistemologie.* Frankfurt: Suhrkamp, 58–82.
Lukes, Stephen (ed.) (1986), *Power.* Oxford: Blackwell.
Lyotard, Jean-François (1979/1984), *The postmodern condition. A report on knowledge.* Manchester: Manchester University Press.

MacIntyre, Alasdair (1981/1990), *After virtue.* London: Duckworth Press.
MacMillan, Ian, McCaffery, Mary Lynn, and van Wijk, Gilles (1985), Competitor's responses to easily imitated new products – Exploring commercial banking product introductions. *Strategic Management Journal,* 6: 75–86.
Magnussen, Anne M. (1992), Reformforslag i domstolene: Effektivisering eller administrativt hærverk? *Nordisk Administrativt Tidsskrift,* 2: 149–168.
Mann, Michael (1986), *The sources of social power,* vol. 1: *A history of power from the beginning to AD 1760.* Cambridge, UK: Cambridge University Press.
Mansfield, Edwin, Schwartz, M. Mark, and Wagner, Samuel (1981), Imitation costs and patents: An empirical study. *The Economic Journal,* 91: 907–918.
Maratos, O. (1973), The origin and development of imitation in the first six months of life. Paper presented at the Annual Meeting of the British Psychological Society, Liverpool.
March, James G. (1981), Decisions in organizations and theories of choice. In: Van de Ven, Andrew, and Joyce, William F. (eds.), *Perspectives of organizational design and behavior.* New York: Wiley, 205–244.
March, James G. (1984), How we talk and how we act: Administrative theory and administrative life. In: Sergiovanni, Thomas J., and Corbally, John E. (eds.), *Leadership and organizational cultures.* Urbana, IL: University of Illinois Press, 18–35.
March, James G. (ed.) (1988), *Decisions and organizations.* Oxford, UK: Blackwell.
March, James G. (1991), Organizational consultants and organizational research. *Journal of Applied Communications Research,* 19: 20–31.
March, James G., and Olsen, Johan P. (eds.) (1976), *Ambiguity and choice in organizations.* Bergen, Norway: Universitetsforlag.
March, James G., and Olsen, Johan P. (1983a), Organizing political life: What administrative reorganization tells us about government. *American Political Science Review,* 77: 281–296.
March, James G., and Olsen, Johan P. (1983b), The new institutionalism: Organizational factors in political life. *The American Political Science Review,* 78: 734–749
March, James G., and Olsen, Johan P. (1989), *Rediscovering institutions. The organizatonal basis of politics.* New York: The Free Press.
March, James G., and Olsen, Johan P. (1993), *Institutional perspectives on governance.* Bergen: LOS-senter, Notat 9315.
March, James G., and Sevón, Guje (1984), Gossip, information, and decision-making. In: Sproull, Lee S., and Larkey, Patrick D. (eds.), *Advances in information processing in organizations.* Greenwich: JAI Press, 95–107. [Reprinted in:

March, James G. (ed.) (1988), *Decisions and organizations*. Oxford: Blackwell, 429–442.]

Marcus, George (1992), Past, present and emergent identities: Requirements for ethnographies of late twentieth-century modernity world-wide. In: Lash, Scott, and Friedman, Jonathan (eds.), *Modernity & identity*. Oxford: Blackwell, 309–330.

Margolis, Howard (1987), *Patterns, thinking and cognition. A theory of judgment.*. Chicago: University of Chicago Press.

Mauss, Marcel (1925/1967), *The gift: Forms and functions of exchange in archaic society*. New York: Norton.

Max, John A.O. (1991), *The development of local government in Tanzania*. Dar Es Salaam: Educational Publishers.

Mbembe, Achille (1993), Raubtiere und Reformen. Niedergang des Staates und Risiken der Demokratisierung. *Lettre International*, (22): 58–59.

McCloskey, Donald N. (1990), *If you're so smart. The narrative of economic expertise*. Chicago: University of Chicago Press.

Medin, Douglas L., Goldstone, Robert L., and Gentner, Dedre (1993), Respect for similarity. *Psychological Review*, 100: 254–278.

Merton, Robert K. (1965/1985), *On the shoulders of giants. A Shandean postscript.* New York: Harcourt and Jovanovich.

Meyer, John W. (1986a), Myths of socialization and of personality, In: Heller, Thomas C., Sosna, Morton, and Wellbery, David E. (eds.), *Reconstructing individualism: Autonomy, individuality and the self in Western thought*. Stanford, CA: Stanford University Press, 208–221.

Meyer, John W. (1986b), Social environments and organizational accounting. *Accounting, Organizations and Society*, 11: 345–356 .

Meyer, John W. (1990a), Comments on institutionalism in sociology. Paper presented at the SCANCOR conference on Institutionalism, Utö, Sweden, August.

Meyer, John W. (1990b), [Personal communication, May 16].

Meyer, John W. (1994), Rationalized environments. In: Scott, W. Richard, and Meyer, John W. (eds.), *Institutional environments and organizations*. Thousand Oak, CA: Sage, 28–54.

Meyer, John W., and Rowan, B. (1977), Institutionalized organizations: Formal structure as myth and ceremony. *American Journal of Sociology*, 83: 340–363.

Meyer, John W., and Scott, W. Richard (1992), *Organizational environments: Ritual and rationality.* 2nd updated edition. Newbury Park, Beverly Hills, CA: Sage.

Meyer, John W., Boli, John, and Thomas, George M. (1987), Ontology and rationalization in the western cultural account. In: Thomas, George M., Meyer, John W., Ramirez, Francisco O., and Boli, John (eds.), *Institutional structure: Constituting state, society, and the individual.* Newbury Park, CA: Sage, 12–37.

Mezias, Stephen J. (1990), An institutional model of organizational practice: Financial reporting at the Fortune 200. *Administrative Science Quarterly*, 35: 431–457.

Middleton, John, and Tait, David (eds.) (1958), *Tribes without rules. Studies in African segmentary systems*. London: Routledge.

Miller, George A., Galanter, Eugene, and Pribram, Karl H. (1960), *Plans and the structure of behavior*. New York: Holt, Rinehart and Winston.

Mintzberg, Henry (1979), *The structuring of organizations*. Englewood Cliffs, NJ: Prentice Hall.

Mitchell, W.J.T. (1986), *Iconology. Image, text, ideology*. Chicago: University of Chicago Press.

Mitroff, Ian, and Mohrman, Susan (1987), The slack is gone: How the United States lost its competitive edge in the world economy. *Academy of Management Executive*, 1: 65−70.

Mohr, Lawrence B. (1969), Determinants of innovation in organizations. *American Political Science Review*, 63: 111−126.

Morgan, Gareth (1980), Paradigms, metaphors and puzzle-solving in organization theory. *Administrative Science Quarterly*, 25, 605−622.

Morgan, Gareth (1986), *Images of organizations*. Beverly Hills, CA: Sage.

Morishima, Michio (1982), *Why has Japan 'succeeded"?* Cambridge, UK: Cambridge University Press.

Moszynski, Peter (1993), Crushing a culture. *Focus on Africa* 4(4): 10−17.

Mühlmann, Wilhelm E. (1966), *Max Weber und die rationale Soziologie*. Tübingen: Mohr.

Münch, Richard (1984), *Die Struktur der Moderne. Grundmuster und differentielle Gestaltung des institutionellen Aufbaus der modernen Gesellschaft*. Frankfurt/ Main: Suhrkamp.

Mytinger, Robert E. (1968), *Innovation in local health services: A study of the adoption of new programs by local health departments*. Washington: US Department of Health.

Nedelmann, Barbara (1987), Georg Simmel as an analyst of autonomous processes: The merry-go-round of fashion. Paper presented at the Symposium Georg Simmel and Contemporary Sociology, Boston.

Nelson, Benjamin (1949), *The idea of usury. From tribal brotherhood to universal otherhood*. Princeton: Princeton University Press.

New York Stock Exchange (1982), People and productivity.

Nohria, Nitin, and Berkley, James D. (1994), Whatever happened to the take-charge manager. *Harvard Business Review*, 72: 128−139.

Nystrom, Paul C., and Starbuck, Williams H. (1984), Organizational façades. *Academy of Management Proceedings*, 182−185.

Nystrom, Paul H. (1928), *Economics of fashion*. New York: Ronald Press Company.

Ohmae, Kenichi (1985), *Triad power: The coming shape of global competition*. New York: Free Press.

Oliver, Christine (1992), The antecedents of deinstitutionalization. *Organization Studies*, 13/14: 563−588.

Olowu, Dele (1988), Bureaucratic morality in Africa. *International Political Science Review*, 9(3): 215−229.

Olsen, Johan P. (1988), The modernization of public administration in the Nordic countries: Some research questions. Bergen: The Norwegian Research Centre in Organization and Management. Research Paper no. 2.

Olsen, Johan P. (ed.) (1989), *Petroleum og politikk*. Bergen: Tano.

Olsen, Johan P. (1992), Analyzing institutional dynamics. Bergen: The Norwegian Research Centre in Organization and Management. Research Paper no. 14.

Parsons, Talcott. (1958), Suggestions for a sociological approach to the study of organizations. *Administrative Science Quarterly*, 1: 63–85 and 225–239.

Pascale, Richard T. (1990), *Managing on the edge*. New York: Simon and Schuster.

Pedersen, Marianne (1992), Moderne reformer i etablerte strukturer: Personalpolitikk og virksomhetsplanlegging i justisdepartementet. Manuscript. Bergen: Institute for Administration and Organization Science, University of Bergen.

Perrow, Charles B. (1970), *Organizational analysis: A sociological view*. Belmont, CA: Wadsworth Publishing Company.

Perrow, Charles B. (1986), *Complex organizations: A critical essay*. New York: Random House.

Peteraf, Margaret A. (1993), The cornerstone of competitive advantage: A resource-based view. *Strategic Management Jouyrnal*, 14: 179–191.

Peters, Thomas J., and Waterman, Robert H. Jr. (1982), *In search of excellence: Lessons from America's best run companies*. New York: Harper and Row.

Peterson, Richard A., and Berger, David G. (1975), Cycles in symbol production: The case of popular music. *American Sociological Review*, 40: 158–173.

Pfeffer, Jeffrey (1981), *Power in organizations*. Boston: Pitman.

Pfeffer, Jeffrey, and Salancik, Gerald R. (1978), *The external control of organizations*. New York: Harper and Row.

Piaget, Jean (1945/1951), Play, dreams and imitation in childhood. New York: W.W. Norton.

Pizzorno, Alessandro (1991), On the individualistic theory of social order. In: Bourdieu, Pierre, and Coleman, James S. (eds.), *Social theory for a changing society*. Boulder, Colorado: Westview Press, 209–231.

Polanyi, Karl (1944), *The great transformation*. Boston: Beacon Press.

Porter, Michael E. (1980), *Competitive strategy. Techniques for analyzing industries and competitors*. New York: Free Press.

Porter, Michael E. (1989), Corporate strategy. In: Tushman, Michael, O'Reilly, Charles, and Nadler, David A. (eds.), *Management of organizations: Strategies, tactics, analyses*. New York: Harper and Row, 43–50.

Powell, Walter W. (1991), Expanding the scope of institutional analysis. In: Powell, Walter W., and DiMaggio, Paul J. (eds.), *The new institutionalism in organizational analysis*. Chicago: University of Chicago Press, 183–203.

Powell, Walter W., and DiMaggio, Paul J. (eds.) (1991), *The new institutionalism in organizational analysis*. Chicago: University of Chicago Press.

Quinn, Naomi, and Holland, Dorothy (1987), Culture and cognition. In: Holland, Dorothy, and Quinn, Naomi (eds.), *Cultural models in language and thought*. Cambridge, UK: Cambridge University Press, 3–40.

Ratzel, Friedrich (1885–88/1896), *The history of mankind*. London: MacMillan.

Reinganum, Jennifer F. (1983), Uncertain innovation and the persistence of monopoly. *The American Economic Review*, 73: 741–747.

Reynold, William H. (1968/1973), Cars and clothing: Understanding fashion trends. In: Wills, Gordon, and Midgley, David (eds.), *Fashion marketing*. London: Allen and Unwin, 369–378.

Richardson, Jane, and Kroeber, Alfred L. (1940), Three centuries of women's dress fashion, a quantitative analysis. *Anthropological Records*, 5: 111–153.

Robertson, Roland (1992), *Globalization: Social theory and global culture.* London: Sage.

Robinson, Dwight E. (1958), Fashion theory and product design. *Harvard Business Review*, 36(6): 128−138.

Robinson, Dwight E. (1976), Fashion in shaving and trimming of the beard: The men of the 'Illustrated London News", 1842−1972. *American Journal of Sociology*, 81: 1133−1141.

Rogers, Everett M. (1962), *Diffusion of innovations.* New York: Free Press.

Rogers, Everett M., and Larsen, Judith K. (1984), *Silicon Valley fever. Growth of high-technology culture.* New York: Basic Books.

Rogers, Everett M., and Shoemaker, F. Floyd (1971), *Communication of innovations: A cross-cultural approach.* New York: Free Press.

Rohr, John (1988), Bureaucratic morality in the United States. *International Political Science Review*, 9(3): 167−178.

Rorty, Richard (1980), *Philosophy and the mirror of nature.* Oxford, UK: Basil Blackwell.

Rorty, Richard (1982), *Consequences of pragmatism.* Minneapolis: University of Minnesota Press.

Rorty, Richard (1989), *Contingency, irony and solidarity.* Cambridge, UK: Cambridge University Press.

Rorty, Richard (1991), *Objectivity, relativism and truth. Philosophical papers,* vol. 1. New York: Cambridge University Press.

Rosecrance, Richard N. (1986), *The rise of the trading state: Commerce and conquest in the modern world.* New York: Basic Books.

Rosenberg, Hans (1958), *Bureaucracy, aristocracy, and autocracy: The Prussian experience, 1660−1815.* Cambridge, MA: Harvard University Press.

Rottenburg, Richard (1989), 'Sesam, öffne dich!" Die Außenwelt in der Innenwelt bei den Moro-Nuba von Lebu in Südkordofan/Sudan. *Anthropos*, 84: 469−485.

Rottenburg, Richard (1991), *Ndemwareng. Wirtschaft und Gesellschaft in den Morobergen.* München: Trickster.

Rottenburg, Richard (1994), Orientierungsmuster afrikanischer Bürokratien: Eine Befragung modernisierungstheoretischer Ansätze. In: Laubscher, M.S. (ed.), *Systematische Ethnologie*, vol. 1. München: Anacon, 217−229.

Rumelt, Richard P. (1974), *Strategy, structure and economic performance.* Boston: Harvard University Press.

Rumelt, Richard P. (1984), Towards a strategic theory of the firm. In: Lamb, Robert B. (ed.), *Competitive strategy management.* Englewood Cliffs, NJ: Prentice-Hall, 556−570.

Rumelt, Richard P. (1987), Theory, strategy, and entrepreneurship. In: Teece, David J. (ed.), *The competitive challenge. Strategies for industrial innovation and renewal.* Cambridge, MA: Ballinger, 137−158.

Ryle, John (1994), The groundnuts and the hyena. *Times Literary Supplement*, July.

Røkenes, Arild (1993), *Nødvendig tilpasning eller tidstypisk trend ? En studie av bemanningsreduksjoner i bankvesenet.* Tromsø: Institute of Political Science, University of Tromsø.

Røvik, Kjell Arne (1982), *Administrativ nydannelse i et sterkt strukturert system: En studie av tiltaksorganisering i Tromsø i perioden 1973−1980.* Tromsø: Institute of Political Science, University of Tromsø.

Røvik, Kjell-Arne (1992a), *Den syke stat: Myter og moter i omstillingsarbeidet*. Oslo: The Norwegian University Press.

Røvik, Kjell-Arne (1992b), Institusjonaliserte standarder og multistandardorganisasjoner. *Norsk Statsvitenskapelig Tidsskrift*, 8(4): 261–284.

Røvik, Kjell-Arne (1992c), *Hva OU-basen forteller oss om omstillingsaktiviteten i norske kommuner*. Tromsø: Institute of Political Science, University of Tromsø. Research Paper no. 3.

Sahlin-Andersson, Kerstin (1989), *Oklarhetens strategi*. Lund: Studentlitteratur.

Sahlin-Andersson, Kerstin (1990), *Forskningsparker och företagsrelationer*. Stockholm: Regionplanekontoret.

Sahlin-Andersson, Kerstin (1991), Science parks as organized fields. Stockholm: EFI Research Paper.

Sahlin-Andersson, Kerstin (1992), The social construction of projects. In *Scandinavian Housing and Planning Research*, 9: 65–78.

Sapir, Edward (1937), Fashion. *Encyclopedia of the social sciences*, vol. 6: 139–144.

Saxenian, Annalee (1988), The Cheshire cat's grin. Innovation and regional development in England. *Technology Review*, 91(2): 67–75.

Schumpeter, Joseph A. (1935), *The theory of economic development*. Boston: Harvard University Press.

Schütz, Alfred (1971), The well-informed citizen. In: *Collected papers*, vol. II. The Hague: Martinus Nijhoff, 120–134.

Schütz, Alfred (1953/1973), Common-sense and the scientific interpretation of human action. In: *Collected papers*, vol. I. The Hague: Martinus Nijhoff, 3–47.

Schütz, Alfred, and Luckmann, Thomas (1973), *The structures of the life-world*. Evanston, IL: Northwestern University Press.

Scott, W. Richard (1987a), *Organizations: Rational, natural and open systems*. Englewood Cliffs, NJ: Prentice-Hall.

Scott, W. Richard (1987b), The adolescence of institutional theory. *Administrative Science Quarterly*, 32: 493–511.

Scott, W. Richard, and Meyer, John W. (1991), The rise of training programs in firms and agencies. In: Staw, Barry (ed.), *Research in Organizational Behavior*, *13*. Greenwich, CT: JAI Press, 297–326.

Scott, W. Richard, and Meyer, John W. (1994), *Institutional environments and organizations. Structural complexity and individualism*. Thousand Oaks, CA: Sage.

Sederberg, Peter (1984), *The politics of meaning. Power and explanation in the construction of social reality*. Tucson: The University of Arizona Press.

Sellerberg, Ann-Marie (1987), *Avstånd och attraktion: Om modets växlingar*. Stockholm: Carlssons.

Sellerberg, Ann-Mari (1994), *A blend of contradictions: Georg Simmel in theory and practice*. New Brunswick, NJ: Transaction.

Selznick, Philip (1949), *TVA and the grass-roots. A study of the sociology of formal organizations*. Berkeley, CA: University of California Press.

Selznick, Philip (1957), *Leadership in administration. A sociological interpretation*. New York: Harper & Row.

Sevón, Guje (forthcoming), The joints in joint R&D ventures. In: Kreiner, Kristian, and Sevón, Guje (eds.), *Constructing R&D collaboration. The enactment of EUREKA*. Helsinki: Swedish School of Economics.

Sigrist, Christian (1967), *Regulierte Anarchie. Untersuchungen zum Fehlen und zur Entstehung politischer Herrschaft in segmentären Gesellschaften Afrikas.* Olten and Freiburg: Walter.

Simmel, Georg (1904/1973), Fashion. In: Wills, Gordon, and Midgley, David (eds.), *Fashion marketing.* London: Allen and Unwin, 171−191.

Singh, Jitendra vir, Tucker, David, and House, Robert J. (1986), Organizational legitimacy and the liability of newness. *Administrative Science Quarterly,* 31: 171−193.

Sjöstrand, Sven-Erik (1985), *Samhällsorganisation.* Lund: Doxa.

Sjöstrand, Sven-Erik (1993), Institutions as infrastructures of human interaction. In Sjöstrand, Sven-Erik (ed.), *Institutional change. Theory and empirical findings,* New York: M.E. Sharpe, 61−74.

Smelser, Neil (1962), *Theory of collective behavior.* New York: The Free Press.

Smith-Lovin, Lynn, and Brody, Charles (1989), Interruptions in group discussions. The effects of gender and group compositions. *American Sociological Review,* 54(3): 424−435.

Spender, J-C. (1989), *Industry recipes.* Oxford: Blackwell.

Spetz, Gunnel (1988), *Vägen till nej. Anade och oanade konsekvenser av en OS-satsning.* Stockholm: EFI.

Spybey, Tony (1984), Traditional and professional frames of meaning for managers. *Sociology,* 18(4): 550−562.

Spybey, Tony (1992), *Social change, development and dependency: Modernity, colonialism and the development of the West.* Cambridge, UK: Polity Press.

Starbuck, William H., and Nystrom, Paul C. (1981), Why the world needs organizational design. In: Nystrom, Paul C., and Starbuck, William H. (eds.), *Handbook of organizational design.* New York: Oxford University Press, iv-xxii.

Stava, Per (1990), Ny nemdstruktuř erfaringer med hovedutvalgsmodellen og veien videre. In: Baldersheim, Harald (ed.), *Ledelse og innovasjon i kommunene.* Oslo: Tano, 156−173.

Strand, Hillevi (1994), *Kvalitetsarbeid i en nordnorsk fiskeindustribedrift.* Tromsø: The Norwegian School of Fishery.

Strang, David, and Meyer, John W. (1994), Institutional conditions for diffusion. In: Scott, W. Richard, and Meyer, John W. (eds.), *Institutional environments and organizations.* Thousand Oaks, CA: Sage, 100−112.

Streck, Bernhard (1995), Männerhaus und Betrieb. In: Oppen, Achim von, and Rottenburg, Richard (eds.), *Organisationswandel in Afrika.* Studien 2, FSP Moderner Orient, Berlin: Das Arabische Buch, 37−51.

Swidler, Ann (1986), Culture in action. *American Sociological Review,* 51: 273−286.

Taps, Judith, and Martin, Patricia Y. (1988), Gender composition and attributional accounts: Impacts on women's influence and likability in task groups. Paper presented at the Southern Sociological Society Meeting, March.

Tarde, Gabriel (1902), *La psychologie economique,* 2 vols. Paris: Felix Alcan.

Tarde, Gabriel (1900/1903), *The laws of imitation.* Gloucester, MA: P. Smith.

Taylor, Tony (1985), High-technology industry and the development of Science Parks. In: Hall, Peter, and Markusen, Ann (eds.), *Silicon landscapes.* Boston: Allen and Unwin: 134−143.

Thomas, George M., and Meyer, John W. (1984), The expansion of the state. *Annual Review of Sociology*, 10: 461–482.

Thomas, George M., Meyer, John W., Ramirez, Francisco O., and Boli, John (eds.) (1987), *Institutional structure: Constituting state, society, and the individual.* Newbury Park, CA: Sage.

Thompson, James D. (1967), *Organizations in action. Social science bases of administrative theory.* New York: McGraw-Hill.

Thorburn, Thomas (1974), *Förvaltningsekonomi.* Stockholm: Prisma.

Tiller, Tom (1990), *Kenguruskolen: Det store spranget.* Oslo: Gyldendal.

Tolbert, Pamela S. (1988), Institutional sources of organizational culture in major law firms. In: Zucker, Lynne G. (ed.), *Institutional patterns and organizations. Culture and environment.* Cambridge, MA: Ballinger, 101–113.

Tolbert, Pamela.S., and Zucker, Lynne (1983), Institutional sources of change in the formal structure of organizations: The diffusion of civil service reform, 1880–1935. *Administrative Science Quarterly*, 28: 22–39.

Touraine, Alain (1974), *The post-industrial society.* London: Wildwood House.

Trist, Eric, and Bamford, Kathryn W. (1951), Some social and psychological consequences of the long-wall method of coal-getting. *Human Relations*, 4: 3–38.

Van de Ven, Andrew, and Polley, David (1990), Learning processes during the development of an innovation. Paper presented at the Annual Meeting of the Academy of Management, San Francisco.

Veblen, Thorstein (1899/1953), *The theory of the leisure class: An economic study of institutions.* New York: Mentor.

Veiledning i virksomhetsplanlegging (1988), Oslo: Statskonsult.

Wall Street Journal (1993), The best laid plans: Many companies try management fads, only to see them flop. July 6: A1+.

Wallerstein, Immanuel (1974), *The modern world-system: Capitalist agriculture and the origins of the European world-economy in the sixteenth century.* New York: Academic Press.

Wallerstein, Immanuel (1979), *The capitalist world-economy.* Cambridge, UK: Cambridge University Press.

Warne, Albin (1929), *Till folkskolans förhistoria i Sverige.* Stockholm: Svenska Kyrkans Diakonistyrelses Bokförlag.

Warren, Roland L. (1967), The interorganizational field as a focus for investigation. *Administrative Science Quarterly*, 12: 396–419.

Warren, Roland L., Rose, Stephen M., and Bergunder, Ann F. (1974), *The structure of urban reform. Community decision organizations in stability and change.* Lexington, MA: Lexington Books.

Weber, Max (1916/1973), Einleitung in die Wirtschaftsethik der Weltreligionen. In: *Soziologie, Universalgeschichtliche Analysen, Politik.* Stuttgart: Kröner, 398–440.

Weber, Max (1920/1972), The protestant ethic and the spirit of capitalism. 2nd edition. London: Allen and Unwin.

Webster's (1986), *New third international dictionary of the English language*, Springfield, MA: Merriam-Webster.

272   References

Weick, Karl E. (1969), *The social psychology of organizing.* Reading, MA: Addison-Wesley.
Westney, D. Eleonor (1987), *Imitation and innovation. The transfer of western organizational patterns to Meiji Japan.* Cambridge, MA: Harvard University Press.
Wills, Gordon, and Christopher, Martin (1973), Introduction. In: Wills, Gordon, and Midgley, David (eds.), *Fashion marketing.* London: Allen and Unwin, 1–11.
Woodward, Joan (1965), *Industrial organization: Theory and practice.* Oxford, UK: Oxford University Press.

Yager, Edwin G. (1981), The quality-control circle explosion. *Training and Development Journal,* 35: 98–105.
Yearley, Steven (1994), Social movements and environmental change. In: Redclift, Michael, and Benton, Ted (eds.), *Social theory and global environment.* London: Routledge, 150–168.
Young, Agnes Brook (1937), *Recurring cycles of fashion 1760–1937.* London: Harper.
Young, Agnes Brook (1937/1973), Recurring cycles of fashion. In: Wills, Gordon, and Midgley, David (eds.), *Fashion marketing.* London: Allen and Unwin, 107–124.

Zey-Ferrel, Mary (1981), Criticisms of the dominant perspective on organizations. *The Sociological Quarterly,* 22: 181–205.
Zucker, Lynne G. (1977), The role of institutionalization in cultural persistence. *American Sociological Review,* 42: 726–743.
Zucker, Lynne G. (1983), Organizations as institutions. In Bacharach, Samuel (ed.), *Advances in organization theory,* vol. 2. Greenwich, CT: JAI Press, 1–47.
Zucker, Lynne G. (1987), Institutional theories of organizations. *Annual Review of Sociology,* 13: 443–464.

About the Authors

Eric Abrahamson is an Associate Professor at the Department of Management, Columbia University. His research interests are organizational theory, interorganizational culture, diffusion and management of technology. His main publications are "Important dimensions of strategic issues: Separating wheat from chaff" (with Jane Dutton and Eric Walton, *Journal of Management Studies*, 1988); "When do bandwagon diffusions roll? How far do they go? And when do they roll backwards?" (with Lori Rosenkopf, *Academy of Management Best Paper Proceedings*, 1990); "When and how are technically inefficient innovations diffused or technically efficient innovations rejected?" (*Academy of Management Review*, 1991); "Champions of changes and shifts in strategy-making" (with Ari Ginsberg, *Journal of Management Studies*, 1991); "Forging the iron cage: Interorganizational networks and the production of macro-culture" (with Charles Fombrun, *Journal of Management Studies*, 1992); "Institutional and competitive bandwagons: Using mathematical modelling as a tool to explore innovation diffusion" (with Lori Rosenkopf, *Academy of Management Review*, 1993); "Management fashion" (*Academy of Management Review*, 1996); "The emergence and presence of employee-management rhetorics" (*Academy of Management Journal*, 1996).

Barbara Czarniawska-Joerges holds the Chair in Management at Lund University, Sweden. Her research focuses on field studies of complex organizations, interorganizational management, the status of organizational knowledge and the connections between organization theory and fiction. She has published in the area of business and public administration in Polish, her native language, as well as in Swedish and English, including *Controlling Top Management in Large Organizations* (1985), *Ideological Control in Nonideological Organizations* (1988), *Economic Decline and Organizational Control* (1989), *Exploring Complex Organizations* (1992) and *The Three-Dimensional Organization: A Constructionist View* (1993). Her articles have appeared in *Problemy Organizacji, Ekonomista, Oeconomica Polona, Organizacja i Kierowanie, Erhervs økonomisk Tidsskrift, Problemi di Amministrazione Pubblica, Scandinavian Journal of Management, Economic and Industrial Democracy, Organization Studies, Journal of Management Studies, Accounting, Organizations and Society, Management Communication, Consultation, International Studies of Management & Organization, Finnish Administrative Studies* and *Accounting, Management and Information Technol-*

ogies. She was also a guest editor of special issues of *ISM&O* (1989/1990, 3 and 4); *Industrial and Environmental Crisis Quarterly* (1994, 1) and *Scandinavian Journal of Management* (1994, 2).

Anders Forssell is a Research Fellow at Stockholm Center for Organizational Research. His research interests are organization forms and transformations; modernity and its influence on organizations and organizational life. His main publications in Swedish are *Reform som tradition* (Reform as a tradition; together with Nils Brunsson and Hans Winberg, 1990) and *Moderna tider i sparbanken* (Modern times in the saving banks, 1992). In English: "Being modern and business-minded" (*Cooperative Yearbook*, 1990) and "How to be modern and business-like: An attempt to understand the modernization of Swedish saving banks" (*International Studies of Management & Organization*, 1989).

David Jansson is a journalist and an affiliated Research Fellow at Stockholm School of Economics. His research interests are: the role of rationality in organizations and institutional change. His main publication in Swedish is *Spelet kring investeringskalkyler* (The game of investment calculus, 1992). In English: "The pragmatic uses of what is taken for granted" (*International Studies of Management & Organization*, 1989), reprinted in I. Hägg and P. Segelod (eds.), *Issues in empirical investment research* (1992).

Bernward Joerges is a Professor of Sociology at the Technical University Berlin and a Senior Researcher at Wissenschaftszentrum Berlin. His research focuses on science studies, large technical systems, technology in everyday life and energy conservation. He has published books and articles on these topics in German and in French. In English, he has co-edited *Public Policies and Private Actions: A Multinational Study of Local Energy Conservation Programmes* (1987) and *Consumer Behavior and Energy Policy* (1984, 1986). His articles have appeared in the *Soziale Welt, Leviathan, Zeitschrift für Kulturaustausch, Zeitschrift für allgemeine Wissenschaftstheorie, Zeitschrift für Soziologie, Journal of Economic Psychology, Journal of Consumer Policy, Technology and Culture, Journal of the Theory of Social Behaviour, Management Communication, International Studies of Management & Organization, Social Studies of Science* and *Futures.*

John W. Meyer is a Professor of Sociology at Stanford University. His research focuses on organization theory, the sociology of education, and (his current research focus) the nature of contemporary global society and its impact on national states and other organizations. In this latter area, along with many articles, he has published (with G. Thomas, J. Boli, and F. Ramirez) *Institutional structure: Constituting state, society and the individual* (1987), and (with D. Kamens, A. Benavot, Y. Cha, and S. Wong) *School knowledge for the masses* (1992). In the field of organizations, along with many articles, he has published (with W. R. Scott) *Organizational environments: Ritual and rationality* (1983/1992), and *Institutional environments and organizations* (1994).

Richard Walter Rottenburg is a Reader at the Department of Anthropology at the Viadrina University (Frankfurt an der Oder). His main research interests are the anthropology of modern organizations in Africa and Europe and the ethnography of Sudan. He acts as a consultant to the German Bank for Reconstruction and Development (KfW), Frankfurt am Main. Some of his publications include: "Three spheres in the economic life of the Moro Nuba in South Kordofan" (in F. Kramer and B. Streck, eds., *Zwischenberichte des Sudanprojekts*, 1983); "Feldbeobachtungen in Unternehmen − Ethnographische Explorationen in der eigenen Gesellschaft" ("Field work in business organizations. Ethnographic explorations at home", with J.M. van de Graaf, in R. Aster, ed., *Teilnehmende Beobachtung*, 1989); "Gegenseitigkeitserwartungen in Unternehmen" ("Expectations of reciprocity in business organizations", in H. Merkens, ed. *Strategie, Unternehmenskultur und Organisationsentwicklung zwischen Wissenschaft und Praxis*, 1990); "Der Sozialismus braucht den ganzen Menschen" ("Socialism needs the entire person", *Zeitschrift für Soziologie*, 1991); *Ndemwareng. Wirtschaft und Gesellschaft in den Morobergen* (Ndemwareng. Economy and society in Moro Mountains, 1991); "Zur Herausbildung von Denkstilen in Unternehmen" (("On the emergence of thought styles in business organizations" in H. Merkens, ed., *Herausforderungen für Unternehmens-kulturentwicklung und Organisationslernene in den neuen Bundesländern und Westberlin*, 1993); "From socialist realism to postmodern ambiguity: East German companies in transition" (*Industrial and Environmental Crisis Quarterly*, 1994).

Kjell Arne Røvik is a Professor of Public Administration at he Department of Political Science, University of Tromsø. His research focuses on learning in organizations, organization development and the diffusion of management tools. His most recent publications in Norwegian are *Læringssystemer og Læringsatferd* (Learning Systems and Learning Behavior, 1988); *Fra Teori till Teknikk: Private Organisasjonsutviklingsfirmaer i Offentlig Sektor* (From theory to technique: The use of organizational consultants firms in public administration, 1991); *Den "Syke" Staten* (The "sick" state, 1992); "Institusjonaliserte standarder og multistandard-organisasjoner" (Institutionalized standards and multi-standard organizations), *Norsk Statsvitenskapelig Tidsskrift*, 1992, and "Vitenskap eller moter? En kunskapssosiologisk analyse av konsulenters organisasjonskompetanse" (Science or fashion? On organizational consultant's knowledge), *Nordisk Administrativt Tidsskrift* , 1992.

Kerstin Sahlin-Andersson is an Acting Chair in Public Management at the Stockholm School of Economics. She is the director of SCORE (Stockholm Center for Organizational Research). Her research concerns large projects and the meaning of the extraordinary in organizational action; the entrance of new actors in existing organization fields; the change of organizational identities. Her major publications in Swedish are *Beslutsprocessens komplexitet* (The complexity of decision making, 1986); *Oklarhetens strategi* (Ambiguity as strategy, 1989). In English:"Science parks as organized fields" (EFI Research Paper, 1991); – "The social construction of projects" (*Scandinavian Housing and Planning Research*, 1992); "The use of ambiguity", in I. Hägg and P. Segelod (eds.), *Issues in empirical investment research* (1992), and "Group identities as the building blocks of organizations: a story about nurses' daily work" (*Scandinavian Journal of Management*, 1994).

Guje Sevón holds the Chair in Organization and Management at the Swedish School of Economics and Business Administration in Helsinki. Her publications in English include "Cognitive maps of past and future economic events" (*Acta Psychologica*, 1984); "Gossip, information, and decision making" (together with James G. March, in *Advances in information processing in organizations,* 1984; reprinted in J.G. March, ed., *Decision making in organizations,* 1988); "The municipality pinch: Slack reduction in state and firms" (together with Elisabeth Sundin, *Scandinavian Journal of Management Studies*); *New directions in research on decision-making* (ed. together with B. Brehmer, H. Jungermann, and P. Lourens, 1986); "Behavioral perspectives on theories of the firm" (together with J.G. March; in *Handbook of economic psychology,* 1988); "Rationalization of action through value development" (in S. Maital, ed., *Applied behavioral economics,* 1988); "Children's economic socialization" (*Journal of Economic Psychology,* 1990). She was also a guest editor (together with D. Leiser and Ch. Roland-Lévy) of the *Journal of Economic Psychology,* 11 (4), 1990.

Tony Spybey is a Principal Lecturer in Sociology at the University of Plymouth. His current research interest is the rise of Western society, its impact on the rest of the world and the outcome, as globalization, in the twentieth century. His main publications are: "Interorganizational networks" (with D. Dunkerley and M. Thrasher, *Organization Studies*, 1981); "Traditional and professional frames of meaning for managers" (*Sociology*, 1984); "Frames of meaning: The rationality in organizational cultures" (*Acta Sociologica*, 1984); *Management and society in Sweden* (with P. Lawrence, 1986) "'Post-Confucianism', social democracy and economic culture" (together with S. Clegg, and W. Higgins; in S. Clegg and S.G. Redding, eds., *Capitalism and contrasting cultures*, 1990); Frames of meaning as a concept of organization" (*International Studies of Management & Organization*, 1990); *Social change, development and dependency* (1992); *Globalization and World Society* (1994).

Subject and Author Index